schools

Schools

and

Inequality

inequality

inschools

Schools

and

Inequality

equality

James W. Guthrie
George B. Kleindorfer
Henry M. Levin
Robert T. Stout

Foreword by John W. Gardner

The MIT Press
Cambridge, Massachusetts,
and London, England

Schools and Inequality

James W. Guthrie
George B. Kleindorfer
Henry M. Levin
Robert T. Stout

Foreword by John W. Gardner

Contents

Tables

Foreword

Equality was an honored word in the American vocabulary long before the founding of the nation. We have always talked as though we believed in it, and perhaps most of us do.

But despite our earnest professions, the path to equality has been long and hard. In 1776 we said, "All men are created equal"; however, eighty-nine years passed before we freed the slaves. Another fifty-five years passed before we granted women the vote. And we still have the gravest problems of inequality.

We have always known that deeply rooted customs, habits, and impulses of social oppression made equality difficult to achieve. In the 1930s we faced up to some of the more obvious economic barriers to equality of opportunity.

Then, in the 1960s, the nation began an even deeper and more painful probing of the circumstances that make for inequality. We began to understand how deeply some of the victims of poverty are trapped. We began to understand how race prejudice has erected countless obstacles—some obvious and some exceedingly subtle—to equal opportunity. We began to understand the multitudinous ways in which mental illness, mental retardation, and physical handicaps blight individual lives and how much can be done to remove the blight.

The latest chapter in our effort to understand the realities of inequality is an immensely important one. Extremely capable students of society are beginning to lay bare the manner in which the very workings of the system create inequities and thwart the drive toward equal opportunity. We were slow to reach this stage because our social machinery is intricate. It requires exceptionally skilled analysis —plus patience and stamina—to demonstrate the ways in which our system is failing to serve our higher purposes. Reformers have traditionally been drawn to more exhilarating chores. Perhaps it is a mark of our maturity that men of deep commitment to social values can and will turn to the arduous kind of analysis represented in this study. We owe a great debt to the authors of this volume.

John W. Gardner

May 13, 1970

Preface

Equality of educational opportunity is an extraordinarily difficult objective to achieve. One reason this is so is the critical problem of definition. What constitutes such equality? How do you know when you have achieved it?

As social scientists and educators we nave not arrived at any final answers to these questions. We have, however, adopted a strategy that we feel is useful in moving toward an answer. That strategy is systematically to define what equality is **not**—in other words, to focus upon inequality. The effort here is to employ the research tools at our disposal to hack away at the protective briars and tangled growth that camouflage those educational practices that we suspect reasonable men, once knowing of them, would agree are unequal. If successful, we are free to move to another thicket and expose another inequity. Such practices may never lead to an ideal definition of "equality," but we hope that they may serve to eliminate or significantly reduce a number of the most glaring inequalities.

One purpose of this book is to expose the inequalities that presently surround the manner in which school resources are distributed. We contend that under present circumstances the general tendency is for children from wealthy homes to have high-quality educational services available to them, whereas their peers from less fortunate circumstances have access only to low-quality educational services. This then is the problem to which we invite the attention of thoughtful men. We hope that they will concur that such a situation is contrary to most any definition of "equality of educational opportunity."

The second purpose of this book is to serve as an example of useful social science research for those individuals who presently are seeking legislative and judicial remedies for educational inequalities. The mid-1960s marked the beginning of a significant increase in the level of attention devoted to equality of educational opportunity. It was during this period that Congress enacted the 1964 Civil Rights Act, the Economic Opportunity Act, and the Elementary and Secondary Education Act. This legislation appeared to have great significance for educational reform, but progress was not quick in coming.

Subsequently, a number of authors began to argue that the courts also offered an avenue by which inequities could be alleviated.[1]

[1] The two best examples of such works are Arthur E. Wise, **Rich Schools: Poor Schools** (Chicago: University of Chicago Press, 1969) and John E. Coons, William H. Clune, and Stephen D. Sugarman, **Private Wealth and Public Education** (Cambridge: Harvard University Press, 1970).

These writers contend that present-day school finance inequalities can be construed to be in violation of the Equal Protection Clause of the Fourteenth Amendment of the United States Constitution.

We believe that this argument possesses a great deal of merit, it may be that the courts will be persuaded to act on the matter, or it may be that the logic of the interpretation will nevertheless be effective in convincing state legislatures themselves of the need to act. In any event, it is our position that the specific arguments made to courts and legislative bodies should embody research of the type illustrated by this book. Our efforts no doubt can be improved upon, but we hope, nevertheless, that they may serve as a model that will enable reformers to span the gap between legal theory and the practicalities of educational change.

A third purpose of this book is also tied to the task of defining equality of educational opportunity. Numerous past studies have framed such a definition in terms of parity of dollar expenditures. If different states, different school districts, and different schools are spending different amounts per pupil, then it is held that opportunities gaps exist that should be rectified. Most such reform efforts have been well intentioned, but their results have been less than decisive. Evidence suggests that expenditure disparities persist in every state, and in some states the discrepancy between the highest-spending and lowest-spending districts is in excess of 300 percent.

One factor that perhaps accounts for the failure of these reform movements has been their inability to demonstrate that equal dollars are indeed tied to "equality of opportunity." Even to an unsophisticated layman, it is obvious that the relationship between dollars spent and how much students learn is neither clear nor constant. Under such murky conditions of cause and effect, why should anyone become very disturbed? Is it not possible that a child who is genuinely motivated can compensate for the lack of science laboratories, new books, and computer-assisted instructional programs? The "little red schoolhouse" previously produced results, and it did not cost $1,500 a year per pupil to run. Why then should we worry about the fact that today not every child has the same amount spent for his schooling? In other words, if reformers are to be concerned about equality of opportunity through the schools, then they must begin to explore systematically the patterns of resource dispersal in the schools and how these patterns affect children's education.

This book is a preliminary effort in that direction. A conceptual

chain has been set up that links (1) the level of financial input to
(2) the quality of services delivered to (3) the level of student achievement to (4) the postschool performance of pupils. Available evidence
has been amassed in support of each hypothesized link in this chain.
We are far from convinced that we have constructed the perfect
conceptual chain or equipped it with all the correct evidentiary links,
let alone logically soldered the links tightly shut. We hope that our
successors can improve on our efforts at every step of the way.
Nevertheless, we do hope that the formulation of the problem in
this fashion may be helpful in reaching conclusions as to what
should be done to eliminate present disparities and thereby bring
us close to the goal of equal educational opportunity.

In pursuing the purposes just described, we were joined by the
National Urban Coalition. In addition to its overall concern for solving
the problems of our cities, that organization was specifically interested in supporting an objective study relevant to a Michigan court
case of national significance for education. The Board of Education
of the School District of the City of Detroit had filed a complaint
alleging that Michigan's governmental arrangements for education
violated both the state constitution and the Equal Protection Clause
of the United States Constitution's Fourteenth Amendment. The litiga-
tion necessitated a high degree of information and analysis regarding
the character of school services in the state. Given this concurrence
of interests, we accepted the National Urban Coalition's offer of
assistance to conduct a study of schools and inequality.

Yet another overlap was our desire to study the state with the most
adequate supply of data about its educational system. The year prior
to our study, Michigan had completed a remarkably thorough examination of its educational system. In addition, a substantial number
of the state's schools and students had been tapped for the Equality
of Educational Opportunity Survey conducted in 1965 by the U.S.
Office of Education. Consequently, it appeared as if a study in
Michigan, more than any other state, would suffice to meet the many
prerequisites for an assessment of schools and their consequences.

Our efforts in conducting the study were aided by literally hundreds
of individuals. We are particularly grateful to James A. Kelly, Associate Professor, Teachers College, Columbia University, formerly an
Executive Associate at The National Urban Coalition, for his many
contributions in facilitating this study. Without his perspective and
persistence there would not have been such a study. Similarly, we

are appreciative of the encouragement and support of The National Urban Coalition and its former Chairman, John W. Gardner.

In attempting to conceptualize the study and arrive at suitable research procedures we were assisted by a number of notable educators and scholars. H. Thomas James, President of the Lyle M. Spencer Foundation, Arthur P. Coladarci, Acting Dean of the Stanford University School of Education, Dean Alan K. Campbell and Professor Jesse Burkhead of the Maxwell Graduate School, Syracuse University, J. Alan Thomas, Dean, and Arthur E. Wise, Assistant Professor, Department of Education, University of Chicago, and Charles S. Benson, Professor, Guy Benveniste, Associate Professor, and Rodney J. Reed, Assistant Professor, Division of Policy Planning and Administration, School of Education, University of California at Berkeley, were all instrumental in this respect.

In addition to these individuals, a number of professional colleagues contributed directly to the content of the report. Jack W. Osman, Associate Professor, Department of Economics, San Francisco State College, provided a general description of state school finance arrangements and a specific analysis of Michigan school aid formulas. Denny Stavros of the Research Division in the Detroit schools helped by increasing our understanding of the relationship between student socioeconomic status and availability of informal educational opportunities. A working paper on school programs designed to increase the educational achievement of low socioeconomic status students was prepared by William D. Rohwer, Professor, School of Education, University of California at Berkeley. Stephen Michaelson, Assistant Professor, School of Education, Harvard University, provided valuable assistance in analyzing data from the Equality of Educational Opportunity Survey. Forest Harrison, formerly a Research Associate in the Division of Policy Planning and Administration in the School of Education, University of California at Berkeley, now an Assistant Professor at the Claremont Graduate School, and Michael Woodroofe and Norman Starr at the University of Michigan provided advice about statistical procedures. Computer programming and other tasks connected with electronic data processing were provided by Charles E. Hansen, Girard C. Pessis, Stephen Rhoads, and Marvin Tener.

Research assistants were invaluable in our data gathering and in the day-to-day work that makes a research effort possible. In this respect we are grateful for the efforts of Stephen R. Blum, David

Burke, Daniel Davis, Rey A. Carr, Marvin C. Gentz, Dennis Mulkulski, Harriet Shogan, Dennis Spuck, and Margaret R. Welco.

We wish especially to express our gratitude to Norman Drachler, Superintendent of the School District of the City of Detroit, who was helpful in conceptualizing the study, suggesting and obtaining sources of data, and criticizing the final product in a most scholarly and constructive manner.

Finally, we are indebted to the editorial, secretarial, clerical, and artistic assistance of Marion L. Crowley, Linda E. Dillon, Ramona S. Fellom, Jan Etta Griffin, Linda M. Hayward, Charles Hamilton, Jacqueline C. Janzen, Delores A. Moody, Paula S. Morelli, and Chris Vandkraiss. Dorothy W. Swatt and Gerald C. Hayward were particularly helpful in assembling the final volume.

In their own fashion, each of the foregoing individuals established high standards of quality to be met by this study, and each contributed his or her utmost to enable us to meet those standards.

J. W. G.
G. B. K.
H. M. L.
R. T. S.

Berkeley, Stanford, and
Claremont, California

1

Introduction

Let us begin by perfecting the system of education as the proper foundation whereon to erect a temple to liberty, and to establish a wise, equitable, and durable policy, that our country may become indeed an asylum to the distressed of every clime—the abode of liberty, peace, virtue, and happiness. . . .

"A Plan for the General Establishment of Schools Throughout the United States," Robert Coram, 1971[1]

---

[1] Reprinted in Frederick Rudolph, ed., **Essays on Education in the Early Republic** (Cambridge, Mass.: Harvard University Press, 1965).

This is a study of opportunity. We should quickly add that it is about educational opportunity, but the complexities of our era weld the two together rather closely. As technology advances and the demand for unskilled labor decreases, sweat, elbow grease, and a strong back seldom suffice any longer as the primary requisites for a good, useful, or happy life. Increasingly today people must acquire the mental skills that will allow them to cope with the complex choices and situations of conflicting value which they will no doubt encounter with increasing frequency in the future. Our educational institutions must at least provide students with basic skills so that they will indeed have the opportunity to meet these future decisions as free, self-determined men and women rather than as people lacking the elementary intellectual ability required for the carrying on of day-to-day affairs.

Schooling should constitute one of the first rungs on the ladder to the achievement of this goal. We think that progress up the ladder depends heavily upon access to high-quality educational services. However, access to such services is not provided equally. **There are individuals and groups whose chances for a good life are being seriously and systematically curtailed by the low quality of schooling that our society makes available to them.** This study describes these unequal educational conditions and proceeds to analyze many of their causes and consequences. In addition, in Chapter 7 we provide a new perspective for solving the problems of inequality.

The primary thesis of this book is that the quality of schooling provided to an individual and his subsequent educational achievement and postschool performance are determined to a substantial degree by his social and economic circumstances. Simply put, at one extreme children from wealthy families tend to have waiting for them the highest quality of available educational services. This provides them with an opportunity to maximize their intellectual potential and thereafter to apply their learning in a fashion that will lead to high income, high social status, possession of many material goods, and access to a wide range of personally pleasing experiences. At the other extreme, a child from a socially less advantaged and economically depressed home typically has waiting for him low-quality school services that inhibit development of his intellectual capacities and that subsequently curtail his ability to earn a living, accrue comforts, and feel fulfilled.

Moreover, the processes connected with inequality frequently have prolonged consequences, consequences that may persist for generations. Having had the benefits of good schooling and parlayed them into a good life, the individual from a wealthy family is then capable of providing his own offspring with a headstart into the same privileged place in the same system. The cycle of advantaged position thus tends to perpetuate itself. Conversely, the poor, poorly educated individual from a lower social class is not able to place his children in an environment that will facilitate their being well schooled and successful.

Our Predecessors
The idea of a linkage among socioeconomic status, school services, school achievement, and success in later life is not a new one. A number of notable writers have previously observed the inadequate educational opportunities available to the poor and have elaborated upon the condition. Among the first modern sociologists to examine these relationships systematically was Willard Waller, in his classic work, **The Sociology of Teaching.** In 1932 Waller wrote:
Differences of position in the community determine important differences in the school. The child's status as the son of a particular person affects his status in the school and his attitude toward school. The daughter of an influential man in the community does not expect to be treated in the same way as an ordinary child. . . .

The children of poor and humble parents experience the situation with the opposite emphasis. They are those whom the teachers do not favor; they are the ones excluded from things exclusive.[2]

In the midst of World War II, William Lloyd Warner, Robert J. Havinghurst, and Martin B. Loeb observed the social setting of American schools and wrote:
The American school also reflects the socioeconomic order in everything that it does; in what it teaches, whom it teaches, who

[2] Willard Waller, **The Sociology of Teaching** (1932; reprinted, New York, Wiley, 1961), pp. 36 and 38.

does the teaching, who does the hiring and firing of the teachers, and what the children learn in and out of the classroom.

The curricula of the secondary schools provide early pathways to success and failure, they operate in a different way on the several class levels, and they are used in a different way by the children of the higher and lower levels. It is apparent that the high-school curriculum is a mechanism that helps perpetuate our class order.[3]

At the beginning of the sixties, John W. Gardner, in his book entitled **Excellence**, acknowledged that "most of the obvious positive steps toward [achieving] true equality of opportunity have been taken."[4] However, he then proceeded to describe some of the subtleties which continued to cause disparity:

Despite our system of free schools, poverty can still be a profound handicap and wealth a clear advantage. The families at the lowest economic level must all too often live in a slum or near-slum area where the schools do not attract the best teachers. The prosperous citizen can afford a house in an expensive suburb which has a fine school. The good suburban schools are sociologically not unlike the good independent prep schools. The chief difference is that in the suburb, establishing residence is a part—and a very expensive part—of the price of admission (the other part being heavy school taxes). In a way the private prep school is more democratic because it takes a number of scholarship students of truly impoverished parents. There is no possibility of such an arrangement in Scarsdale. A youngster cannot attend the Scarsdale schools unless his parents live in Scarsdale; and that is something that impoverished parents do not commonly do.[5]

In the same year John Gardner's comments were published, James Bryant Conant's now famous book, **Slums and Suburbs**, appeared. Conant's observations were the product of his extensive survey of educational conditions around the nation. His book describes the startling contrast to be found between the quality of education received by children in slums and children in affluent suburbs. He suggests curriculum reforms, teacher training changes, revised graduation requirements, and so on. However, he frames these specific recommendations with the general statement:

[3] William Lloyd Warner, Robert J. Havighurst, and Martin B. Loeb, **Who Shall be Educated** (New York: Harper, 1944), p. xi. (The emphasis is ours.)
[4] John W. Gardner, **Excellence** (New York: Harper & Row, 1961), p. 38.
[5] **Ibid.**, p. 39.

The contrast in the money spent per pupil in wealthy suburban schools and in slum schools of the large cities challenges the concept of equality of opportunity in American public education.[6]

In 1965 Charles S. Benson wrote **The Cheerful Prospect,** in which he describes disparities in the provision of school services and puts forward a comprehensive plan for reforming U.S. education. Benson acknowledges the general low quality of education historically made available to rural students. He then proceeds to state:

In earlier days it was thought to be the rural youth who suffered from educational deprivation, and some of the first state aid schemes were established to channel public revenues toward the support of schools in farm districts. Now attention has shifted to the problem of the slum school in our great cities, a problem brought to light by the high rate of unemployment among educationally deficient urban young people. But our laissez-faire system of public education is not as selective as this in breeding inequalities. Within one state it is possible to find quite startling differences in provision among middle-sized cities, none of which could be described as having any notable amount of slum-school conditions.[7]

The Cheerful Prospect and other books we have quoted are notable for their display of keen insight, clear-cut description, and just plain wisdom. We have obtained many valuable ideas ourselves from them. Nevertheless, in order to understand more fully the requirements for equal educational opportunity and to assist in introducing effective educational reforms, it is important to know the extent and effects of present educational inequities. Accordingly, we need to pursue systematic procedures in order to obtain more precise information. This book represents such an effort.

The Conceptual Framework for the Study

Our purpose is to understand schools, the social and economic forces that influence them, and the influence they in turn have upon their students. This is a task that is laced with complexities. Natural scientists are frequently able to perform controlled experiments in which they can eliminate from consideration all but one possible influence and then test to see its effects. Such opportunities are not

[6] James Bryant Conant, **Slums and Suburbs** (New York: McGraw-Hill, 1961), p. 145.
[7] Charles S. Benson, **The Cheerful Prospect** (Boston: Houghton Mifflin, 1965), p. 2.

readily available to the researcher interested in explaining human social behavior. In addition to our understandable and healthy trepidations about experimenting with people, human processes typically are so complex as virtually to defy controlling all other possible influences while examining one behavioral facet at a time. These complexities have hampered systematic efforts to examine and document schooling inequalities and their consequences.

We, of course, were beset by the same complexities as our predecessors. We have attempted to overcome them by several means. The first of these was by mentally defining or conceptualizing as accurately as possible the phenomena we wanted to study and then attempting to establish relationships among these phenomena. As we will describe later, the essence of our research involved testing these relationships. Here, however, we want to make clear the conceptual framework that underlies our research efforts.

We postulated the existence of four conceptual components, which can be diagrammed as shown in the accompanying figure.

We hypothesized that each component in this chain presently influences its successor. However, we do wish to insert a word of caution here. Quality of available school services is known to be affected by factors in addition to the socioeconomic status of the students being served; academic achievement of students is influenced by conditions other than those that obtain in school, and pupils' postschool opportunity obviously does not depend only on academic achievement while in school. **Thus, no claim is being made that each component in the accompanying diagram is determined solely by its predecessor;** such would be entirely too simple an explanation.

Nevertheless, after acknowledging the existence of additional influences, we hold that each conceptual component in the diagram is a major determinant of its successor. This chain of causal linkage

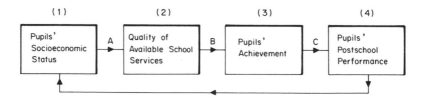

is represented by the three lettered arrows in the diagram.[8] Each of these linkages has been framed as a separate proposition to guide our research. The propositions are as follows:

A. **Socioeconomic Status and School Services.**[9] The quality of school services provided to a pupil is related to his socioeconomic status, and that relationship is such that lower-quality school services are associated with a pupil's being from a lower socioeconomic stratum.

B. **School Services and Pupil Achievement.** A relationship exists between the quality of school services provided to a pupil and his academic achievement, and that relationship is such that higher-quality school services are associated with higher levels of achievement.

C. **Pupil Achievement and Postschool Opportunity.** The postschool opportunities of a pupil are related to his achievement in school, and that relationship is such that higher achievement is associated with "success" and lower achievement is associated with lack of "success."

Setting for the Study

The state of Michigan was selected as the location for the study. Michigan is characterized by a demographic pattern that appears increasingly typical of industrialized states. It contains several major population centers consisting of core cities with surrounding suburbs. In addition, a significant minority of its citizens still live in rural areas with low population densities. Its economy is consistent with this demographic pattern. There is a mixture of heavy manufacturing, the nucleus of new space age industries, substantial agricultural production, and significant extractive and recreational enterprises. In all of

[8] The fourth arrow illustrates a feedback loop wherein the process sequence is presumed to have effects over generations. The father's postschool success influences his children's social position, and so on for their children.
[9] An independent variable that could be used in addition to or in place of "socioeconomic status" is race or minority group membership. That is, many of the disparities we hypothesize as occurring as a consequence of an individual's being of lower socioeconomic status might also be hypothesized as occurring as a consequence of an individual's being a member of a minority racial or ethnic group. The primary reason for not pursuing such a line of inquiry was lack of suitable data across school district boundaries. In addition, however, "socioeconomic status" is a more inclusive concept that encompasses those minority groups whose members tend to appear in disproportionate numbers in lower socioeconomic strata as well as members of the majority.

Table 1.1 Selected 1960 Census Figures for the United States and Five Largest States

Demographic Dimension	United States	Michigan	California	New York	Pennsylvania	Illinois
Total Population	179,323,175	7,823,194	15,717,000	16,782,000	11,319,000	10,081,000
% Urban	69.9	73.4	86.4	85.4	71.6	80.7
% Rural	30.1	26.6	13.6	14.6	28.5	19.3
% Nonwhite	11.42	9.41	8.0	8.9	7.6	10.6
% White-Collar Workers	41.1	40.1	47.3	46.9	39.5	42.3
% Agricultural Workers	6.58	3.12	4.5	1.8	2.6	4.4
% Earning $2,000 or Less	13.04	9.41	8.0	7.7	9.5	9.0
% Earning $10,000 or More	15.05	17.0	21.8	19.9	13.9	20.4
% Housing Owner-Occupied	61.9	74.4	58.4	44.8	68.3	57.8
Median Family Income	$5,660	$6,526	$6,726	$6,371	$5,719	$6,566
Median Years of School Completed	10.6	10.8	12.1	10.7	10.2	10.5
Cities over 10,000	1,688	67	159	78	98	112
Cities over 100,000	130	5	14	8	5	3

these features Michigan appears similar to the most populous states, particularly in the north and northeast. The 1960 census figures in Table 1.1 provide a brief demographic profile of the state.

In terms of the structure and operational nature of its school system, Michigan is typical of most states. The state constitution directs the legislation to "maintain and support a system of free public elementary and secondary schools. . . ." The charge is translated into the reality of educational services by a multilevel administrative network consisting of a state board of education, a state department of education, and 650 local school districts. The diversity of the latter is rather remarkable: they range from Lilliput-like little red schoolhouses to the colossus-sized School District of the City of Detroit with some 300,000 pupils in over 300 schools. The state school finance arrangements also allow for diversity. For example, in 1967–1968, per-pupil expenditure figures ranged from a high in excess of $1,000 to a low of only slightly more than $400. Within the framework of state law, policy for each of these districts is established by a school board of locally elected citizens. A comparison of Michigan's school statistics with those of other states is displayed in Table 1.2.

Along a number of significant demographic and educational dimensions, Michigan bears a sufficient resemblance to large states, particularly in the north and northeast sections of the nation, to allow us to assert that it is not an atypical or unrepresentative setting for our study. We feel confident in saying that what we find to be true in Michigan will also be true to a substantial degree in a majority of the other states.

Sources of Information
The United States probably collects more social statistics on itself than does almost any other nation. In the realm of education, however, we yet have much progress to make. We collect a fair amount of facts about numbers of children in school and matters dealing with revenues for education, but we compile very little information that enables us to examine what is going on in schools. Relatively speaking, Michigan is an exception to this generalization. And, as we mentioned in the Preface, availability of data about schools is one of the reasons for our selecting this state for our study. Despite this comparatively rich informational lode, we still needed to utilize a wide variety of sources, both within the state and without, in order

Table 1.2. Selected School Statistics for the United States and Five Largest States, 1967–1968

Characteristic	United States	Michigan	California	New York	Pennsylvania	Illinois
Total Public School Enrollment	43,940,000	2,059,000	4,446,000	3,320,000	2,261,000	2,202,000
Nonpublic Enrollment as % of Public School Enrollment	15.02%	17.62%	9.64%	27.78%	29.20%	26.39%
Total Number Public School Teachers	1,842,600	78,800	169,700	162,300	96,500	96,900
Total Number Public Schools (1963–64)	104,015	4,418	6,189	4,561	4,752	4,567
Mean Expenditure per Pupil	$684	$753	$803	$1,053	$658	$704
Total Expenditure as % of Personal Income	4.85%	5.19%	5.53%	4.99%	4.01%	3.75%
Median Years of Schooling— Persons 25 +	10.8	10.6	12.1	10.7	10.2	10.5

to identify and accumulate data for our research. Because of these complexities, we will describe here only the major sources of information used in testing our research propositions. In later chapters, we will provide specific details where they enhance understanding of our procedures.

Michigan School Finance Study

Our major source of information was an official statewide educational survey conducted for the Michigan legislature and published in 1968.[10] The survey was directed by Professor J. Alan Thomas of the University of Chicago, and it is described by the State Superintendent of Instruction as "the most comprehensive study of elementary and secondary education" in the state's history. Within Michigan the survey is popularly known as the "Thomas Report," after its director. We too will refer to it by this shorthand label.

The Thomas Report gathered data from almost all public (and many nonpublic) schools and school districts in Michigan. Out of a total (in 1967) of 533 unified school districts (kindergarten through twelfth grade), 517 (97 percent) responded to requests for information. For purposes of our research, a 10 percent random sample of Michigan's unified school districts was drawn and used as a basis for generalizing about the state. There were 533 such districts in 1967, fifty-two of which were selected for study. In addition, Detroit was added on the basis that it was the only district of its magnitude in the state and contained approximately 13 percent of all Michigan's public school students. Moreover, given the concern for urban problems in the United States, we thought it best to include the state's major big city school district.

Equality of Educational Opportunity Survey

The Thomas Report served as the primary source of information for making comparisons of school service quality between **school districts.** However, for making comparisons among individual schools and individual students, this source was supplemented by information collected in Michigan for the Equality of Educational Opportunity Survey (EEOS). This study was authorized by Congress in a provision of the 1964 Civil Rights Act and was conducted by the U.S. Office of Education. The EEOS is generally considered to be the most

---

[10] J. Alan Thomas, **School Finance and Educational Opportunity in Michigan** (Lansing: Michigan Department of Education, 1968).

comprehensive data collection effort ever undertaken in the history of U.S. education.[11]

The sampling procedures employed in the EEOS resulted in the inclusion of fourteen Michigan school districts equally divided between the categories "metropolitan" and "nonmetropolitan."[12] For these fourteen districts, data were analyzed for 5,284 sixth-grade pupils enrolled in eighty-nine elementary schools. From the same districts and schools, we analyzed information on the characteristics of almost 1,300 teachers and eighty-nine principals, as well as educational programs and school facilities.

The Equality of Educational Opportunity Survey was concerned with assessing the incidence of educational inequality by race and ethnic group. Consequently it employed a research sample containing more individuals from minority group populations than is typical of the United States as a whole. These procedures are reflected in a Michigan sample that somewhat overrepresents schools and students from Detroit. As a consequence, the EEOS sample is not strictly representative of students and school-service conditions throughout the entire state of Michigan (though the Thomas data are). We chose to analyze these data because they comprise the only means by which full comparisons can be made among individual schools and among individual students. Despite their limitations, the EEOS data are the best available.

Overview

The chapters that follow are devoted primarily to a systematic examination of the study's three research propositions. In addition, however, we have proceeded further (1) to examine the social and governmental conditions that provide the contextual setting for schools and (2) to include an alternative perspective on the problems of providing schooling for poor children.

Chapter 2 opens with a discussion of the concept of socio-economic status and our means for rendering that concept suitable for empirical investigation. From there the chapter proceeds to discuss the characteristics of our sample of students, schools, and

[11] This is the survey upon which the so-called Coleman Report is primarily based. See James S. Coleman et al., **Equality of Educational Opportunity** (Washington, D.C.: U.S. Government Printing Office, 1966).
[12] The survey grouped schools into these categories on the basis of whether or not they were located in a standard metropolitan statistical area (SMSA) as defined by the Census Bureau.

school districts. The chapter concludes with a definition of the
other concepts employed in the study and a description of the
procedures used in analyzing data statistically.

Chapter 3 describes the levels of analysis at which we examined
Proposition A, social status and school services. The chapter
reviews the scholarly literature on the topic and then turns to a
discussion of our analyses of Thomas Report and EEOS data for
the state of Michigan.

Chapter 4 examines Proposition B. It begins by placing research
on school effectiveness in a historical context and then reviews and
analyzes existing research on the subject. The chapter concludes
with a presentation of our own analyses of the ability of school
services to affect students' performance.

Chapter 5 examines Proposition C by first defining what is meant
by "postschool performance" and then analyzing research that
relates that concept to topics such as individual lifetime earnings,
occupational choice, social mobility, political participation, and social
deviancy.

Chapter 6 describes governmental arrangements and economic
conditions in Michigan that determine the quality of education
available to a student. We examine the school finance statutes and
attempt to explain how these provisions operate to provide low-
quality services to children from lower social classes.

Chapter 7 opens with a discussion of the concept of capital
embodiment, proceeds to describe discrepancies in embodiment
between low- and high-social-class children at the time they first
enter school, and concludes with a discussion of alternative
strategies for delivering and financing school services.

2

Definitions, Data, and Analytical Design

What is far superior to theories without facts or facts without theories, is obviously that happy combination of fact and theory in which the facts are illuminated by the theories and the theories are tested by the facts.[1]

[1] Harold A. Larrabee, **Reliable Knowledge** (Boston: Houghton Mifflin Co., 1948), p. 166.

In the three research propositions stated in the preceding chapter
we attempted to make clear our basic thesis, namely, that
socioeconomic status discrimination exists in the means by which
school services are provided, and that such discrimination has both
short-term and long-term consequences for the individuals involved.
Now we wish to specify more clearly the "facts" and methods we
shall use to test that thesis. We shall begin with a discussion of
socioeconomic status, our particular measures for that variable, and
the socioeconomic profiles of our sample. We then shall define
briefly what we mean by school services, pupil achievement, and
postschool performance. We conclude with a description of our
data processing methods and statistical procedures.

Socioeconomic Status

By **socioeconomic status** (SES) we refer to the results of a
complicated social rating process, a process that appears to take
place in some form wherever humans live together in groups.[2] In
layman's language, the equivalent terms for socioeconomic status
may be expressions such as "social class" and "social order." We
will use the more technical phrase "socioeconomic status"
primarily because it is consistent with the sociological research
upon which we wish to draw.[3] However, so that a reader can carry a
more vivid mental image when we begin to speak, for example, of
"high SES" and "low SES" students, we describe in detail on page
24 some of the life-style characteristics of the students in our
sample. Before turning to that description, however, we first wish
to define our use of the term "socioeconomic status" and then
explain our measures for it.

There is little disagreement regarding the existence of a social
hierarchy or the idea that an individual's position in such a system
significantly influences his perceptions and behavior. There is,
however, controversy among social scientists as to which
characteristics of individuals and groups are most important in the

[2] Much has been written on the topic of social stratification, but in our view
the most comprehensive coverage of relevant theoretical concepts and
empirical findings is contained in the work by J. A. Kahl, **The American
Class Structure** (New York: Rinehart, 1959).
[3] Also, we have chosen not to emphasize the term "social class" because
in sociological research it is a technical term generally reserved to describe
more rigid and clearly defined social ranking systems than that which operates in the United States.

hierarchy. Various writers have grappled with these difficulties and have arrived at different conclusions.

Karl Marx deduced from his analysis of history that the primary determinant of social status was one's relationship to the means of production. He held that those individuals who stood in the same relationship formed a "class." Classes of individuals enjoyed the benefits, or suffered the exploitative consequences, of a particular economic system to varying degrees, and these variations served as the basis for the social hierarchy.[4] The German sociologist Max Weber criticized Marx's views as being overly simple; he contended that economic position was of itself insufficient to explain fully the interaction patterns of groups of individuals. He demonstrated that even within specific economic groupings there were varying "styles of life." Moreover, in addition to life style, Weber held that "power" was not a simple function of economic conditions; it must be taken into account separately in explaining social hierarchies.[5]

Marx and Weber are notable for their theoretical insights and logical formulations, but systematic empirical inquiry regarding the nature of the social stratification process awaited the fieldwork of American sociologists such as William Lloyd Warner and August B. Hollingshead. Beginning in the early 1930s, these men and their colleagues conducted a series of community studies that continue to serve as a useful starting-point for research into the structure of American society.[6] Their methodology consisted of living in a community and ascertaining its stratification structure by requesting residents to rate one another in terms of their position in the town's social hierarchy. Warner labeled this method **evaluated participation (EP)** and explained that his investigations were

posed on the proposition that those who interact in the social system of a community evaluate the participation of those around

[4] An explanation of Marx's views on social stratification is contained in Karl Marx and Friedrich Engels, **Manifesto of the Communist Party** (New York: International Publishers, 1932).
[5] Weber's views are described in "Class, Status and Power," in **From Max Weber: Essays in Sociology,** translated and edited by H. H. Gerth and C. Wright Mills (New York: Oxford University Press, 1946).
[6] The first of these community studies, **Yankee City,** was of a New England town then containing some 17,000 inhabitants. This was followed by **Old City,** a study of a southern town of about 10,000, and **Jonesville,** a midwestern town of 6,000. Hollingshead was the author of **Elm Town's Youth,** an early 1940 study of adolescents in Morristown, Illinois. An insightful description of the Negro section of Chicago, **Black Metropolis,** by F. S. St. Clair Drake and Horace R. Cayton, is part of the same generation of studies.

them, that the place where an individual participates is evaluated, and that the members of the community are explicitly or implicitly aware of the ranking and translate their evaluations of such social participation into social-class ratings that can be communicated to the investigator.[7]

Despite some advantages, evaluated participation has methodological shortcomings.[8] It is cumbersome and sometimes impractical to employ. J. A. Kahl gives the following explanation of this difficulty:

Procedures for placing individuals from interviews are laborious and expensive, and depend upon the efforts of highly skilled interviewers. Furthermore, they cannot be used in large cities where people do not know many of their townsmen by name, and they are difficult to use for comparative studies which draw their subjects from several different towns, for it is hard to decide when the strata of one town are equal to those of another.[9]

To meet the difficulty, attempts were made to construct indexes that could be applied rapidly but that would still correlate highly with the results of a field interview procedure such as EP. A number of such indexes have been developed, but the only one that has been validated thoroughly is Warner's **index of status characteristics** (ISC). From the wide range of possible ingredients, a combination of six items was found to provide the highest correlation with the results of the evaluated participation process. They are (1) occupation, (2) amount of income, (3) source of income, (4) house type, (5) dwelling area, and (6) education.

In using the ISC, an individual is rated on each dimension, and the ratings are computed in accordance with a formula to provide a

---

[7] William Lloyd Warner, Marcia Meeker, and Kenneth Eels, **Social Class in America** (Chicago: Science Research Associates, 1949), p. 35.

[8] The use of the evaluated participation technique did not always result in identical findings. In some community studies social stratification was found to be more complex than in others, and it was difficult to determine if this complexity was a consequence of the measuring procedures or an accurate reflection of reality. For example, in **Yankee City**, Warner discovered a six-class structure, whereas, in **Elmtown**, Hollingshead's analyses revealed but five strata. However, even with its imperfections, there is general agreement that the evaluated participation process has proved to be of practical value in attempting to understand the social structure of our society.

[9] Kahl, **American Class Structure**, p. 41.

unitary socioeconomic status score. In validation studies of the ISC, this score has been found to correlate between 0.72 and 0.96 with status ratings arrived at by EP.[10]

In a subsequent research attempt to identify simple but precise predictors of socioeconomic status, Kahl and Davis employed a factor analytic technique to examine a range of potential status indicators. They found that the individual's occupation was the best single proxy measure of his social rank. That is, a rating of an individual on a scale of occupational prestige provided the most powerful prediction of his overall socioeconomic status.[11]

The Thomas Report and EEOS collected somewhat different information on the dimension of socioeconomic status. Consequently, we followed different procedures in arriving at SES measures for the two sets of data. In each instance, however, we attempted to operate in a manner that was consistent with the logic and findings of Warner and his associates.

Thomas Report SES Measures

The Thomas Report queried school principals as to the character of their school's attendance area on three demographic dimensions: (1) average annual income of residents, (2) occupational type, and (3) type and value of housing. Our procedure was to assign each principal's response a number and then form a weighted average of each of these numbers for the district, the weight assigned to each principal being the number of students enrolled in his school. These averages then served as three "subjective" indexes of school districts' SES and allowed us to rank the fifty-two districts in our sample from low to high in terms of their SES.

Elementary school principals tend to be quite knowledgeable about the social makeup of the population their schools serve, and we expected their estimates to be relatively accurate. Nevertheless, their information was the result of individuals' perceptions, with all the attendant problems of reliability. Consequently, we felt the need

[10] Ibid., p. 43.
[11] J. A. Kahl and James A. Davis, "A Comparison of Indexes of Socio-Economic Status," **American Sociological Review,** 20 (June 1953), 317–325. Additional description and analysis of the relationship of occupation to social status is contained in Albert J. Reiss, **Occupations and Social Status** (New York: The Free Press of Glencoe, 1961).

to buttress it with two more objective measures based on information from the 1960 census.[12]

The first of these "objective" SES indicators was derived by matching census tracts as best as possible to school district boundaries and multiplying for each district the median years of schooling in the adult population by the median family income. The resulting number also served as a basis for comparing school districts' SES.

A second "objective" measure of districtwide SES was derived from data regarding the **proportion of pupils from poverty-impacted families** (PPP), those with incomes of $3,000 and less.[13] Our procedure here was taken as an inverse indicator of the district's SES; that is, the lower the percentage of students from "poverty" families, the higher the district mean SES.

In order to discern the range and general SES distribution of the fifty-two districts in our sample, we ranked districts on their SES scores, divided them into eight equal segments, and then calculated the median SES score for each of these octiles. Tables 2.1 and 2.2 display the results of this procedure for our two "objective" measures of SES.

A Digression for Format

Tables 2.1 and 2.2 illustrate the manner in which we display a number of our findings. Consequently, we need to explain the format we use and the notations that accompany that format. All

[12] The 1960 census information was collected about eight years prior to the Thomas Report data with which we compare it. Thus, its accuracy can be questioned. The social nature of many neighborhoods does evolve over time. This evolution, however, does not appear to occur as rapidly or as widely as it sometimes seems. Tryon reported research results, from comparing 1940 and 1950 census information from the same neighborhoods, that indicate that the SES level remains relatively stable over ten-year intervals. He reports a correlation coefficient of 0.90 for census tract characteristics over time. People may move out of particular neighborhoods, but their replacements tend to be of the same SES. Robert C. Tryon, "Biosocial Constancy of Urban Social Areas," paper read before The American Psychological Assn., 1955, as reported in David Krech, Richard S. Crutchfield, and Edgerton L. Ballachey, **Individual in Society** (New York: McGraw-Hill, 1962), p. 325.

[13] This figure can readily be recognized as the poverty level definition embodied in the 1967 amendments to Title I of the Elementary and Secondary Education Act. Under conditions of full appropriations, federal school aid funds are to be distributed to states and school districts in proportion to the number of their pupils from families with annual income of this amount or less.

Table 2.1. Districtwide SES Score Octile Medians (Education × Income)[16]

	Low SES						High SES	
Octile	1	2	3	4	5	6	7	8
Median	35	44	49	60	64	66	79	98

Table 2.2. Districtwide SES Score Octile Medians (Percent Poverty Pupils)[17]

	High SES						Low SES	
Octile	1	2	3	4	5	6	7	8
Median	7.3	10.6	14.1	17.2	22.1	25.7	29.4	33.1

variables used in the study have been numbered sequentially. If
the information for the variable was obtained from Thomas Report
data, the variable number is preceded by the letter "T." If the
information was obtained from EEOS data it is preceded by the letter
"E."[14] All variables are listed, and a substantial portion of the
computer displays[15] are contained in Appendix B. Within Appendix
B there are three sections. Section 1 contains statistical tables
relating to interdistrict comparisons (Thomas Report variables).
Section 2 displays tables of interschool comparisons (EEOS variables) and Section 3 shows interstudent comparisons (EEOS
variables).

Here is an example of how the notation system operates. The SES
distribution displayed in Table 2.1 was arrived at by octiling the
Thomas Report sample according to variable number 181 and then
computing the median score on the same variable, 181, for the
subjects in each octile. This comparison can be found in the
Thomas Report section of Appendix B. Consequently, our notation

[14] The questionnaires employed to collect Thomas Report data can be obtained from the Michigan Department of Education. EEOS questionnaires are
printed in the Coleman Report Appendices. An explanation of the manner
in which each questionnaire response was cited for purposes of this research
can be obtained from the authors. Space limitations do not permit the inclusion of such detailed information in this book.
[15] Because of an error several additional computer runs were found to be
significant after Appendix B had been prepared. A discussion of these runs
is included in the text. They may be obtained on request from the authors.
[16] T, 181 V. 181.
[17] T, 182 V. 182.

Table 2.3. Median SES (OEI) Rank for Each of Eight Strata[18]

	Low SES							High SES
Octile	1	2	3	4	5	6	7	8
Median	42	53	61	66	81	101	124	158

reads "T, 181 V. 181." The appendix location of all comparison tables and statistical displays will be noted accordingly.

We conducted a number of statistical tests to assess the degree to which our "subjective" and "objective" measures of SES were similar. From these analyses, all five measures appear to be closely related. (The lowest rank order correlation coefficient obtained in comparing all possible paired combinations of the five variables was 0.57. Most of the other correlations were substantially higher.) Because of this relatively high degree of association, most of what we describe in our comparisons of school districts in Chapter Three will be based on only two SES indicators, the "objective" measures obtained from census information.

SES Measures from the EEOS

Students in the EEOS Michigan sample were asked a number of questions about their parents and homes that were in keeping with components of Warner's index of status characteristics. From responses to these questions we constructed two indexes of student socioeconomic status. One of these indexes was constructed by combining information about a student's father's occupation and education. The other SES index was a symbolic measure of the level of material possessions in the student's home.

We will refer to the first SES measure as the **occupation-education index** (OEI). The process by which this index was calculated can be seen from the following example. If a black student responded to EEOS question number 12 (a question about father's occupation) that his father was a farm worker, we then referred to 1960 census occupational information to find that the mean annual income for nonwhite farm workers was $1,679.[19] If he responded to question number 11 (a question about father's schooling) that his father had

[18] E, 179 V. 179.
[19] The levels of mean annual income for occupational categories are listed separately for whites and nonwhites.

little or no schooling, we used the weight assigned to this schooling level (4) and multiplied it by the father's income level. Thus, SES = education × income = 6,716 units.

Using this method, SES values were computed for each student in the EEOS Michigan sample. SES scores were then ranked from low to high and divided into eight groups of equal size. Each of these octiles then came to represent a socioeconomic stratum, and the eight strata taken together became the socioeconomic baseline against which we examined the distribution of school services. The median SES score was calculated for each octile so as to illustrate the range of the distribution and the degree to which the eight strata were different. The total possible spread is from 1 to 176. The strata median SES scores for our sample are displayed in Table 2.3. The breadth of the range indicates that our student sample represents a substantial portion of the total SES spectrum.

A second measure of socioeconomic status was derived from an EEOS query as to the number and kinds of material possessions in the student's home. The EEOS posed nine questions asking a student whether or not his home contained specific material items (refrigerator, automobile, television, and so on). Responses to these queries were compiled into a scale for each student running from a low of one to a high of nine.

Possession scales have been used previously in studies of social stratification[20] and in the applied research surveys of those interested in the potential consumer market for various manufactured products. We employed a possession scale as a measure of socioeconomic status because it seems reasonable to assume that the type and quantity of material objects an individual owns reflects his position in the social and economic hierarchy as people perceive it. For our sample of 5,284 sixth grade students we found a statistically significant relationship between our first described scale (OEI) and the **index of possessions** (IP). Moreover, when these two main measures were compared separately with other student SES measures (mother's education level, number of books in the home, number of rooms in the home, and so on), they both tended to bear significant statistical relationships to the same attributes. This co-correlation also reinforces the commonality of the two measures.

[20] The research work described in Stuart F. Chapin, **Contemporary American Institutions** (New York: Harper, 1935), was the first to employ such a scale systematically.

Social Strata Contrasts

In order to gain a more complete understanding of the students in
our sample, we constructed a "profile" of life style attributes for the
highest and lowest SES octiles. This analysis was done by ordering
students' SES scores according to rank, dividing them into octiles,
and then computing for each octile the median student's response
on EEOS questions regarding parents, siblings, conditions at home,
and so on. Rank ordering into octiles was done both by OEI and the
IP. The complete tabulations from this analysis can be seen in
Appendix B. What we present below is a generalized description
for sixth grade students. Our effort here is to describe those life
style characteristics that distinguish low- and high-status students
from one another.

Low SES Students[21]

A typical low SES student is about the same age as or slightly older
than his higher-status schoolmates (eleven years for sixth graders).
However, he is more likely than they to be nonwhite. (The lower SES
octiles generally contain many more Negro, Mexican-American,
Puerto Rican, American Indian, and Oriental children than do the
higher strata.) He comes from a home that has more persons living
in it, particularly more children, but with relatively few rooms.
Often, his father does not live with the family. He is either
fatherless or has a stepfather. Regardless of who it is, the individual
who serves as his father is probably a school dropout whose
employment is likely to be of an unskilled nature and low paying.

The child's mother may have attended high school for one or two
years, but typically she did not graduate. Also, she is likely to hold
a full-time job that, much more frequently than is the case for her
upper-stratum counterpart, may constitute the major source of
income for the family. The home, in addition to being relatively small
and crowded, contains fewer material objects than upper-stratum
homes.

This picture of the low SES students' relative deprivation is
verified by his teacher, who reports that his home environment is
generally poor and that he comes to school ill clothed and ill fed.
The composite picture is one of a child who is likely to arrive at

---

[21] These profiles were constructed for sixth grade students by E, 168 and
179 V. 154, 155, 157, 158, 159, 160, 161, 162, 163, 164 and 170. (See
explanation of format on page 20.

school each day hungry and unhappy and not particularly prepared
for a day of learning.

High SES Students[22]

This student's teacher reports that his home environment is generally
good, and every question he answers about himself confirms the
teacher's impression. He lives with his real father, who is likely to
have attended college and to be in a managerial or professional
occupation. Family income is steady and tends to be above $10,000
annually. His mother is likely to have graduated from high school,
but, in contrast to the low-status student, the family's economic
circumstances do not press her into seeking employment outside
the home. The house in which he lives is relatively more spacious
and occupied by fewer people. Moreover, there are more material
possessions, including more that may stimulate his intellect. These
more comfortable circumstances are accompanied by relative
stability. He is only half as likely as his low SES sixth grade peer to
have transferred among schools. In short, his chances of leaving
for school each morning with his physical needs satisfied and his
mind psychologically honed for a day of learning are substantially
better than that of his low SES schoolmate.

Schoolwide SES

When we extended our analysis to compare schools we needed a
means by which to represent the SES of an entire school. Our
procedure for doing this was to calculate the average of each SES
indicator for the students in each school and allow these scores to
represent the entire school. As was the case with individuals, we
arrived at a view of the social stratification of the eighty-six
elementary schools in our EEOS sample by arranging them in octiles
on the IP scale and obtaining the median in each octile. The resulting
intraoctile medians are displayed in Table 2.4.

   As can be seen by inspecting the display in Table 2.4, the range
of schoolwide SES is not as great as that for individual students.
This, of course, is a consequence of both the diversity of students'
social backgrounds in any one school and our averaging procedures.
We do not bother to present life style profiles for schools because
they are very much in keeping with the foregoing characterizations
for individual students.

[22] Constructed from the measures listed in footnote 21.

Table 2.4. Schoolwide IP Score Octile Medians[23]

	Low SES						High SES	
Octile	1	2	3	4	5	6	7	8
Median	6.1	6.8	7.2	7.5	7.8	8.0	8.3	8.6

Other Definitions

SES constitutes one of our primary independent variables; consequently, we have spent considerable time attempting to define the concept and to explain the means by which we measured it. However, our arguments also hinge on three additional clusters of variables, and we will now attempt to describe them.

School Services

By this term we refer to the processes and objects connected with schools that are designed to affect the outlook and behavior of students. This is a broad category that ranges all the way from the physical appearance of school buildings and their environmental settings, whether in a city slum, rural isolation, or suburban splendor, to the difficult-to-measure actions of persons such as teachers, counselors, and principals.

We review a number of research studies that have previously assessed the effectiveness of a variety of school service variables. In addition we conduct our own analyses. Our measures of school services are taken from literally hundreds of questions employed by the EEOS and Thomas survey teams. The components measured by these queries can be classified generally into five categories. (1) administrative services, (2) equipment and facilities, (3) curricular and instructional arrangements, (4) staff characteristics, and (5) student environment. The specific items within each of these categories will be presented in later chapters.

Pupil Achievement

Here again we have a comprehensive term. Of course, the question of what students should obtain from schooling is fundamentally a matter of values. It is our view that schools should (whatever else they are to do) impart to students certain cognitive skills along with the self-confidence necessary to use them. There exist many dimensions of student performance, some of which are more easily measured than others. Our measures consist of students' scores on standardized tests (for example, verbal ability, and reading and

[23] E, 168 V. 168.

mathematics achievement). We do not wish to mislead the reader into believing that we think that these are the only outcomes of schooling. We acknowledge the need for schools to concentrate on a wide range of skills and attitudes, as well as cognitive understandings. Nevertheless, our measures of school performance touch directly on several of what we view as the schools' primary functions, reading, mathematics, and feelings of self-confidence.

Postschool Performance

By this label we refer to the wide range of activities and events with which an individual has contact upon leaving school. This category includes matters such as lifetime earnings, occupational attainment, political participation, social and economic mobility from generation to generation, social deviancy, and chances for further schooling. Our attempt here is to assess the effect that skills learned in school have upon such phenomena. Neither the EEOS nor the Thomas Report addresses this question. Consequently, our information on this subject is derived from a compilation of findings from other studies that have touched upon the topic.

Statistical Procedures

Suppose we wish to examine our proposition A, that the quality of school services available to students depends on their socioeconomic status. Suppose, for example, that we use as subjects our eighty-nine elementary schools in the EEOS sample. Let us for these schools contrast EEOS variable 8, the age of the school building, with the average school value of EEOS variable 179, student socioeconomic status. An examination of the relationship between these two variables has a direct bearing on the confirmation or rejection of our research proposition.

The computer printout comparing these two variables is shown in the accompanying diagram. First, let us explain the meaning of the

Octiles According to Variable 179 6–SES Level							
Medians from Variable 8 Age of Building							
Octile	1	2	3	4	5	6	7	8
Median	7	7	5	6	7	6	4	4
NTRUE = 81							
STUDENT T = −2.21513							

upper four lines in this display. These four lines are printed to provide
illustrative material for our discussions. The information required for
a statistical test of the relationship between the two variables,
average school SES and school building age, is provided in the last
two lines of the display. In order to obtain the upper four lines we
ordered the schools in our EEOS sample from lowest to highest
according to the average of the SES index for the students in each
school. Then we divided the schools into octiles so that each octile
has higher values of average SES than the one preceding it. The
octiles are numbered from 1 (lowest SES) to 8 (highest SES).
Each octile can then be considered as a separate group of schools.
For each of these octile groups we calculate the median age of
school building. The median can be easily obtained by ordering the
schools within each octile from lowest to highest according to the
age of the school building. The school in the middle of this ordered
group has the median building age for the octile. These medians are
printed in the computer printout display above. In order to interpret
the display we must look to the definition of variable number 8.
Table 2.5 shows how this variable was constructed. From the
computer printout we see that the median value of variable
8 for octile 1 (the lowest SES octile) is 7, and for octile 8 (the
highest SES octile) the median value is 4. The value of 7 corresponds to a school building age of forty years or older whereas a
value of 4 corresponds to an age between ten and nineteen years.
The computer printout display also shows us the distribution of the
medians for the schools in the intermediate octiles.

Table 2.5. Construction of EEOS Variable 8, Age of School Building

Variable Value	EEOS Question (Principal's Questionnaire)
	10. About how old is the main classroom building of your school plant?
1	(A) Less than 1 year old
2	(B) 1–4 years
3	(C) 5–9 years
4	(D) 10–19 years
5	(E) 20–29 years
6	(F) 30–39 years
7	(G) 40 years or older
blank*	Other

* The answer was disregarded and the school dropped from the analysis in
the particular run in question.)

The choice of the octiling variable is determined in most cases by the nature of the particular research proposition being examined. Under each proposition there is a separate set of "independent" and "dependent" variables. These terms are used here in an intuitive causal sense rather than a rigorous statistical sense; that is, under the proposition the latter variables (dependent variables) are described as being determined by the former (independent variables).[24] In statistics, strictly speaking, there are no dependent or independent variables; rather, there are only covariates. In our work octiling is done with the independent variable and the medians are determined from the dependent variable. For example, in Proposition A the intuitive causal sense is that socioeconomic status is the independent variable. Hence, in our example we octile by EEOS variable 179 and median by EEOS variable 8.

Listed in the fifth line of the computer printout display is an item labeled "NTRUE". This is the number of subjects considered in the particular analysis at hand. In our example the subjects were eighty-one schools. This is eight less than the total number of schools in the EEOS sample. The data from these eight remaining schools were not in a form that allowed us to include them in this particular computer run; that is, they fell under the classification "blank" in the construction of variable 8.

Let us now discuss the statistic, STUDENT T, given at the bottom of each display.[25] To obtain this statistic we first rank the schools in our example from one to eighty-one according to the value of the schools' average SES. Then we rank them from one to eighty-one according to the value of the schools' age. Thus we have two sets of ranks; SES rank and building age rank. The STUDENT T is computed from NTRUE and the correlation between these two sets of ranks. For a given NTRUE the magnitude of the STUDENT T increases from zero as the magnitude of the rank correlation increases from zero.

Suppose that our hypothesis is that there is no association between SES and building age. Statisticians call this the "null hypothesis." If this hypothesis is true we would expect that there would exist very little or no correlation between the SES rank and the building age rank. Accordingly, for a given NTRUE the STUDENT T should be near zero. Under the assumption of the truth of the null

[24] The dependence is never assumed to be exclusive in our hypotheses; that is, there may be other variables which affect the dependent variable.
[25] A detailed description of the statistical procedures is given in Appendix A.

hypothesis, statisticians have derived and tabled the probability distribution for the statistic STUDENT T. If for a given random sample we find from the probability distribution that in fact the observed magnitude of the STUDENT T has a very small probability of occurring then we reject the null hypothesis. More speciflcally we choose a threshold value for STUDENT T such that the probability under the null hypothesis of achieving a magnitude of STUDENT T over that threshold is only one in twenty.[26] Then if a magnitude of STUDENT T greater than the threshold is observed we reject the hypothesis that, in our example, school SES and building age are **not** related. Any value of STUDENT T over the threshold is said to be **significant.**

The threshold value of STUDENT T for NTRUE = 81 is about 1.99. We see from our computer printout display that STUDENT T = −2.21513, which is greater in magnitude than the threshold. Thus we reject the hypothesis that average school SES and school building age are unrelated, and we thereby accept the opposite hypothesis.

The direction of the relationship between the two variables is indicated by the sign of STUDENT T. In our example this sign is negative, indicating that increasing SES values are associated with decreasing building ages.

[26] We used a two-tailed test at the 0.05 level.

3

Socioeconomic Status and School Services

An important part of the American Dream was low social or economic status would not be a serious barrier to the education of any child of adequate intelligence.[1]

[1] Kenneth B. Clark, Foreword to Patricia Cayo Sexton's **Education and Income** (New York: Viking, 1964).

In this chapter we test our first proposition, that:

The quality of school services provided to a pupil is related to his socioeconomic status, and that relationship is such that lower-quality school services are associated with a pupil's being from a lower socioeconomic status household.

The history of educational reform can be viewed as a struggle to determine who will have access to schooling. From this nation's beginning, tensions have existed between those who view education as an instrument for maintaining inherited social class differences, and those who believe schools should be a vehicle by which to overcome such distinctions through individual achievement. Historically, few have argued that schools are obliged to provide society with identical products. Rather, the general view has been, and still is, that the provision of equal access to schooling is a societal duty. However, as Mann makes clear in the following statement, the early definition of such access was a minimal one:

The sole mark of equality in the [1918] educational mosaic was the legal right of every child to receive some schooling . . . the quality varied immensely, not only from state to state, but also from district to district in any given state and even among schools within the same district.²

More than a half century later, as we demonstrate in this chapter, the quality of available school services in Michigan still varies from district to district, from school to school, and from child to child.

Research Antecedents

It would be tedious to present a full accounting of all past research efforts, journalistic portrayals, and citizens' complaints relating to Proposition A. However, a partial catalogue of the systematic research efforts of others does provide useful background for our Michigan results. Because of the dynamics of discrimination against some ethnic groups, much related research deals with both social class and ethnicity. Thus the following review has two focal points: (1) inequity between socioeconomic levels and (2) inequity between ethnic groups. Both kinds of research provide background for our results, even though our primary concern is with the relationship between school services and socioeconomic status. To facilitate

---

² Mann, Arthur, "A Historical Overview: The Lumpenproletariat, Education, and Compensatory Action," in **The Quality of Inequality: Urban and Suburban Public Schools**, ed. Charles U. Daly (Chicago: The University of Chicago Center for Policy Study, 1968), p. 15.

understanding, we have classified the findings of other studies by
the patterns of inequity they examine: (1) interdistrict, (2) interschool,
and (3) interstudent. We take up each of these categories in sequence.

Interdistrict Inequity

There have been very few systematic, large-scale tests of interdistrict
inequities. However, there are three recent studies, two done in
California and the other in Michigan, that are worthy of note. On the
basis of an examination of 392 school districts in California, Benson
concludes:

**Thus, it would appear that districts wherein a large proportion of
children enter school with environmental advantages are the districts best provided with school resources and that districts in
which a relatively large proportion of children enter school under
environmental handicaps are least well provided with the means
through which these handicaps could be overcome.**[3]

The drama of Benson's findings is somewhat dampened by the
fact that he had access to data on only a limited number of school
services. We suspect that had he had more information, he would
have uncovered an even more extensive pattern of discrimination.

Another recent California study was conducted by Charles Hansen.
He examined the quality of school services in surburban and urban
school districts throughout the San Francisco Bay area. He found
that on almost every dimension high SES districts provided higher-
quality services to students. Moreover, within districts, particularly
the heavily urban school district of Oakland, he found discrimination
against low SES students. There appeared to be more money spent
on instructional materials for poorer students, but when **total** instructional expenditures (including teachers' salaries) were considered,
the expenditure pattern shifted dramatically. More experienced and
more educated teachers in high SES schools accounted for the significantly higher dollar costs in the education of high SES students.[4]

Perhaps the most detailed research antecedent is the previously
mentioned study conducted by J. Alan Thomas for the Michigan
Department of Education.[5] In it Thomas concludes:

[3] Charles S. Benson et al., **State and Local Fiscal Relationships in Public
Education in California**, a report of the Senate Fact Finding Committee on
Revenue and Taxation published by the Senate of the State of California,
(March 1965), p. 58.
[4] Charles E. Hansen, "Central City and Suburb: A Study of Educational
Opportunity" (unpublished doctoral dissertation, University of California,
Berkeley, 1969).
[5] J. Alan Thomas, **School Finance and Educational Opportunity in Michigan**
(Lansing: Michigan Department of Education, 1968).

The most favorable opportunities (in terms of . . . school services
. . .) are available to students who live in districts of (a) high per-
pupil state equalized valuation, (b) high expenditures per pupil
for education, (c) large size as measured by enrollment, (d) high
social class in terms of levels of income, quality of residence,
and a preponderance of higher status occupations.[6]

Although some of the data employed in this study were collected
by Thomas, we have had a greater opportunity to perform more
detailed analyses. Consequently, the results presented later in this
chapter expand substantially upon those that he reports.

Despite some limitations of scope, the Benson, Hansen, and Thomas
findings suggest strongly that low SES districts provide fewer and
lower-quality services than do high SES districts.

Interschool Inequity

Our primary intent is to demonstrate that school service disparities
exist between districts and that such disparities work to the
disadvantage of low SES students. Nevertheless, the dynamics
behind these disparities are more pervasive; they also operate to
precipitate inequities between individual schools. Several studies
demonstrate that services tend to be distributed in such a way that
schools with larger concentrations of poor children receive fewer
services than do schools with a preponderance of children of higher
socioeconomic status. Dollard's study of a city in the South was one
of the first systematic explorations of this type of inequity. His
conclusion was that in "Southerntown" almost all facets of public life
and services were directed at establishing and perpetuating a
castelike distinction between whites and Negroes.[7] Thus, educational
services were consciously distributed in a fashion favorable to white,
and therefore, for the most part, higher social-class children.

In 1961, Patricia Cayo Sexton repeated and expanded Dollard's
findings in a large northern city.[8] By ranking schools according to
the income levels of families residing within attendance boundaries,
she was able to examine the range and quality of school services
among "Big City's" 240 elementary schools. She discovered
significant differences in class sizes, percentages of uncertified
teachers, building ages, substandard facilities, and availability of
free meals. These differences all tended to favor schools serving

---

[6] Ibid., p. 63.
[7] John Dollard, **Caste and Class in a Southern Town** (New Haven: Yale
University Press, 1937).
[8] Sexton, **Education and Income.**

children of higher socioeconomic status. Similar differences were demonstated among the seventeen high schools in "Big City."

In 1964 the National Opinion Research Center of the University of Chicago undertook a research effort for the U.S. Office of Education.[9] This study was designed to assess the social and political forces that surrounded school board decisions about racial desegregation in fifteen large northern and southern cities. In almost every case, the preliminaries of the political process had included a study by citizens or school officials of the relationship between school services and ethnicity. Each study demonstrated that Negro (poor) children received fewer services than white and affluent children. A subsequent study of medium-sized northern cities where school desegregation had taken place revealed that here, too, citizens' groups had demonstrated inequities in the distribution of school services.[10]

The most ambitious research effort that bears on inequities among schools is the so-called Coleman Report.[11] Coleman and his colleagues described a number of school services that were inequitably distributed among white and Negro children. This information, combined with the evidence of racial separation by schools, supports the contention that the quality of educational services is distributed inequitably among schools. Further analyses of the data from the Coleman Report by Mayeske and others provide additional evidence of systematic differences in the delivery of school services. These differences range from the provision of free lunch and milk programs to the average verbal ability of teachers, and all the differences tend to favor children of higher socioeconomic status.

Two other examinations of school inequities are worthy of note. The first, by Katzman, was a study of fifty-six elementary schools in Boston.[12] In it he demonstrates that services such as staff persons

[9] Robert L. Crain, **The Politics of School Desegregation** (Chicago: Aldine, 1968).
[10] Robert T. Stout and Morton Inger, **School Desegregation: Progress in Eight Cities**, a report to the U.S. Commission on Civil Rights, 1966.
[11] James S. Coleman, **et al.**, **Equality of Educational Opportunity** (Washington, D.C.: U.S. Office of Education, 1966). See also George W. Mayeske, **et al.**, Technical Note Number 61, **Correlational and Regression Analyses of Differences between the Achievement Levels of Ninth Grade Students from the Educational Opportunities Survey** (Washington, D.C.: U.S. Office of Education, National Center for Educational Statistics, March 11, 1968).
[12] Martin T. Katzman, "Distribution and Production in a Big City Elementary School System," **Yale Economic Essays,** (Spring 1968), pp. 201–256.

per child, percent of tenured teachers, and amount of teacher turnover are distributed in such a fashion as to favor children of higher socioeconomic status. The other study by Thornblad concentrated on the elementary schools of Chicago and presents essentially the same conclusions.[13] School services in the low income sections of the city are not equal to those provided to students in middle and high income areas.

Interstudent Inequity

Perhaps the first significant research in the contemporary examination of interstudent inequity was conducted by the Lynds[14] and by Warner, Meeker, and Eels.[15] In the small northern cities in which they chose to examine social stratification, they described both the obvious practices and the subtle techniques by which local school officials gave advantaged treatment to the sons and daughters of middle-class and wealthy citizens.

Subsequent research has focused on the mechanism of tracking, or homogenous grouping, by which children are separated within a school according to some supposed academic or occupational criteria. A thorough study of the consequences of this practice was undertaken in Berkeley, California.[16] Prior to the total racial desegregation of the Berkeley public schools, tracking of students in junior high schools and the single senior high school was accompanied by almost complete separation of white and black children within any school. Because in Berkeley ethnicity and socioeconomic status tend to be related, racial separation also accomplished an effective separation by social class. Thus, white students of higher socioeconomic status were placed in "advanced" classes, and black, lower-status students were placed in "general" or "remedial" classes. The process was accompanied by other forms of discrimination, such as in college counseling and participation in extracurricular activities.

A more recent documentation of the consequences of certain forms of grouping or tracking is contained in the court record for

[13] Eric C. Thornblad, "The Fiscal Impact of a High Concentration of Low Income Families upon the Public Schools" (unpublished doctoral dissertation, University of Illinois, Urbana, 1966).
[14] Robert S. Lynd and Helen M. Lynd, **Middletown in Transition** (New York: Harcourt, Brace, 1937).
[15] William Lloyd Warner, Marcia Meeker, and Kenneth Eels, **Social Class in America** (Chicago: Science Research Associates, 1949).
[16] Berkeley Unified School District, Board of Education, Citizens Committee, "De Facto Segregation in the Berkeley Public Schools" (Berkeley, California: Berkeley Unified School District, November 19, 1963, mimeographed).

the case of **Hobson** v. **Hansen.**[17] In his suit against the public schools
of Washington, D.C., Julius Hobson alleged that the tracking system
discriminated against Negro and poor children by placing them in
the lowest academic tracks. Thus, he argued, they were deprived of
access to higher-quality services within the schools they attended.
In the opinion of the court, his allegation was valid, and he was
granted a favorable decision. The Washington, D.C. schools were
ordered to alter the procedures that led to the discriminatory
dispensation of school services.

The research evidence we have reviewed to provide background
for understanding our findings is clearly consistent with Proposition
A. Our task now is to test whether the proposition holds at several
levels when subjected to careful examination with a large body of
data gathered systematically in the state of Michigan.

Interdistrict Disparities
The continuing issue of this chapter is the extent to which low SES
is associated with fewer, or less adequate, school services in
Michigan. The primary questions are (1) whether school districts can
be distinguished from one another when the SES of children in the
district is averaged to establish the criterion, and (2) if so, whether
that criterion allows us to predict the quality of services that will be
provided for children in a district. In order to answer these questions
it is convenient to classify services into some reasonable set of
clusters. Consequently, we have chosen to discuss school services
under five major headings: (1) administrative services, (2) equipment
and facilities, (3) curricular and instructional arrangements, (4) staff
characteristics, (5) student environment.

Administrative Services
The availability of accurate information about the internal and external
environment is a clear prerequisite to intelligent decision making
in any organization. Industrial organizations go to great lengths to
obtain accurate information as a basis for rational policy planning.
Since obtaining and analyzing such information is an expensive
process, we would expect high SES districts to be in a better position
to allocate resources to these functions than are low SES districts.
Indeed, this is the case in Michigan. While no districts in our sample
spent much for research, high SES[18] districts did spend higher

[17] **Hobson** v. **Hansen,** 369 F. Supp. 401 (D.D.C. 1967).
[18] As we discussed in Chapter 2, our measures of SES are closely related
to one another. Thus, to speak of SES is typically to speak of a cluster of
indicators rather than any single indicator.

percentages.[19] Again, while no group of districts spent a significant amount for testing and evaluative functions, high SES districts nevertheless made higher percentage allocations than did low SES districts.[20] Finally, high SES districts are more likely than their low SES counterparts to have access to an electronic computer for use in administrative and research tasks, and the highest SES districts have used computers for the longest period of time.[21] This latter phenomenon also may be an indicator of a district's ability to introduce innovative practices, and later we shall present other data that indicate a pattern with respect to the adoption of innovations.

Equipment and Facilities

In addition to inequities with respect to administrative services, there exist inequities that might be thought of as affecting all learning activities. The first of these is the general availability, in adequate quantities, of materials that supplement basic texts. Low SES districts, according to responses of school principals, are less likely to have adequate supplies of supplementary materials.[22] A second measure of a general effect on curriculum is obtained from an index of available instructional aids. Such aids include projectors, science laboratories, reading laboratories, closed-circuit television, and the like. High SES districts have more of these than do low SES districts.[23]

Curricular and Instructional Arrangements

Perhaps one of the most important clusters of service provided by a school district is the breadth of its curricular offerings. In one sense, these represent options to students that may be either expansive or restrictive in nature. That is, with a broad curriculum, students have experiences available to them that may serve subsequently to increase their schooling or postschool opportunities. This expansion of alternatives would seem to be an important function of education, and has, in fact, been a definition of education for many writers.

In Michigan, there are important differences among districts in the curricular alternatives available to students. In high SES districts, a higher percentage of students are enrolled in foreign language courses than in low SES districts. In the lowest SES districts only 14 percent of the high school students, on the average, are so enrolled,

[19] T, 171 V. 11.
[20] T, 171 V. 12.
[21] T, 169 V. 215; 170 V. 215; 171 V. 215; 182 V. 215; 265 V. 215.
[22] T, 265 V. 185. This relationship holds only when the state equalized assessed valuation per pupil is considered as the measure of SES. This indicates the dependence of materials adequacy on availability of funds.
[23] T, 169 V. 188; 170 V. 188; 181 V. 188.

Table 3.1

Octiles According to Variable 181		Socioeconomic Scale					
Medians from Variable 241		Percentage Enrollment in High School Foreign Language					
Octile	1	2	3	4	5	6	7	8
Medians	14	14	20	16	26	23	28	44
NTRUE = 48							
STUDENT T = 4.44							

while in the highest SES districts 44 percent are enrolled in high school foreign language courses.[24] Table 3.1 displays these data across all eight SES categories.

If college attendance is taken as an important option for an individual, then we have evidence to suggest that there is less possibility for students in some districts than in others. In fact, in low SES districts, children may be encouraged to take courses that generally preclude college attendance. Low SES districts have higher proportions of students enrolled in business education,[25] home economics,[26] and agriculture courses.[27] With respect to this last phenomenon, it is possible than it is a product of the rural nature of many low SES districts. However, the measure of district SES used (average family income) is not a particularly precise indicator of rural composition.[28] Thus, independent of a district's location, the phenomenon holds true.

The options of children in low SES districts are reduced in another fashion. Low SES districts provide fewer instructional innovations than do those that are high on the socioeconomic scale. For example, with respect to an index of innovation in instructional arrangements such as team teaching, modular scheduling, and provision for independent study by students, low SES districts are substantially less innovative.[29]

A more direct measure of curricular innovation is an index of innovation in the teaching of science. High SES districts are more likely to have adopted one or more programs such as the Biological

[24] T, 170 V. 241; 171 V. 241; 181 V. 241.
[25] T, 170 V. 243.
[26] T, 169 V. 245; 170 V. 245; 171 V. 245; 181 V. 245; 182 V. 245.
[27] T, 170 V. 242.
[28] T, 170 V. 174.
[29] T, 170 V. 225; 181 V. 225; 182 V. 225.

Table 3.2

Octiles according to Variable 181				Socioeconomic Scale				
Medians from Variable 217				Adoption of Innovation in Science Instruction				
Octile	1	2	3	4	5	6	7	8
Median	0	1	2	1	3	2	3	3
NTRUE = 45								
STUDENT T = 2.97								

Table 3.3

Octiles according to Variable 181				Socioeconomic Scale				
Medians from Variable 46				Services to Children with Special Needs				
Octile	1	2	3	4	5	6	7	8
Median	8	10	7	15	18	14	16	15
NTRUE = 50								
STUDENT T = 4.36								

Science Curriculum Study, the Chemical Bond Approach Project, and the Physical Science Study Committee.[30] In fact, as shown in Table 3.2, the median low SES district has adopted none of these programs, while the median high SES district has adopted three.

Not only are low SES districts less able to provide services in the regular curriculum, but also they are less able to provide services to children with special needs. On a summary index of provision of services to children with special needs, such districts offer fewer services to fewer numbers of children.[31] This index includes provision of services to the blind, deaf, crippled, and homebound as well as children in need of speech correction and children judged to be mentally retarded. Table 3.3 provides a display of the differences among districts.

Because of the way this score is constructed, the differences among districts represent important qualitative disparities. A score of 20 means that for ten possible services, the district is able to provide service to all needy children. A score of 10 indicates that while the

[30] T, 169 V. 217; 171 V. 217; 181 V. 217; 182 V. 217.
[31] T, 170 V. 46; 181 V. 46; 182 V. 46.

services may be available to some needy children, they are not available to all. A score of 0 signifies that no services are available to any needy children. Thus, among the lower SES schools, few services are available, and those only to some fraction of the children who need them. Moreover, in high SES districts more often than in low SES districts, special services are likely to be offered in the summer months as well.[32] Given these two conditions, it is not surprising to discover that high SES districts are more likely to make provision for children unable to benefit from the regular program.[33] Table 3.4 indicates that among the lower SES districts about one-half make such provisions, while among the districts higher on the scale almost all do.

Somewhat in keeping with their deficiencies in providing remediation, low SES districts are also less able to provide services to children who possess special talents. Using an index of services to children who are gifted verbally, quantitatively, or artistically, low SES districts are seen to provide fewer such offerings than high SES districts.[34]

Staff Characteristics

Perhaps the most important school service component is embodied in the capabilities of district staff members.[35] Our measures of such capabilities are gross, but they suggest significant differences. An indirect indicator of teacher quality is continuing education.[36] High

Table 3.4

Octiles according to Variable 181				Socioeconomic Scale			
Medians from Variable 180				Percent of Districts Providing Services to Children Unable to Benefit from Regular Program			
Octile	1	2	3	4	5	6	7	8
Median	45	56	91	67	80	60	100	92

NTRUE = 48
STUDENT T = 2.48

[32] T, 169 V. 47.
[33] T, 170 V. 180; 181 V. 180.
[34] T, 181 V. 186.
[35] One indicator of their importance is that 65 to 85 percent of school district operating budgets are spent for staff salaries.
[36] Continuing education is defined as formal university offerings as well as school district inservice courses.

SES districts outranked low SES districts in the enrollment of
teachers in formal graduate courses during the year preceding the
Thomas survey.[37] In addition, these districts had proportionately
higher budgets for provision of inservice training of teachers[38] and
provided more days of released time to teachers for inservice
activities.[39] Thus, teachers in high SES districts are more likely to
have exposure to current ideas and knowledge than are teachers in
low SES districts. Finally, superintendents of districts in the former
category have more years of formal schooling than do
superintendents of districts in the latter category.[40]

In addition to personal qualifications, an important indirect
measure of the quality of service is the allocation of the school staff.
From staff allocation patterns we can infer a district's ability to
support staff specialization. While some staff specialization is a
function of the sheer size of a district,[41] the cost of providing
specialization is prohibitive in many cases. In Michigan, school
principals in low SES districts, at all grade levels, are more likely
to be teaching principals than in high SES districts.[42] This fact is an
indication of the relative inability of low SES districts to afford a staff
position that has exclusive and specialized functions. Department
chairman in such schools are less likely than those in high SES
districts to be released from regular teaching duties for some period
each day in order to fulfill their obligations as chairmen.[43] While this
phenomenon may be partly a function of school size (since the ratio
of teachers to faculty chairmen ratio is higher in high SES districts),[44]
it also indicates an inability to absorb the cost associated with
fulfillment of an institutionalized speciality. We can infer that as a
result, departments in low SES districts enjoy few of the benefits that
can be derived from an administrator who devotes time to evaluation,
coordination, communication, and other support activities.

The allocation patterns for regular teachers also indicate a lack of
specialization in low SES districts. Teachers in low SES districts

[37] T, 170 V. 176; 181 V. 176; 182 V. 176.
[38] T, 169 V. 13.
[39] T, 169 V. 14; 170 V. 14; 171 V. 14; 181 V. 14; 182 V. 14.
[40] T, 169 V. 28; 181 V. 28; 182 V. 28.
[41] Economies of scale determine, in part, whether a district can afford a
specialized staff, particularly in high schools.
[42] T, 181 V. 25; 181 V. 27; 182 V. 27.
[43] T, 170 V. 210; 182 V. 210.
[44] T, 170 V. 211; 181 V. 211; 182 V. 211.

Table 3.5

Octiles according to Variable 181				Socioeconomic Scale				
Medians from Variable 208				Percent of Teachers with More than Three Daily Lesson Preparations				
Octile	1	2	3	4	5	6	7	8
Median	15	15	5	5	5	5	5	5

NTRUE = 48
STUDENT T = −2.56

Table 3.6

Octiles according to Variable 181				Socioeconomic Scale				
Medians from Variable 181				Socioeconomic Scale				
Octile	1	2	3	4	5	6	7	8
Median	35	44	49	60	64	66	79	98

NTRUE = 51
STUDENT T = 150.08

teach more hours[45] and make more separate subject matter preparations per day.[46] This latter fact is displayed in Table 3.5.

Student Environment

The Thomas Report data that bear upon patterns of student interaction, though not as rich as those from the EEOS, do provide clues as to the nature of such interaction. Table 3.6 indicates that, in our sample of school districts, differentials between octiles by SES are large, and that within each octile the children are of similar SES. This finding is in keeping with evidence that has accumulated over the last four or more decades of research and that has touched upon the subject of student associations. In our sample, children in low SES districts come in contact with a great many more low SES children than is the case for children in high SES districts.[47]

Another way in which this phenomenon operates can be observed for each octile from the percentage of children whose families earn $3,000 or less per year. While no grouping of districts is free of poverty, some are clearly more free than others. Table 3.7 displays

[45] T, 181 V. 206.
[46] T, 170 V. 208; 181 V. 208.
[47] T, 181 V. 181.

Table 3.7

Octiles according to Variable 181				Socioeconomic Scale			
Medians from Variable 182				Percent of Children from Poverty Homes			
Octile	1	2	3	4	5	6	7	8
Median	37.6	29.6	27.4	22.2	20.4	14.1	8.8	8.3
NTRUE = 51								
STUDENT T = −20.63								

the median percent of children in a district whose families earn less than $3,000 per year.[48] As we proceed from left to right, from octile 1 to octile 8, SES increases, but the percent of children from poverty homes decreases.

Table 3.7 demonstrates that SES is a predictor of the likely patterns of association among children. That is, in the median low SES district, a child has one chance in three of associating with another child whose family earns $3,000 a year or less. In the median high SES district, the probability of such an association is only one chance in twelve. In Chapter 4 we shall review the available literature, which indicates that where poverty is concentrated, student achievement is depressed. Thus, in the lowest SES octile of the Michigan sample, children from poverty homes are schooled in an atmosphere of concentrated poverty and denied the opportunity to view and participate in an alternative style of life.

Conclusion

Throughout this section we have provided evidence to prove that major inequities exist among school districts. The data demonstrate that high SES districts provide more services and services of higher quality. By contrast, the educational program in a typical low SES district has the effect of severely reducing the opportunities of children who must attend school there.

Interschool Disparities

The examination of interschool inequity is based on analyses of EEOS data. As in the preceding sections we shall discuss clusters of services.

Equipment and Facilities

As shown in Table 3.8, low SES schools tend to be housed in older buildings.

[48] T, 181 V. 182.

Table 3.8

Octiles according to Variable 179				Socioeconomic Index				
Medians from Variable 8				Building Age				
Octile	1	2	3	4	5	6	7	8
Median	7	7	5	6	7	6	4	4
NTRUE = 81								
STUDENT T = −2.71								

According to the procedures by which these data were coded, a score of 7 in the table represents a school age of forty years or more. At the other extreme, a score of 4 signifies a school age of between ten and ninteen years. Thus, the difference in actual years of building age is at least twenty years and possibly greater. Low SES schools also tend to be on small building sites,[49] and because they have larger numbers of students than high SES districts,[50] they are more crowded.[51]

In addition to the tendency for low SES schools to be old and crowded, they seem to be poorly equipped.[52] Moreover, such schools have available fewer library books per 1,000 students.[53] At the extremes of social class, the inequity of available library books is especially great. The lowest SES schools are able to provide 1.7 library books per child, while the highest SES schools provide 5.4 library books per child. Thus, although no children in the sample schools are being inundated with available books, children in low SES schools suffer the greatest scarcity.

Health Services
Low SES children are more subject to disease and malnutrition than are high SES children. However, low SES schools are somewhat less likely to have a room specifically set aside as an infirmary or room for the care of children who become ill.[54] In addition, these same schools are no more likely to provide a school nurse.[55] This lack is exacerbated by the fact that, according to teachers, more

[49] E, 179 V. 7; 168 V. 7.
[50] E, 179 V. 121; 168 V. 121.
[51] E, 179. 137.
[52] E, 179 V. 131.
[53] E, 179 V. 13.
[54] E, 168 V. 29.
[55] E, 168 V. 40.

Table 3.9

Octiles according to Variable 179				Socioeconomic Index				
Medians from Variable 115				Percent of Teachers Reporting That Students Come to School Poorly Fed and Clothed				
Octile	1	2	3	4	5	6	7	8
Median	62	42	25	37	25	18	0	0
NTRUE = 86								
STUDENT T = −6.88								

students in low SES schools come to school poorly fed and clothed[56] (see Table 3.9).

Not only are low SES schools less able to provide services for the physical health of children, but also, despite greater need, they are no better able to provide the services of a school psychologist.[57]

Curricular and Instructional Arrangements

Low SES schools generally provide more remediation services than high SES schools. In schools in the former category there are about two remedial reading teachers per 1,000 students, while in the latter category this figure is reduced to about one part-time reading specialist.[58] In addition, in the higher SES schools there are generally no special remedial classes in math or reading,[59] reflecting, perhaps, the lack of need.

At the extremes, however, low SES schools tend to be less able to offer services for speech correction.[60] Such schools provide fourteen man days of speech correction per week per 10,000 students, whereas the highest SES schools provide twenty-seven man days of speech correction per week per 10,000 students. In addition, low SES schools provide fewer special classes for such student problems as low IQ, inability to speak English, speech impairments, physical handicaps, and behavior and adjustment problems.[61]

Although teachers in low SES schools report that there are too

[56] E, 179 V. 115; 168 V. 115.
[57] E, 179 V. 36; 168 V. 36.
[58] E, 179 V. 37.
[59] E, 179 V. 78; 179 V. 79.
[60] E, 179 V. 36.
[61] E, 179 V. 80.

many student absences[62] and too much student turnover,[63] such schools have no more attendance officers than do high SES schools.[64] Moreover, teachers appear to do no more counseling in low SES schools.[65] Thus, if we could compute the availability of services as a function of probable need, low SES schools would be shown to be even more dramatically devoid of support.

We have seen that these schools are somewhat less able to provide for the remedial needs of children. Likewise, they appear to be less able to provide services for the positive development of students' talents. For example, low SES schools provide fewer days of music teaching per 10,000 students.[66] They are also less likely to provide any students with an accelerated curriculum.[67]

Staff Characteristics

One might expect that those who decide school policy would make special efforts to staff schools in poor districts with exceptionally able persons. This does not appear to be the case for our sample of schools. The administrators of low SES schools do not appear to be significantly different from other principals. They have been principals about the same length of time[68] (although their tenure in their present schools is somewhat shorter);[69] they are about the same age[70] (although principals of schools in the highest octiles are younger), are of the same racial background (Caucasian),[71] and have about the same amount of formal education[72] (primarily in education courses rather than in traditional academic disciplines).[73]

The most significant difference between personnel is that teachers in low SES schools have lower scores on a measure of verbal facility. This is shown in Table 3.10.

Because of the nature of this test, the range between the lowest and the highest scores represents a significant difference in ability. The standard deviation is about 1.5 raw score points. Thus, approximately 68 percent of all teachers will score between 23 and

[62] E, 179 V. 120; 168 V. 120.
[63] E, 179 V. 129; 168 V. 129.
[64] E, 179 V. 41; 168 V. 41.
[65] E, 168 V. 138.
[66] E, 179 V. 34.
[67] E, 168 V. 75.
[68] E, 179 V. 58; 168 V. 58.
[69] E, 179 V. 59.
[70] E, 179 V. 60; 168 V. 60.
[71] E, 168 V. 64.
[72] E, 179 V. 62; 168 V. 62.
[73] E, 179 V. 63; 168 V. 63.

SES and School Services

Table 3.10

Octiles according to Variable 179				Socioconomic Index			
Medians from Variable 141				Verbal Ability Score of Teachers			
Octile	1	2	3	4	5	6	7	8
Median	23.5	23.5	24.4	24.7	24.4	24.5	25.0	25.6

NTRUE = 86
STUDENT T = 3.84

26. The low octile's median of 23.5 signifies a dramatically reduced verbal ability compared to the high octile score of 25.6. This relationship holds even though teachers in low SES schools have a slightly higher number of course credits in graduate work.[74]

Another, somewhat more subtle, component of a school's contribution to a child is composed of the attitudes of teachers toward their jobs and students. Teachers in low SES schools would be less likely than their colleagues in high SES schools to repeat teaching as a career if they had a chance to choose again.[75] Not surprisingly, in view of the environment in which they teach, they would be more likely to choose another school if given the chance.[76] These two findings are reinforced by the teachers' perceptions of the low general reputation of their schools[77] and reflect their perceptions of the students with whom they work. Teachers in poor schools have low estimates of the academic abilities of their students. While 15 percent of the teachers in the highest SES schools believed that there was too much competition among students for grades, no teachers in the lowest SES schools complained of such a problem.[78] Teachers in the latter group of schools are more likely to indicate that the home environments of children are poor.[79]

Perhaps more important, these same teachers frequently described their students as not being interested in learning.[80] Over one-half the teachers in the lowest SES schools reported that they felt this way, while none of the teachers in the highest SES schools gave similar responses. Finally, when asked to estimate student academic

[74] E, 179 V. 93.
[75] E, 179 V. 105; 168 V. 105.
[76] E, 179 E. 106; 168 V. 106.
[77] E, 179 V. 109; 168 V. 109.
[78] E, 179 V. 118; 168 V. 118.
[79] E, 179 V. 114; 168 V. 114.
[80] E, 179 V. 124; 168 V. 124.

abilities, teachers in the former group of schools consistently
provided lower estimates than did teachers in the latter group.[81]
Student Environment
Perhaps the most obvious phenomenon in this category is that the
population of students and teachers in low SES schools is transient.
More students transfer in [82] and more students transfer out[83] than in
high SES schools. Teachers confirm this finding in their subjective
reports that there is too much student turnover in low SES schools[84]
(see Table 3.11). While none of the teachers in the highest IP octile
believes there is too much student turnover, one-half of the teachers
in the lowest IP octile believe this to be the case. On a related dimension, Table 3.12 illustrates the median percent of teachers who report
that there are too many student absences.

Just as they indicate that there are too many transient students,
teachers in low SES schools report that there is too much teacher
turnover.[85] Apparently, the typical opening day experience for

Table 3.11

Octiles according to Variable 168				Index of Possessions			
Medians from Variable 129				Percent of Teachers Reporting There Is Too Much Student Turnover			
Octile	1	2	3	4	5	6	7	8
Median	50	31	33	33	11	7	3	0

NTRUE = 86
STUDENT T = −7.66

Table 3.12

Octiles According to Variable 168				Index of Possessions			
Medians from Variable 120				Percent of Teachers Reporting There Are Too Many Student Absences			
Octile	1	2	3	4	5	6	7	8
Median	52	48	35	22	12	15	11	0

NTRUE = 86
STUDENT T = −7.19

[81] E, 179 V. 103; 168 V. 103; 179 V. 139; 168 V. 139.
[82] E, 168 V. 47.
[83] E, 168 V. 48.
[84] E, 179 V. 129; 168 V. 129.
[85] E, 179 V. 133, 168 V. 133.

teachers and students in a low SES school is one of a group of relative strangers coming together. A great deal of time and energy must be expended before these strangers can function as a group. However, the available time for establishing effective social relationships is severely reduced by the high degree of student turnover and absenteeism.[86]

Whether as a consequence of the transiency or the result of a variety of other problems, low SES schools seem to be environments in which conflict occurs more frequently. Teachers complain about having to spend too much time on discipline[87] and losing too much time because of class-time interruptions.[88] Finally, conflict among students and between students and teachers is accompanied by conflict among teachers.[89] Also, teachers in low SES schools believe that they receive inadequate support from the parents of their students.[90]

Although our image is melodramatic, we are tempted to picture the teacher in such a school as feeling alone and subject to tremendous emotional and physical strain. This environment does not seem to support close emotional and intellectual relationships between and among a community of scholars and their eager charges. As far as the student is concerned, this social environment is equally unsympathetic, and perhaps hostile, to his needs as a pupil and a young human being.

Interstudent Disparities

Having demonstrated that districts of low socioeconomic status provide fewer services than do those of high socioeconomic status and that the same is true at the interschool level, we turn now to an examination of Proposition A using data for individual students, rather than districtwide or schoolwide averages,as the focus of our analysis. Here we rely upon the EEOS, rather than the Thomas Report, for our information. Our findings are similar to those concerning interdistrict and interschool disparities, but in order to be complete we include them.

Equipment and Facilities

One of the more striking phenomena associated with the environment

[86] E, 179 V. 120; 168 V. 120.
[87] E, 179 V. 123; 168 V. 123.
[88] E,179 V. 132; 168 V. 132
[89] E, 179 V. 127.
[90] E, 179 V. 126; 168 V. 126; 179 V. 130; 168 V. 130.

of low SES students is limitation of physical space. Generally, their families live in fewer rooms than more affluent families, in houses and apartments that tend to be clustered in close proximity to one another. And, in addition, there is lower access to open, or park, space. These conditions of high density are extended into the schools. Low SES children attend schools that are more crowded and have fewer acres for the school site.[91] This tendency is aggravated by the fact that low SES children attend schools with larger student enrollments, so that the available square footage per child is much smaller. The problem is illustrated by three objective measures. Poor children attend schools with more makeshift rooms, such as those in halls or basements,[92] schools in which there are fewer classrooms per 1,000 students,[93] and schools in which there are more students per class. [94] Moreover, when asked for their subjective views, teachers of low SES students more frequently report that their classes are too large.[95]

However, the crowding in classrooms may be offset to some extent by the greater incidence of cafeterias,[96] gymnasia,[97] and athletic fields[98] in schools attended by low SES students. These facilities may also reflect the ages of the buildings, since such facilities are less often provided in newer elementary schools.

Crowding is compounded by the fact that the buildings attended by poor children are considerably older than those attended by more affluent children.[99] In fact, at the extremes, there is about twenty years difference in the age of buildings. From trends in school architecture we can infer that the older the building, the more likely it is to have limited outside window exposure, less well illuminated halls and rooms, fewer sound-dampening characteristics, and to be generally less pleasing aesthetically.

In addition to being crowded, poor children do not have access to the same range or quality of other facilities and materials available to higher SES children. For example, the lower the SES of the child, the less likely he is to attend a school in which there is set aside a

[91] E, 179 V. 7; 168 V. 7.
[92] E, 179 V. 11; 168 v. 11.
[93] E, 179 V. 88; 168 v. 88.
[94] E, 179 V. 121; 168 V. 121.
[95] E, 179 V. 137; 168 V. 137.
[96] E, 179 V. 15.
[97] E, 179 V. 16, 168 V. 16.
[98] E, 179 V. 23.
[99] E, 179 V. 8; 168 V. 8.

room specifically used as an infirmary.[100] Teachers of poor children, more often than other teachers, report they have poor equipment with which to work,[101] although there is an indication that more movie projectors are available.[102] And, more importantly, poor children have available fewer library books than more affluent children[103] and less often have a sufficient number of textbooks.[104] This lack may be partially offset by the higher probability that low SES students attend schools within walking distance of a public library.[105]

Curricular and Instructional Arrangements

If a number of physical facilities are less adequate and less available for poor than for affluent children, so it is also with instructional services. As we have pointed out, more poor children attend schools with no infirmary. In addition, they are less likely to attend a school that provides a school nurse[106] and the services of a school psychologist.[107] These disparities occur despite the fact that the incidence of physical and mental ailments is higher among low SES children, and their teachers describe them as coming to school in inadequate clothing and with inadequate diets.[108]

Although low SES children appear to have less access to health services than do other children, they are somewhat better provided with academic remediation. Low SES students have greater access to special classes for academically handicapped children,[109] special classes for remedial work in mathematics,[110] and special classes for remedial work in reading.[111] However, the availability of this last service is partially reduced by the fact that teachers of remedial reading have more students.[112] Also, the students themselves have less access to services for speech correction.[113]

On the other hand, low SES students have less access to accelerated courses than do high SES students.[114] In addition, while

[100] E, 179 V. 29; 168 V. 29.
[101] E, 179 V. 131; 168 V. 131.
[102] E, 168 V. 24.
[103] E, 179 V. 13; 168 V. 13.
[104] E, 179 V. 26.
[105] E, 179 V. 68; 168 V. 68.
[106] E, 179 V. 40; 168 V. 40.
[107] E, 179 V. 36; 168 V. 36.
[108] E, 179 V. 115; 168 V. 115.
[109] E, 179 V. 80; 168 V. 80.
[110] E, 179 V. 78; 168 V. 78.
[111] E, 179 V. 79; 168 V. 79.
[112] E, 168 V. 81.
[113] E, 179 V. 35; 168 V. 35.
[114] E, 179 V. 75; 168 V. 75.

high SES students are less likely to be in academic or ability tracks or groups,[115] they are more likely to experience changes from one to another when they are so categorized,[116] indicating, perhaps a greater number of options for high SES students.

Low SES and high SES students appear to have equal access to exposure to life's aesthetic experiences. Poor children have available fewer days of music teaching,[117] but more days of art teaching[118] and a greater number of extracurricular activities.[119] Although we do not know the nature of such extracurricular activities, we have found that low SES students are more likely to have teachers who believe that the schools place too much emphasis on athletics.[120]

Staff Characteristics

It is apparent that low SES students receive no more, and may receive fewer special services, than affluent children. In addition, there are differences in the persons from whom they receive these services. Principals of poor children tend to be more experienced,[121] but to have less tenure in their present schools,[122] to be older,[123] and to have somewhat higher salaries.[124] Also, principals of poor children are seen by teachers as less effective leaders than the principals of higher SES children.[125]

Another way to estimate the nature and intensity of the discrepancies between low and high SES students is on the basis of teacher perceptions of the school environment. We have already indicated problems of physical crowding, but there are other indicators. Low SES children are more likely to have teachers who believe that the school's reputation is poor,[126] that parents are uninterested in what goes on,[127] and that there is too much teacher[128] and administrator turnover.[129]

[115] E, 168 V. 72.
[116] E, 1968 V. 74.
[117] E, 179 V. 34; 168 V. 34.
[118] E, 179 V. 33.
[119] E, 179 V. 77; 168 V. 77.
[120] E, 179 V. 119; 168 V. 119.
[121] E, 179 V. 58; 168 V. 58.
[122] E, 179 V. 59; 168 V. 59.
[123] E, 179 V. 60; 168 V. 60.
[124] E, 179 V. 67; 168 V. 67.
[125] E, 179 V. 125; 168 V. 125.
[126] E, 179 V. 109; 168 V. 109.
[127] E, 179 V. 117; 168 V. 117; 179 V. 126; 168 V. 126; 179 V. 130; 168 V. 130.
[128] E, 179 V. 133; 168 V. 133.
[129] E, 179 V. 134; 168 V. 134.

In addition, teachers of low SES students report a social environment in which few social interactions appear to be pleasant, or perhaps even bearable. They say more often than other teachers that there is racial conflict among students,[130] that there should be a better racial mixture of students,[131] that they have to spend too much time on student discipline,[132] that there are too many uncalled-for interruptions during class periods,[133] that they have too little freedom in textbook selection, curriculum development, and student discipline,[134] and that the teachers around them do not seem able to work amicably together.[135]

As we have seen, teachers of low SES children are less likely than others to work in supportive environments. It is not surprising, then, to discover that they are dissatisfied with their jobs, and to some extent, their careers. If given a choice, teachers of low SES students are less likely to say that they would chose teaching as a career if they could start over[136] and more likely to say that they would transfer to another school if given the chance.[137] This general displeasure is compounded by the fact that the teachers of poor children are less likely to have chosen to teach in the schools they are now in than are the teachers of more affluent children.[138] Thus, teachers of low SES students, because of the conditions accompanying their employment, are more likely to be dissatisfied with their jobs and their schools.

We have presented evidence on interstudent disparities to show that low SES children have greater educational needs but receive fewer special services and attend more crowded, conflict-prone schools than do other children. Moreover, teachers of such children have smaller amounts of teaching and preparation time.[139] Finally, and perhaps of most concern, teachers of poor children appear to have less verbal ability than the teachers of more affluent children.[140]

Summary

We began this chapter with the assertion that high-quality school

[130] E, 179 V. 116; 168 V. 116.
[131] E, 179 V. 122; 168 V. 122.
[132] E, 179 V. 123; 168 V. 123.
[133] E, 179 V. 132; 168 V. 132.
[134] E, 179 V. 128; 168 V. 128.
[135] E, 179 V. 127; 168 V. 127.
[136] E, 179 V. 105; 168 V. 105.
[137] E, 179 V. 106; 168 V. 106.
[138] E, 179 V. 98; 168 V. 98.
[139] E, 179 V. 135; 179 V. 136; 168 V. 136.
[140] E, 179 V. 141; 168 V. 141.

services are provided for high SES students and low-quality school services are provided to low SES students. The accumulated evidence of related research provided us with substantial support for this assertion. We have added an extensive analysis of school service data collected in Michigan. The conclusion of our analysis is that the quality of school services is tied tightly to the child's social and economic circumstances.

Information from Michigan provided one of the most comprehensive sources of data available for testing Proposition A. Consequently, it has been possible to address the question in a number of ways. We have been able to demonstrate that, regardless of the level of analysis, socioeconomic status is an excellent predictor of available school services.

Our most significant finding is that the relationship between SES and the provision of school services holds for entire **school districts.** What this means is that in Michigan, where social and economic conditions tend to cause a clustering of poor families, school districts in which poor children live typically cannot provide services equal to those of other districts, in which residents enjoy greater personal wealth.

Similarly, we discovered that **individual schools** that enroll large numbers of poor children tend to provide fewer and lower-quality services than schools that enroll small numbers of poor children. Finally, inequities among **individual students** exist to the effect that poor children are provided with lower-quality services than wealthy children, almost regardless of the school districts in which they live, or the schools that they attend.

We have chosen to address ourselves to the relationship between socioeconomic status and school services on three levels. Our data are consistent and broad in scope. On the basis of this information, we have no doubt that our original assertion is true; to be an elementary school child of lower socioeconomic status is to experience an extraordinary probability of discriminatory treatment High-quality school services are provided to children from wealthy homes. Poor-quality school services are provided to children from poor homes.

4

School Services and Pupil Performance

. . . equality of educational opportunity through the schools must imply a strong effect of schools that is independent of the child's social environment. . . . [1]

[1] James S. Coleman et al., **Equality of Educational Opportunity** (Washington, D.C.: United States Government Printing Office, 1966), p. 325.

We have shown that the quality of many available school services and formal educational opportunities is linked to the student's socio-economic status. Poor children tend to go to school in older, more crowded buildings, have fewer special services available to them, come into contact with older, less satisfied, frequently less capable teachers, and are surrounded by fellow students with learning disabilities and low motivation. Now, what does all this mean? What, if any, difference do these disparities make? Does the school performance of low SES children suffer as a consequence of such disparities? These questions convey our central concern in this chapter. More specifically, we focus here upon research Proposition B, which holds that

A relationship exists between the quality of school services provided to a pupil and his academic achievement, and that relationship is such that higher-quality school services are associated with higher levels of achievement.

At the end of this chapter we will present our findings from Michigan on this proposition, but first we wish to review some related research findings and attempt to explain why efforts in this general area of research have been characterized often by frustration and failure.

A Digression for Historical Perspective

For many years, at least since public schooling became an endeavor involving many millions of dollars, laymen, educators, and researchers have been interested in making the enterprise more effective, and hopefully more efficient. This concern has been reflected in a large number of research studies dealing with school effectiveness. Early efforts were conducted for the most part by professional educators. This work is probably best characterized by the "cost-quality studies" of the late Paul R. Mort of Teachers College, Columbia University.[2] These studies used expenditure levels as gross measures of the quality of a school. The "outputs" of schools were measured on a number of dimensions. In some of the studies, the

[2] A review of the cost-quality line of inquiry and some of its successors is provided by William E. Barron's chapter "Measurement of Educational Productivity" in **The Theory and Practice of School Finance**, ed. Warren E. Gauerke and Jack R. Childress (Chicago: Rand McNally, 1967), pp. 279–308. An earlier review of such efforts is provided in Paul R. Mort, "Cost Quality Relationships in Education," in **Problems and Issues in Public School Finance**, ed. R. L. Johns and Edgar L. Morphet (New York: National Conference of Professors of Educational Administration, 1952).

dollar inputs were related to actual measures of pupil performance. In other studies, assessment of school effects stopped short of pupil performance measures and took instead some process variable such as the rate at which the schools adopted innovative instructional practices or new curricular ideas.[3] The studies rather consistently concluded that those districts that spent more dollars per pupil were the most "effective"; their students performed the best on test scores, attended college more frequently, and so on. These findings provide a strong case for increasing school expenditures if one desires higher levels of student performance.

The simplified cost-quality studies, however, contain a serious failing. They do not take into sufficient account the student's capabilities prior to entry into the school or the types of experiences that the student participates in outside of school. In short, such studies do not control adequately for the background and environment of the pupil. What their findings tend to demonstrate is that the high-expenditure districts, the Scarsdales, Grosse Pointes, and Palo Altos of this nation, produce large numbers of high-performance students. However, given the nature of the environment from which these students typically come, the level of education of their parents, the efforts frequently spent in their homes to prepare them for school, and the many cultural and educational advantages they have by virtue of their community setting, it would be surprising indeed if such high-expenditure schools did not produce highly capable students.

In time the weaknesses of the cost-quality type of research became evident to investigators, and a new line of inquiry began. This time, the primary researchers were trained in methods of sociological research. Their findings, best illustrated, perhaps, in studies conducted by Alan B. Wilson and James S. Coleman,[4] tend to emphasize the significance of the student's social context over school services as determinants of pupil performance.

The general tenor of such sociological studies has been to demonstrate that a student's achievement is tied very tightly to his socio-

[3] See, for example, Orlando Frederick Furno, "The Projection of School Quality from Expenditure Level" (unpublished doctoral dissertation, Columbia University, 1956).
[4] In this context, one can take, for example, either the Coleman Report, to which we have already referred, or an earlier study by the same author, "The Adolescent Subculture and Academic Achievement," **The American Journal of Sociology,** 65 (1960), 337–347. An excellent example of Wilson's research is "Residential Segregation of Social Classes and Aspirations of High School Boys," **American Sociological Review,** 24 (1959), 836–845.

economic status. For example, the authors of the Coleman Report
wrote of differences between ethnic groups as to "sensitivity" to
the effects of school quality.[5] On balance, however, in the view of
Coleman and his fellow authors, the school service variables suc-
ceeded in explaining such a small portion of the variation in pupils'
performance that they were moved to write:

**Taking all these results together, one implication stands out above
all: That schools bring little influence to bear upon a child's
achievement that is independent of his background and general
social context; and that this very lack of independent effect means
that the inequalities imposed upon children by their home, neighborhood, and peer environment are carried along to become the
inequalities with which they confront adult life at the end of
school.[6]**

Critics of the Coleman Report hold that this conclusion is not
necessarily warranted.[7] They attack the report on three levels: (1)
inadequacy of the measurements utilized, (2) imprecise manipulation
of those measures, and (3) inappropriate statistical techniques. The
first of these criticisms, they say, is exemplified by the report's
measures of school facilities, volumes per student in the school
library and (for grades nine through twelve) the presence or absence
of science laboratories. These writers contend that so few and such
simple measures are insufficient in any attempt to understand the
significance of the school in explaining pupil performance.

The second criticism, according to the opposition, is exemplified
by the treatment accorded the statistic, "instructional expenditures
per pupil." Each student was assumed by the report to be benefiting
from an annual instructional expenditure equal to the mean for his
school district. The use of such an average masks intradistrict disparities, and from evidence displayed elsewhere in the report such
disparities appear to be substantial. By averaging expenditures and

---

[5] Negroes, Indian-Americans, Mexican-Americans, and Puerto Ricans tended
to respond more dramatically to contact with good teachers and enriched
programs than did white students.
[6] Coleman et al., **Equality of Educational Opportunity**, p. 325.
[7] For a more detailed explanation of the limitations of Coleman Report findings, see Samuel S. Bowles and Henry M. Levin, "The Determinants of
Scholastic Achievement: An Appraisal of Some Recent Findings," **Journal
of Human Resources**, 3 (Winter 1968). Also, see "More on Multicollinearity
and the Effectiveness of Schools," **Journal of Human Resources**, 3 (Summer
1968), by the same authors.

curtailing the range of their distribution, the report weighted the data against the possibility of finding a significant relationship.

The third major criticism involves the report's statistical analyses. The issue here is that the report's authors employed a form of regression analysis, which is inappropriate if there exists a high degree of intercorrelation among "independent" variables. The Coleman Report attempted to explain variance in achievement scores by adding successively different independent variables to the analysis. The outcomes of this approach are highly sensitive to the order in which the explanatory variables are entered whenever the explanatory variables are interrelated.

The critics maintain that the report's measures of socioeconomic conditions and school services are highly interrelated and do not meet the criterion of independence. Their argument is similar to our Proposition A: the factors that influence distribution of school services are such that high-quality school services tend to be made available to students from higher socioeconomic strata and lower-quality school services to students from low socioeconomic strata. If in a regression analysis "independent" variables are in fact highly intercorrelated, whichever variable cluster (socioeconomic status or school services) is first placed in the equation will have the highest explanatory power. The first-entered cluster will have exhausted the major portion of whatever variance exists to be explained by the total of the two variable clusters together. The analysis involved in the Coleman Report chose to place socioeconomic status variables into the equation first; not unexpectedly they "discovered" that this cluster explained substantially more variance than did the school service cluster. Had they reversed the entry position of the two clusters, they would have found schools to be the major contributor to pupil performance.[8]

The studies that have emphasized or overemphasized the influence of social environment at the expense of school services, if taken on their face, have the effect of discounting the significance of schooling. At the other extreme, the cost-quality–type study has frequently been oversimplified and construed to mean that schools will solve the problems of low pupil performance if only we spend just a little more money. Clearly, in order to assess the determinants of intellectual achievement, or any other kind of student performance, adequate

[8] Bowles and Levin, "The Determinants of Scholastic Achievement."

account must be taken of both the social context enveloping the student and the character of the school services to which he is exposed.

Ideally, such an assessment should be of a "value added" nature. That is, we should like to determine what the child "knew" before he came to school, what he "knew" when he completed school, and how much of the difference was the unique contribution of the school. In order to conduct such an ideal study, the researcher would need to control methodologically for the possible influence of a host of out-of-school factors such as the student's innate intellectual capacity, family and home background, and neighborhood environment. Obviously such experimentation is impossible.[9]

A Perspective on Schooling

Before launching into research findings regarding the effects of various school services upon measures of pupil achievement, it seems appropriate to step back for a moment and attempt to gain a reasoned view of what it is that schools do and what it is that affects what schools do. Nowhere is it defined with precision, but schools in American society are expected to transform pupils on a large number of dimensions. A wide variety of attitudes, skills, and knowledge are supposed to be given to each pupil by the educational system. We do not yet understand well what mechanisms inside the human body enable one to "learn" these things. We do know, however, that whatever the process, or processes, they are extraordinarily complex. We can see this when we witness the wide range of ways in which children typically respond to the same events and stimuli. Children comprehend and express that comprehension in different ways, at different rates, and to varying degrees.

We do not, at least at this point, wish to become embroiled in what appears to be a specious argument as to whether the abilities of children are more sensitive to biological or environmental influences.[10] Suffice it here to say that almost all of the typical individual's biologically inherited components and a very substantial share of

[9] For further elaboration upon the difficulties inherent in assessing the effects of schools see Charles E. Werts and Robert L. Linn, "Analyzing School Effects: How to Use the Same Data to Support Different Hypotheses," **American Educational Research Journal**, 6 (May 1969), 439–447.

[10] See, for example, the article by Arthur R. Jensen, "How Much Can We Boost IQ and Scholastic Achievement?" **Harvard Educational Review**, 39 (Winter 1969) and the critical reactions to it in the subsequent issue, Vol. 39, No. 2 (Spring 1970).

those that are environmentally shaped have taken hold prior to his first experiences with any formal education. Now, once having acknowledged the potential influence of genes and preschool environment, it seems reasonable to assume that the scope of variation in human performance that remains for the school to affect uniquely is somewhat limited. Moreover, it must be remembered that schools do not occupy the entire span of even the most ardent student's time. Even on a school day, and these usually take up less than one-half of all the days in a year, a student is likely to be in the company and under the influence of his peers and parents for a longer period of time than he is engaged in school activities. Nevertheless, it still seems reasonable to expect the schools to have an effect; indeed, we will soon describe some of these effects.[11]

But What Part of "School" Makes a Difference?

The term "school" is a deceptive generic label. **Webster's New World Dictionary** contains no less than ten different contemporary definitions.[12] An etymological approach scarcely provides more precision. At its Latin roots, "school" refers to leisure, or the manner and location in which leisure took place. The difficulty with this ambiguity is that it complicates our efforts to assess the "difference" that "school" makes. Only the most naive could possibly believe that the sheer fact of being physically present in a building labeled SCHOOL renders an individual knowledgeable or skilled. Presumably, some sort of pedagogical process must be undergone before educational objectives are met. But just what are these processes? Where is it in the school that we should look? Is it the edifice itself? Is it the blackboards, the teacher, the textbooks, the movie projector, or the principal? Is it all of these things, or is it something else again?

[11] Bowles presents an interesting argument for deducing the potential maximum contribution that can be attributed to formal education. He estimates that the hypothetical limit of the range of school effectiveness is about 0.7 to 0.8 of a standard deviation on any particular measure of learning. That is, given two students of equal capacity, the one receiving poor-quality school services would score at about the twenty-fifth percentile on a performance measure whereas the one receiving high-quality services would score about the seventy-fifth percentile. See Samuel S. Bowles, "Toward an Educational Production Function," paper presented at a Conference on Research in Income and Wealth, November 15–18, 1968, and published in W. Lee Hansen, ed., **Education, Income and Human Capital**, Studies in Income and Wealth, vol. 35 (New York: National Bureau of Economic Research, 1970).
[12] **Webster's New World Dictionary of the American Language**, College Edition (New York: World, 1966), p. 1, 304.

In this quest, we are reminded of the frequent admonition: "Get the facts!" All right, but what facts? Facts about what? What facts are relevant? Without some systematic theoretical guidance, the researcher must resort to an almost random inquiry to isolate the essential ingredients. Our plight is not quite this bad; we will be able to resort to logic and research findings in order to identify school service components worthy of being tested for effectiveness. However, our research would be greatly aided if we had a body of theory, theory about learning and instruction, which could guide us. Psychologists are daily discovering more about the nature of the learning process. We are perhaps still a long way from a unified theory of learning, and we may never complete the task. Nevertheless, bits and pieces of such a theory are beginning to fall into place. What is not yet evolving very rapidly is a theory of instruction.[13] An analogy with the practice of medicine may be helpful in understanding the difference. To have a theory or body of knowledge that explains the origin of some particular disease is crucial to, but by itself insufficient for, treating a patient with that disease. Given knowledge that the patient has cancer, do you treat the illness with drugs, surgery, or radiation? This answer, of course, must rest upon the traits of the individual patient, the location and type of the cancer, the therapeutic processes at hand, and the skill of the physician. Much the same relationship holds between a learning theory intended to explain how to manipulate the environment to take advantage of the processes that "cause" one to be able to read. We are beginning to know moderately well the neurological and psychological mechanisms that interact to enable one to read. What we are just beginning to investigate is the means by which we can aid those processes in the instance of individuals to make readers out of them. Given the biological and environmentally induced differences between individuals, the "treatment" for reading disabilities may well turn out to be complicated severalfold over the techniques necessary to treat cancer.

In the absence of a theory of instruction, educational researchers have tended to construct typologies of ordered school service components and to use available empirical measures to represent

[13] The need for a theory of instruction is forcefully explained in an article by Nathan L. Gage entitled "Theories of Teaching," in **Theories of Learning and Instruction,** The Sixty-Third Yearbook of the National Society for the Study of Education, ed. Ernest R. Hilgard (Chicago: University of Chicago Press, 1964), pp. 268–285.

each of the typology categories. This is the general procedure followed in the research we will review, and, indeed, it is the procedure that we ourselves followed in our study of school service component effectiveness. We do not wish to apologize for this non-theoretical approach or to bemoan our lack of an instructional theory. Our point here is simply that research strategies based on "raw" empiricism are comparatively inefficient, and the continued lack of an instructional theory will hamper efforts to identify the **sine qua non**, the crucial instructional components, of schools.

Inability to construct a unified theory of instruction, however, has not been the only factor deterring identification of effective school service components. Another significant inhibitor of this quest has been the relatively slow development of research strategies and measurement methodologies applicable to education. Measures of results tend to be narrow; that is, they typically consist of a single performance criterion, for example, students' scores on various kinds of standardized achievement tests. Moreover, information about the school milieu is also frequently limited. The limitation here is that only a very few school systems collect information on any sizeable number of dimensions; and, even where such an effort is made, interdistrict comparisons are frequently frustrated by the lack of standardization in the data collected. Despite such handicaps, an increasing body of research is accumulating on the effectiveness of various school service components, and we begin our review of such studies at this point.

Related Research Findings
One of the forerunners in educational input-output analysis is a little-known, but nevertheless significant, study done in 1956 for the Educational Testing Service by William G. Mollenkopf and S. Donald Melville.[14] These researchers gathered aptitude and achievement test scores from a nationwide sample of 9,000 ninth grade students in 100 schools and 8,357 twelfth grade students in 106 schools. Principals in each school responded to a questionnaire that led to the construction of thirty-four variables dealing with socioeconomic characteristics of students and their parents, availability of community educational opportunities, and quality of available school

[14] William G. Mollenkopf and S. Donald Melville, "A Study of Secondary School Characteristics as Related to Test Scores," Research Bulletin 56–6 (Princeton: Educational Testing Service, 1956), mimeographed.

services. Given these three clusters of variables, the authors were able to assess the school's contribution to student performance while attempting to control for out-of-school influences. The authors are particularly careful to caution readers of the difficulty in prohibiting student socioeconomic factors from contaminating any analysis of school service effects. Nevertheless, after controlling as best they could for student SES, they report four school service measures to be significantly related to pupil achievement. These are (1) number of special staff (psychologists, reading specialists, counselors in the school, (2) class size, (3) pupil-teacher ratio,[15] and (4) instructional expenditures per student.

All of these findings suggest the central importance of the school staff and of relatively frequent contact between students and staff. Measure number 4 is somewhat difficult to interpret because instructional expenditures usually include funds for supplies and equipment as well as staff salaries. However, in that the major proportion of this expenditure category is spent on instructional salaries, this measure also hints of the significance of the school's personnel in the learning process. What is necessary now is to compare the results obtained in this study with those obtained in investigations where the controls for out-of-school influences are more adequate.

Another one of the early studies in this field was conducted in 1959 by the State Education Department of New York under the direction of Samuel M. Goodman.[16] This study, known as the Quality Measurement Project, covered a sample of 70,000 seventh and eleventh grade students in 102 school districts selected for their ability to represent all of New York State. Findings here are comparable on two dimensions with the work of Mollenkopf-Melville. After identifying and setting aside the statistical variance accounted for by the socioeconomic status of parents, Goodman reports per pupil instructional expenditures and number of special staff per 1,000 students to be significantly correlated with the achievement test scores of seventh grade students. In addition, two other characteristics were found to be significantly linked to pupil performance; they are teachers'

[15] The second and third measures (class size and pupil-teacher ratio) represent similar but not identical phenomena. For example, it is possible for a school to have a relatively high ratio of pupils to teachers, but if each teacher instructs in six or more classes, average class size may be relatively low. In general, however, where class size is large there will be relatively few staff members for the number of students enrolled.
[16] Samuel M. Goodman, **The Assessment of School Quality** (Albany: The State Education Department of New York, 1959).

experience and a variable described as "classroom atmosphere." Teacher experience was measured as number of teachers in a district with five or more years of employment as a classroom instructor. "Classroom atmosphere" was a measure resulting from an observer's rating of the degree to which the teacher attempted to relate the subject matter under consideration to the interests and ability levels of students. In essence, it appears to be a measure of the degree to which the teacher was student oriented as contrasted with what educators frequently term "subject-matter oriented." In general, Goodman's findings again point to the importance of the school's personnel in the instructional process.

J. Alan Thomas, the author of the Thomas Report, to which we have often referred, conducted an interesting inquiry about school effectiveness in 1962.[17] Thomas utilized Project TALENT information to test the impact of a large number of home, community, and school service variables upon student performance. His sample was composed of 206 high schools in communities of 2,500 to 25,000 in forty-six states. For tenth and twelfth grade students in these schools he had scores on eighteen achievement tests. Data about students, communities, and schools were taken from Project TALENT surveys and the 1960 census. Regression analysis was the statistical treatment utilized, and three measures of school service were found to be significantly related with students' test scores, after taking home and community factors into account. These school service components are (1) beginning teachers' salaries, (2) teachers' experience, and (3) number of volumes in the school library.

Two significant studies of the effects of schools were reported in 1965: one, centered on schools in New York, was done by Herbert J. Kiesling;[18] and the other, centered on schools in California, was done for the California state senate by Charles S. Benson.[19] The Benson

[17] J. Alan Thomas, "Efficiency in Education: A Study of the Relationship between Selected Inputs and Mean Test Scores in a Sample of Senior High Schools" (unpublished Ph.D. dissertation, Stanford University School of Education, 1962).

[18] Kiesling's study was an unpublished Harvard University Ph.D. dissertation. The results of that study are more readily available in an article entitled "Measuring a Local Government Service: A Study of School Districts in New York State," Review of Economics and Statistics, 49 (August 1967), 356–367.

[19] Charles S. Benson et al., State and Local Fiscal Relationships in Public Education in California, a report of the Senate Fact Finding Committee on Revenue and Taxation published by the Senate of the State of California, March 1965.

study relied on data for fifth grade students from 249 school districts. Student performance was measured by standardized reading and mathematics tests. Data were compiled from the 1960 census on twelve socioeconomic and demographic variables of school district residents. Information was gathered from school districts and official statewide reports on eighteen variables relating to school finance and expenditure allocations for school services. Because of a lack of time and the condition of the data, the study utilized only entire school districts, not individual schools, as the unit of analysis. Consequently, because of the averaging that occurs when measures for an entire district are used, the findings contain the potential of understating the importance of school service variables. Nevertheless, stepwise multiple regression analysis revealed teachers' salaries and instructional expenditures per pupil to be positively related to pupils' achievement even when socioeconomic status variables were taken into account. In Benson's words:

The association between the achievement of pupils and the instruction offered by these teachers who are qualified by experience and training to be paid in the upper salary quartile is positive, and the association stands independently of the known connection between the home environment of pupils and their achievement.[20]

For medium-sized school districts (those with enrollments of 2,000 to 4,500 pupils) Benson found that, in addition to variables relating to teachers' salaries, mean salary of administrators was also positively associated with student achievement. Thus, this study also shows the importance of staff members with certain characteristics in influencing the performance of pupils.

The study of Kiesling was based on information collected in the previously described New York State Quality Measurement Project conducted by Goodman. One of Kiesling's major findings is that expenditures per pupil are positively related to student achievement (measured on Iowa Tests of Basic Skills and Iowa Tests of Educational Development). This finding holds specifically for large school districts (those with enrollments in excess of 2,000 pupils), particularly large urban school districts containing relatively large proportions of disadvantaged students. For small districts, particularly small rural districts, the relationship between these two factors was frequently found to be random, and in some instances even to be negative. However, as the author is careful to suggest, the opportunity for

[20] Ibid., p. 56.

various kinds of measurement idiosyncracies to manifest themselves
is substantially greater in small districts. In a research sample made
up of school districts that contain small numbers of students and
very few teachers the characteristics of individuals at the extremes
of the measurement scales take on statistical significance out of
proportion to their number. Moreover, as was the case with the
Benson study, the per-pupil expenditure variable used by Kiesling
was a districtwide average figure and thus contains the potential to
distort significantly the amount of resources spent on any individual
student within a specific district. Nevertheless, one of the study's
findings deserves particular emphasis. In Kiesling's words, "The
relationship of expenditure to performance in large urban districts is
quite strong, with an additional $100 of expenditure being associated
with 2.6 months of [achievement] at the beginning of the expenditure
range and 1.4 months at the end of the range."[21]

In that the total per-pupil expenditure figure for a school district
represents money spent for a wide range of products and services, it
is impossible to state precisely from Kiesling's findings just what
school service component or components are making the difference.
One extrapolation which appears reasonable, however, stems from
the fact that the overwhelming portion of most school districts'
expenditures are for the salary of professional staff. (This figure
typically accounts for from 65 to 85 percent of a school district's
budget.) Consequently, it might be that the higher expenditure figure
represents an ability to purchase services of instructional personnel
who are more effective by virtue of their experience, preparation, and
general ability. These increments in the quality of staff, in turn, reflect
themselves in the achievement test scores of students. This is but a
supposition, however, because Kiesling does not present data directly
related to teacher preparation and experience.

Results of the study **Equality of Educational Opportunity** (the
Coleman Report) were made public in 1966. At the beginning of this
chapter we noted the limitations of the Coleman team's efforts; at
this point it is appropriate also to acknowledge some of the report's
strengths. The Coleman Report represents the most extensive attempt
at assessment of a nation's entire educational system ever made. The

[21] Kiesling, "School Districts in New York State," p. 365. The word "achievement" in this quotation is ours. The journal article has the word "expenditure" at that exact point, but the meaningless nature of the term in that
context leads us to believe that it is a printing error and that our substitution
is consistent with the author's intent.

survey collected information on approximately 660,000 students attending thousands of schools in hundreds of school districts in every region of the United States. In addition, data were gathered regarding the teachers of those students, the characteristics of their schools, the range and diversity of their curriculums, qualifications of the school administrators, and so on. Because of serious measurement errors and inappropriate analytical procedures, we believe that Coleman and his colleagues, though unintentionally, underestimate very greatly the potential significance for pupil achievement of a number of the school service components they examined. Nevertheless, a fact that is worthy of emphasis is that, having biased their analysis against finding effective school service components, the Coleman team reports several such components to be positively and significantly associated with pupils' performance.[22]

The most significant school service variable in explaining student achievement (measured by a vocabulary test) was a teacher characteristic, the teacher's verbal ability. As with the other findings of this nature that we have discussed, care must be used in interpreting the meaning of such a result. What the Coleman team reports is that, after having made an effort to control statistically for home background and community social environment, researchers found that a student's achievement test results tend to increase in direct relation to the verbal ability level of his teacher. Obviously, much more is involved in the instruction of a student than his teacher's skill at responding to verbal-ability test questions. However, if one views teachers' verbal ability as a proxy measure for a number of related skills and qualities, the Coleman Report finding can be interpreted in a meaningful fashion.[23] If the measure of verbal ability is taken to represent the general intelligence level of the teacher, the finding can be

[22] The analysis of the effect of school service components upon pupil performance is discussed in the Coleman Report, pp. 290–332. In addition to the already cited works by Bowles and Levin, anyone who is deeply interested in studies of school effectiveness should read Glen Cain and Harold Watts, "Problems in Making Inferences from the Coleman Report," mimeographed working paper of the Institute for Research on Poverty (Madison: University of Wisconsin, 1968) and John F. Kain and Eric A. Hanushek, "On the Value of Equality of Educational Opportunity as a Guide to Public Policy," mimeographed working paper no. 36 of the Program on Regional and Urban Economics (Cambridge, Mass.: Harvard University, 1968).
[23] For additional information on the relationship of verbal ability to other personal attributes see John C. Flanagan et al., The American High School Student (Pittsburgh: Project TALENT office, University of Pittsburgh, 1964), Chapters 7 and 8.

construed to mean that an intellectually facile instructor is more adept at tasks such as finding means to motivate students, adapting materials to their ability levels, and communicating in ways that make the subject matter more understandable. This is an interpretation that is totally consistent with observation and conventional wisdom.

An interesting adjunct to the Coleman finding about teachers' verbal ability is that the variable appears to have an accumulative effect. It is statistically significant when examined for sixth grade students and thereafter increases in importance when examined for ninth and twelfth grade students. Moreover, its effect tends to vary in accord with the characteristics of the student. It shows consistently positive correlations with the achievement of all students, but it appears to be especially important in explaining the achievement levels of Negro students. To paraphrase the Coleman Report, Negro children appear to respond in a particularly sensitive and positive fashion to a teacher who is skilled verbally.

In the year following issuance of the Coleman Report (1967), three additional studies were published that deal with some facet of the topic of school service effectiveness. Two of these, a study by Marion F. Shaycoft[24] and a study directed by Jesse Burkhead[25] focus on U.S. secondary schools. The third study, known as the Plowden Report,[26] was conducted in England.

The Shaycoft study is unusually informative on several dimensions and somewhat disappointing on others. Its greatest asset results from the procedures employed to measure student performance. The study sample consisted of 6,583 students who were tested by Project TALENT in 1960 when they were in the ninth grade. Subsequently, these students matriculated in 118 different secondary schools (101 of which were comprehensive high schools, the other seventeen specialized vocational high schools).[27] In 1963 this same cohort of

---

[24] Marion F. Shaycoft, **The High School Years: Growth in Cognitive Skills** (Pittsburgh: American Institute for Research and School of Education, University of Pittsburgh, 1967).

[25] Jesse Burkhead, Thomas G. Fox and John W. Holland, **Input and Output in Large City High Schools** (Syracuse: Syracuse University Press, 1967).

[26] This study represents the efforts of a distinguished committee chaired by Lady Plowden. The research study and report were issued by the Central Advisory Council on Education and are officially entitled **Children and Their Primary Schools** (London: Her Majesty's Stationery Office, 1967).

[27] The secondary schools were selected on the basis of a stratification procedure that aimed at constructing a sample that was representative of all secondary schools in the nation.

students was administered a battery of examinations designed for twelfth grade students. The test battery, in addition to the usual generalized test of verbal and quantitative reasoning ability, also included achievement examinations in specific subject areas, for example, foreign language, English, accounting, and literature. Presumably, schools are established to instruct students in moderately well-defined subject matter areas, not to increase some quality as amorphous as "verbal ablity." Consequently, the Shaycoft output measures appear to be more related than those of most studies to the functions and objectives of schools.

A second feature of the Shaycoft study is the use of longitudinal or time series testing. What a student knew about a particular subject was measured in grade nine, and this information was used as a base line against which to assess increments in achievement for the subsequent three years of schooling. This procedure, more closely than most other methods, enables the researcher to gain a picture of the "value added" to the student during the course of his schooling. Moreover, in that the tests were heavily concentrated on school-related subjects, subjects about which one typically does not learn outside of schools, the room for alternative explanations of achievement gains is reduced.

The Shaycoft analyses reveal student achievement gains over the three years to be consistent and of a healthy magnitude. In most instances, twelfth grade achievement gains represented a difference of one standard deviation when compared to ninth grade norms. This is so even when differences in students' socioeconomic status are controlled statistically. It is reasonable to infer from such a finding that for the schools in question some school service characteristics are influencing student achievement. The difficulty, and consequently the disappointment, with the Shaycoft study, is that only a very limited spectrum of school service components was examined. The study concentrated on the availability within schools of particular subject matter offerings. No measures of components such as staff quality, instructional material availability, or equipment and facility adequacy were employed. What can be said is that the availability of a particular curriculum in a school is related significantly to whether or not students grow in knowledge about the subject matter contained in that curriculum. Not surprisingly, for example, when schools did not offer courses in accounting or electricity, then students' scores on achievement tests in these areas were limited.

The effort by Burkhead and his colleagues lacks the richness of the Shaycoft study on the dimension of subject-matter performance measures, but it is much more complete in terms of the school service components it examines. The Burkhead study sample included thirty-nine Chicago public secondary schools (enrolling almost 90,000 students), and twenty-two Atlanta public high schools (enrolling a total of approximately 19,000 students). Results for schools in these two large cities were compared with data from a Project TALENT sample of approximately 180 public high schools in smaller communities. Information regarding students' performance was constructed from scores on a variety of tests of aptitude, reading, and general knowledge and measures of school persistence (the degree to which students do **not** "drop out" of schools). Socioeconomic status measures were derived from 1960 census data about residents in high school attendance areas. School service components consisted of measures such as teacher–man-years per pupil, teachers' experience, and school building age. Statistical techniques were employed in an effort to control for the SES of students. Unfortunately, however, these statistical procedures were essentially the same as those employed by the Coleman Report team, and, thus, tend to understate seriously the potential impact of school service components. Despite methodological limitations biasing the findings against schools, Burkhead reports some school services to be effective.

Findings varied somewhat from Chicago to Atlanta, probably, at least in part, reflecting the lack of standardization in the input and output measures used for schools in the two cities. Moreover, results from analyses of Chicago's schools were somewhat hampered by lack of variation or dispersion in the quality of school services dispensed at the different schools. Nevertheless, in Chicago, newer buildings were found to be associated with lower dropout rates and the teachers' experience was linked to pupils' reading scores. For Atlanta schools, low rates of teacher turnover were found to be positively associated with increments in pupils' scores on tests or verbal ability. For the sample of high schools in small communities, the beginning salary and years of experience for teachers and the age of the school building were found to explain variations in test score results.

The work of England's Central Advisory Council on Education (the Plowden Report) consists of two volumes, Volume I presents the policy recommendations of the Council, and Volume II contains results of the several research studies that serve to support these recommendations.[28] For our purposes, the Plowden Report's most significant research study is the **National Survey of Parental Attitudes and Circumstances Related to School and Pupil Characteristics,** directed by Gerald Peaker. This effort collected information from a stratified random sample of primary school students as to academic performance and school and home characteristics. These data enabled the study team to assess the relative influence upon pupil performance of home and socioeconomic status characteristics and school service components. The primary statistical procedure employed was regression analysis.

Except for the fact that the study limits itself to a concern for elementary school students, its findings and the controversies surrounding them are not very different from those produced by the Coleman Report in this nation. Nevertheless, several school service components are described as contributing in a statistically significant fashion to an explanation of pupil achievement. These components deal with the school building and the teacher. Specifically, age, of building and teachers' experience, academic preparation, and "ability" were found to be postively associated with output measures. These findings are all consistent with and support the results of the other studies we have already reviewed.

Added evidence of the significant role played by teachers in the instructional process is provided by research for a 1968 study by Elchanan Cohn.[29] Cohn was primarily concerned with examining possible economies of scale in public high school operations. His analyses, however, also lend themselves to our search for information about the effectiveness of various school service components. For secondary school students in a sample of 377 school districts in the state of Iowa, Cohn obtained information relative to achievement (as measured by scores on the Iowa Test of Educational Development) and school services (mostly expenditure data and information about teacher characteristics). Using multiple regression analysis, Cohn reports that amount of teacher salary and number of instructional assignments per teacher are associated with increments of pupil

[28] A discussion and critique of both volumes is provided in separate articles by Joseph Featherstone and David Cohen in the **Harvard Educational Review,** 38 (Spring 1968), pp. 317–340.
[29] Elchanan Cohn, "Economies of Scale in Iowa High School Operations," **Journal of Human Resources,** 3 (Fall 1968), 422–434.

achievement, and the direction of the association is in keeping with conventional expectations. The higher the salary and the fewer the number of different teaching assignments for a teacher, the higher the test scores of pupils. In terms of his primary objective, assessing economies of scale, Cohn found high schools with enrollments between approximately 1,250 and 1,650 students to be the most cost-effective.

The extent to which Cohn's study possessed an effective statistical control for certain nonschool inputs (student aptitude and SES) is questionable. Consequently, the results in terms of the unique contribution of school services must be interpreted with caution. Nevertheless, Cohn's findings are consistent with what we have come to expect by comparison with findings from other studies.

A study somewhat similar to Cohn's was reported in 1968 by Richard Raymond.[30] Raymond's sample consisted of approximately 5,000 West Virginia high school students who graduated between 1963 and 1966 and who subsequently matriculated at the University of West Virginia. The freshman year performance of these students was measured by achievement test scores and individual grade point averages. Students were grouped by the counties in which their high schools were located, and measures of school service characteristics were then obtained for county school systems.[31] Four measures of socioeconomic status for the residents of these counties were obtained from 1960 census data. Using these census figures to control for SES, Raymond regressed school service components on the two output measures and found teachers' salaries to explain a significant portion of the variance in students' freshman year scholastic performance. The salaries of elementary school teachers appeared to be particularly powerful variables in explaining differences in student achievement.

The 1968 study of Boston schools done by Martin Katzman,[32] to which we referred in Chapter 3, in addition to examining factors influencing distribution of services among schools in a large urban system, also examined the relationship between school services and

[30] Richard Raymond, "Determinants of the Quality of Primary and Secondary Public Education in West Virginia," **Journal of Human Resources,** 3 (Fall 1968), 450–470.
[31] In West Virginia, as in most southern states, the county serves as the primary unit for organizing local school districts.
[32] Theodore Martin Katzman, "Distribution and Production in a Big City Elementary School System," **Yale Economic Essays,** 8 (Spring 1968), 201–256.

student achievement. He collected data from fifty-six of the Boston school system's elementary school attendance districts. Information was gathered on six dimensions of pupil performance: three measures pertaining to regularity of attendance and school holding power and three scholastic measures (percentage of students taking and percentage passing the entrance examination to the academically elite Boston Latin School, and reading achievement increments as determined by differentials between second and sixth grade examination results).

Using multiple regression analysis in an effort to control for students' SES, Katzman found school service variables to be significantly associated with one or more of the above output measures in the following fashion:

A measure of "crowding" was derived from the number of classrooms that contained more than thirty-five students. That figure represented the modal number of desks in a Boston city school classroom; students in excess of this number were taken to be in some sort of makeshift arrangement. The consequences of crowding were not found to be clear and consistent on the attendance output measures. Noncrowding, however, was associated with increments of reading achievement and number of students passing the Latin School's entrance examination.

The ratio of students to staff members was found to have consistent and significant correlation with school attendance and school persistence output measures.

The size of the attendance district appeared to provide some economies of scale when judged on the output criteria of reading scores and school persistence. That is, the larger the number of children served by an attendance district, the higher their reading achievement increments and the greater the schools' holding power. However, in contrast to these positive consequences of size, some diseconomies of scale were found when the output measures dealt with the Latin School. The larger the attendance district's enrollments, the smaller the proportion of students who sat for and passed the Latin School's entrance examination.

The percentage of permanently employed teachers was found to have minor, but nevertheless positive, effects on all output measures. The greater the percentage of permanently employed, or tenured, teachers, the better the performance of pupils.

Percent of teachers who possessed a master's degree was found to have generally positive effects. This component demonstrated particularly strong relationships with measures of school attendance.

The percent of teachers in an attendance district with from one to ten years of teaching experience was taken as a school service component or input variable. The relationship of this measure to outputs was interesting, but inconsistent. Experience was positively associated with measures of school attendance and holding power, but negatively related to relative increments in reading achievement.

The turnover rate among teachers within an attendance district was demonstrated to have a slight negative association with all the output measures.

Katzman's study adds substantially to the evidence supporting the significant role of school staff in affecting pupil performance. As with almost all such efforts, however, the findings of his study would be even more helpful had he been able to enlarge the scope and refine the input measures considered. The finding for teacher experience provides an interesting example here. To know that the variable "percent of teachers with from one to ten years of teaching experience" is positively linked to increments in holding power but negatively associated with relative increments of reading achievement is to paint a somewhat perplexing picture. If Katzman had had access to complete information we could begin to see more precisely whether these findings result from a preponderance of very new, inexperienced teachers, say in their first year, or of teachers near the nine- and ten-year end of the category.

In 1968, Samuel Bowles presented results of another study on educational production functions.[33] Bowles' findings are based on a sample of twelfth grade Negro male students constructed from data compiled by the Coleman Report survey team. Bowles is careful to circumscribe the validity and generalizability of his findings by referring to the limitations of the sampling and measurement procedures employed in the initial collection of the data. Despite these limitations, we find his results to be of interest; not only do they reaffirm the significance of teacher characteristics, but also they suggest certain additional categories of school service components to be important. Regression analysis was employed, and four measures of a student's home environment were entered into the equation in an effort to control for out-of-school influences. Relative presence of science laboratory facilities, average amount of time a teacher spends in guidance activities, and number of days the school stays in session during a school year are all variables found to be sig-

[33] Bowles, "Toward an Educational Production Function."

nificantly associated with students' scores on tests of verbal ability. The "science teaching laboratory" variable is somewhat similar to "teacher's verbal score" in its need to be interpreted. How can the presence or absence of science laboratories have an impact on student achievement when the latter is measured by general tests of reading and vocabulary? Our answer to this query is to take science laboratories as a proxy measure of school facilities more generally. The logic here is that schools possessing such laboratory facilities are also likely to be relatively well equipped on most other dimensions of school facilities. Conversely, a school lacking science laboratories is also likely to be in a poor position with regard to other facilities used for instruction.

In another place, Bowles reports findings from a study that utilized a sample of twelfth grade Negro students for which Project TALENT information was available.[34] In this instance, the output measures were students' achievement in mathematics and reading and scores on a test of generalized academic ability. Bowles found large class size and "teaching" or ability grouping to be negatively related and amount of teachers' graduate preparation to be positively related to students' performance on reading tests. Only the class size variable was significant at the 0.05 level, however. When mathematics achievement scores were taken as the criterion, ability grouping and age of school building appeared to have a negative influence and expenditures per pupil and teachers' graduate preparations a positive influence. Finally, on the test of general academic ability, class size and ability grouping were again found to be negatively related and teacher preparation level positive. All of these findings came about after statistical controls for students' social environment had been exercised.

In another study coauthored with Henry Levin, Bowles presents more findings about the effectiveness of several other school service components.[35] During the course of their literary debate with James S. Coleman and his colleagues regarding the validity of the survey of **Equality of Educational Opportunity** findings, Bowles and Levin employed Coleman Report data in a regression analysis that attempted to correct for some of the Coleman Report's controversial

[34] Samuel S. Bowles, "Educational Production Functions," final report to the Office of Education under cooperative research contract OEC 1-7-00451-2651 (February 1969).
[35] Samuel S. Bowles and Henry M. Levin, "More on Multicollinearity and the Effectiveness of Schools."

methodological procedures. These analyses were conducted using verbal ability test results as output measures for twelfth grade Negro students. In this effort, they found teachers' salaries and science laboratories to be significantly related to pupil performance. In another regression analysis in the same study, they found teachers' verbal ability to be significantly related to student achievement. These same findings held generally for analyses done for white twelfth grade students, but, for reasons which are not readily explainable, the levels of significance were lower.

Somewhat similar findings stem from a 1968 study done by Eric Hanushek.[36] This study attempts to calculate educational production functions for sixth grade children using standardized achievement test scores as a criterion of output and measures derived from Coleman Report data as inputs. The study centers on white children in 471 elementary schools and Negro children in 232 elementary schools in the metropolitan North. Regression analysis was the statistical procedure utilized, with suitable controls for socioeconomic status. Significant relationships to achievement were found for teachers' verbal ability and years of teaching experience.

Also in 1968, Thomas I. Ribich published the results of a study utilizing information from Project TALENT.[37] Ribich's procedure was to examine only those students who fell into the lowest quintile on measures of socioeconomic status. When this control was exercised for out-of-school influences, it was found that pupils' performance on standardized achievement tests was directly related to expeditures per pupil.

Summary of Effective School Service Components

In the preceding section we reviewed seventeen studies that deal with the effectiveness of school service components. These investigations have been conducted using a variety of sample subjects, input and output measures, and controls for what are commonly presumed to be out-of-school influences upon pupil performance. In order to impose some degree of uniformity upon this diversity, we have attempted to condense the essential components of each investigation into a summary chart (Table 4.1).

[36] Eric Hanushek, "The Education of Negroes and Whites" (unpublished doctoral dissertation, Department of Economics, Massachusetts Institute of Technology, 1968).
[37] Thomas I. Ribich, **Education and Poverty** (Washington, D.C.: Brookings, 1968).

Table 4.1. Summary of Effectiveness Studies on School Service Components

Study Author(s)	Description of Sample	Measure of Pupil Performance (School Output)	Measure(s) of Effective School Service Component(s) (School Input)
1. Mollenkopf and Melville	U.S. 17,000 9th grade (in 100 schools) and 12th grade (in 106 schools), male and female	Aptitude and achievement tests	1. Number of special staff 2. Class size 3. Pupil-teacher ratio 4. Instructional expenditures
2. Goodman	New York, 70,000 7th and 11th grade, male and female in 102 school districts	Achievement test	1. Number of special staff 2. Instructional expenditures 3. Teachers' experience 4. "Classroom atmosphere"
3. Thomas	Project TALENT Sample (national), 10th and 12th grade, male and female	Achievement test	1. Teachers' salaries 2. Teachers' experience 3. Number of library books
4. Benson	California, 5th grade, 249 school districts	Reading achievement test	1. Teachers' salaries 2. Administrators' salaries 3. Instructional expenditures

Study	Sample	Measure	Variables
5. Kiesling	New York, 70,000 7th and 11th grade male and female in 102 school districts	Achievement test	1. Expenditure per pupil (in large school districts)
6. Coleman Report	U.S. sample	Verbal ability test	1. Teachers' verbal ability
7. Shaycoft	U.S., 108 schools, 6,500 9th and 12th grade, male and female	Battery of 42 aptitude and achievement tests	1. Curriculum variables
8. Burkhead	90,000 Chicago high school students in 39 schools, 19,000 Atlanta high school students in 22 schools and 180 small community high schools	Aptitude and achievement tests and school holding power	1. Age of building 2. Teachers' experience 3. Teacher turnover 4. Teachers' salaries
9. Plowden Report	English elementary school students		1. Age of building 2. Teachers' experience 3. Teachers' academic preparation 4. Teachers' "ability"

Table 4.1 (Continued)

Study (Author(s))	Description of Sample	Measure of Pupil Performance (School Output)	Measure(s) of Effective School Service Component(s) (School Input)
10. Cohn	Iowa high school students in 377 school districts	Achievement test	1. Teachers' salaries 2. Number of instructional assignments per teacher 3. School size
11. Raymond	W. Virginia, 5,000 high school students	Freshman year (college) GPA and achievement test scores	1. Teachers' salaries
12. Katzman	Boston elementary school students	School attendance, school holding power, reading achievement, special school entrance examination	1. Pupils per classroom 2. Student-staff ratio 3. Attendance district enrollment size 4. Teachers' employment status 5. Teachers' degree level 6. Teachers' experience 7. Teacher turnover ratio

	Sample	Dependent variable	Independent variables
13. Bowles (1)	U.S., 12th grade Negro males	Verbal ability test	1. Teachers' verbal ability 2. Science laboratory facilities 3. Length of school year
14. Bowles (2)	U.S., 12th grade Negro males	Mathematics and reading achievement test and a test of general academic ability	1. Class size 2. Ability grouping 3. Level of teacher training 4. Age of school building 5. Expenditures per pupil
15. Bowles & Levin	12th grade Negro students and 12th grade white students	Verbal ability test scores	1. Teachers' verbal ability 2. Teachers' salaries
16. Hanushek	6th grade white students in 471 schools and 6th grade Negro students in 242 schools	Verbal ability test	1. Teachers' verbal ability 2. Teachers' experience
17. Ribich	Project TALENT sample	Achievement test	1. Expenditures per pupil

From an inspection of these digested results it is evident that there is a substantial degree of consistency in the studies' findings. The strongest findings by far are those that relate to the number and quality of the professional staff, particularly teachers. Fourteen of the studies we reviewed found teacher characteristics, such as verbal ability, amount of experience, salary level, amount and type of academic preparation, degree level, and employment status (tenured or nontenured), to be significantly associated with one or more measures of pupil performance.

In order for school staff to have an effect upon students, however, it is necessary that students have some access to such persons. And, indeed, we also found that student performance was related to some degree to contact frequency with or proximity to professional staff. This factor expressed itself in variables such as student-staff ratios, classroom size, school or school district size, and length of school year.

In addition to findings in support of the effectiveness of staff, a number of studies under review also present results to suggest that service components such as age of school building and adequacy and extent of physical facilities for instruction also are significantly linked to increments in scales of pupil performance. Finally, as might be expected logically because all the foregoing components translate into dollar costs, we find that measures such as expenditures per pupil and teachers' salary levels are correlated significantly with pupil achievement measures.[38]

In summary, we are impressed with the amount and consistency of evidence supporting the effectiveness of school services in influencing the academic performance of pupils. In time, we would wish for more precise information about which school service components are most effective and in what mix or proportion they can be made more effective. On the basis of information obtained in the studies we have reviewed, there can be little doubt that schools can have an effect "that is independent of the child's social environment." In other words, schools do make a difference.

A New Test of School Service Effectiveness
There are many reasons to believe that the findings of other studies of school service component effectiveness, studies done on other

[38] For a more detailed description of the manner in which teacher quality characteristics translate into dollar costs, see Henry M. Levin, **Recruiting Teachers for Large City Schools** (Columbus, Ohio: Charles Merrill and Sons, forthcoming).

samples in other geographic circumstances, would also hold for a sample of students in Michigan. In an effort to assess performance consequences of the specific inequalities we described in our third chapter, we examined the relationship between school service quality and academic achievement for the sample of Michigan students in the Equality of Educational Opportunity Survey.[39] This examination was conducted using the following procedures.

In order to "control" for social environment or background, students were grouped, as nearly as possible, in terms of their socioeconomic status. Students were ranked on their SES scores (OEI). A computer program was written that sorted out all students who fell into a single SES decile. The entire sample included 5,284 sixth grade students; thus, each decile contained approximately 528 students. Deciles were selected as the appropriate sorting unit on the basis that they allowed for clustering of students into SES groups with a desirable degree of homogeneity. For each decile a rank order coefficient was calculated between individuals' scores on school service component quality measures and their scores on measures of academic achievement. This procedure was repeated ten times until school service component effectiveness was assessed for students in each SES decile stratum.[40]

Measures of pupil performance were threefold. As we have discussed in other places throughout this study, we do not regard cognitive development as the school's only function. We do regard it, however, as one of the school's most important functions. Accordingly, measures of performance consist of pupils' scores on three cognitive area examinations: (1) a test of reading ability, (2) a test of mathematics understanding, and (3) a test of verbal facility.[41]

From knowledge of the research literature on school effectiveness we selected twelve school service components to test against the above-listed output measures. Each of these components was found

[39] This research is reported in greater technical detail in a paper entitled "A Study of School Effectiveness," delivered by the authors at the conference of the American Educational Research Association held in Minneapolis in March of 1970.
[40] A caveat is in order here. The deciling selection technique provides a control for SES, but it does not permit precise assessment of each school service variable's independent influence upon the student performance criterion measure. Univariate analysis in this instance permits the possibility that one school service variable may be acting as a proxy for another. However, even if the underlying or "real" variable is not the one we examine, the likelihood is that it is nevertheless a school service resource and this is the only fact that is essential to our proposition.
[41] These tests were EEOS variable numbers 142, 146, and 148.

Table 4.2 Summary of Michigan School Service Component Effectiveness

EEOS Variable No.	School Service Component	Variable Name	Output Measures	Significant SES Deciles	Direction of Relationship
7		School site size	Math score	5, 8, 10	+
			Reading score	None	
			Verbal score	5, 6	
8		Building age	Math score	4, 6, 7, 8, 9, 10	−
			Reading score	1, 2, 4, 6, 7, 9, 10	
			Verbal score	1, 2, 4, 5, 6, 7, 8, 9, 10	
11		Percent of makeshift classrooms	Math score	7, 9, 10	−
			Reading score	None	
			Verbal score	6, 9	
13		Library volumes per student	Math score	1, 6, 7, 8, 9, 10	+
			Reading score	4, 6, 8, 9	
			Verbal score	6, 7, 8, 9	
43		Size of school (enrollment)	Math score	1, 2, 6, 8, 10	−
			Reading score	1, 6, 10	
			Verbal score	1, 2, 6, 8, 10	

			Sign
47	Percent of students transferring	Math score	4, 6, 7, 8, 9	
		Reading score	1, 2, 4, 5, 6, 7, 8, 9	
		Verbal score	1, 2, 4, 7, 8	−
88	Classrooms per 1,000 students	Math score	2, 6, 8, 9, 10	
		Reading score	2, 6, 8, 9	
		Verbal score	2, 6, 8, 9, 10	+
95	Teachers' experience	Math score	3, 4	
		Reading score	None	
		Verbal score	None	+
105	Teacher attitude (1) (Would you be a teacher again?)	Math score	1, 2, 5, 6, 7, 8, 9	
		Reading score	1, 2, 5, 6, 7, 8, 9	
		Verbal score	1, 2, 3, 5, 6, 7, 8, 9, 10	+
106	Teacher attitude (2) (Do you like the school you are in?)	Math score	1, 2, 5, 6, 7, 8, 9, 10	
		Reading score	1, 2, 5, 6, 7, 8, 9	
		Verbal score	1, 2, 5, 6, 7, 8, 9, 10	+
127	Teacher attitude (3) (Compatibility of teachers in the school)	Math score	1, 2, 6, 7, 8, 9, 10	
		Reading score	4, 6, 7, 8, 9	
		Verbal score	2, 6, 7, 8, 9	+
141	Teachers' verbal ability	Math score	1, 3, 4, 5, 6, 7, 8, 9	
		Reading score	5, 6, 8, 9	
		Verbal score	1, 3, 5, 6, 7, 8	+

to be associated with at least one output measure at the 0.05 level of statistical significance.[42] Table 4.2 summarizes these findings.

School Facilities

Four facility measures were used, and each was found to be significantly associated with all three measures of student achievement. Specifically, the four measures were: school site size, age of school building, number of classrooms per 1,000 students, and percent of makeshift classrooms in the school.[43] School site size is significantly associated with two achievement measures, but this tends to be true only for middle and upper SES deciles. The other three facility measures are significant across all SES levels. This is particularly the case of building age, which is significant in nearly every decile for all three output measures.

Our view of the facility measures is that they should be regarded as illustrative of the wider physical environment of the school. It is difficult to argue straightforwardly that the amount of acreage around a school, the building's age and state of repair (except in the most extreme circumstances), or the presence or absence of sufficient numbers of classrooms directly influence a child's reading and mathematics achievement. However, if we take these measures to be proxies of the total school physical environment with which the student has contact, then the above-described findings fit into place logically. It is conceivable that the adequacy of facilities affects learning in at least two ways. First, it may influence the child's attitudes and subsequently his motivation for learning. Second, a limited physical environment will restrict the range and intensity of curriculum offerings. Regardless of the precise processes involved, however, it appears clear that inadequate physical facilities are linked to lower levels of academic achievement.

Instructional Materials

One measure of instructional materials was employed, and it is significantly correlated with achievement measures.[44] This is the number of library volumes per thousand students. This variable is tied to all three output measures and at all SES decile levels. However, it appears particularly effective with the higher SES students.

Teacher Characteristics

This domain can be divided into two sets of variables: (1) those that

[42] As was the case in the analyses described in Chapter 3, a two-tailed test of significance was also employed in these analyses.
[43] These are, respectively, EEOS variable numbers 7, 8, 11 and 88.
[44] EEOS variable number 13.

assess relatively objective attributes of the teacher, and (2) those which assess teacher attitudes.

Teacher Attributes. This subset of variables contains two measures: (1) teachers' scores on a test of verbal ability and (2) years of teaching experience.[45] Of these, the experience measure is the weakest. It registered a significant association only with the mathematics test output measure and only for two SES deciles at that. The measure of verbal ability, however, is quite another matter. It registered a significant correlation with all three achievement tests and then for many deciles and at almost every SES level. Again, as we discussed previously in this chapter, this verbal score should be interpreted as reflective of a large constellation of a teacher's abilties.

Teacher Attitudes. Three measures of teacher attitude were employed.[46] Two of these assessed the degree to which the teacher was satisfied with teaching as an occupation. The first of these inquired of the respondent, "Suppose you could go back in time and start college again; in view of your present knowledge, would you enter the teaching profession?" The response alternatives allowed teachers to register the degree of assuredness with which they would or would not repeat their career choice. The more sure the teacher was that he or she would again choose teaching as a career, the higher the students' test scores. Much the same result came about when teachers were asked "if you could choose, would you be a faculty member in some school other than this one?" Students whose teachers responded "no," thus indicating satisfaction with their teaching position, had achievement test scores that were significantly higher than those whose teachers displayed dissatisfaction. We interpret these findings to mean that morale does have an effect upon the teaching abilities of the individual involved.

The third attitude measure is based on a question that assessed the teacher's perception of the compatibility of his or her fellow faculty members. Where the teacher viewed other school staff members as working well together, students achieved well. Conversely, where staffs were seen not to work well together, student achievement declined.

Student Characteristics
One measure relating to student characteristics was percentage of

[45] EEOS variable numbers 95 and 141.
[46] EEOS variable numbers 105, 106, and 127.

students transferring in and out of the school each year.[47] This is a
significant variable for all three test measures and in most every
SES decile. Moreover, the finding is in the direction expected; that
is, the greater the amount of student turnover in a school, the lower
students' scores on examinations. This suggests that there are substantial discontinuities connected with switching schools and these
discontinuities are reflected in lower levels of achievement. High
rates of student transfer absorb energy, both the students' and the
teachers', that otherwise could be expended on learning.

A second variable that can be viewed as a student body characteristic measure is enrollment size. This refers to absolute number of
students attending the particular school in which our sample sixth
graders were located. The variable is associated significantly with
all three output measures for almost every SES decile. The direction
of the linkage is negative. That is, the larger the number of students
attending a school, the lower the sample students' achievement test
scores.

This chapter has concerned itself with the domain of school effectiveness. From previously conducted studies, studies that exercised
controls for out-of-school influences, a sizeable number of school
service components has been specifically identified as being capable
of "making a difference" in what happened to pupils in school. These
components include items such as quality of physical facilities,
ability of instructional staff, and adequacy of instructional materials.
The achievement of high quality on each of these service dimensions
costs money. Thus, quite understandably, the dollar amount spent
per pupil also appears frequently as a significant predictor of pupil
performance.

In addition to reviewing the results of other studies, an assessment
of school service effectiveness was conducted using data for school
children in Michigan. The findings of this assessment reinforce
strongly the results of other studies. The "stuff" of schools, when
available in adequate quality and quantity, influences what children
learn. Conversely, relatively inadequate services lead to lower levels
of academic achievement. **Clearly, Proposition B is confirmed.**
What remains to be demonstrated of the three original research
propositions is that differences in academic achievement influence
the opportunities available to a child after he completes his schooling.
This is the topic to which we address ourselves in the next chapter.

[47] EEOS variable numbers 43 and 47.

5

Education and Postschool Opportunity

Education . . . prevents being poor.[1]

[1] Horace Mann, quoted in Arthur Mann, "A Historical Overview: The Lumpenproletariat, Education, and Compensatory Action," in **The Quality of Inequality: Urban and Suburban Public Schools,** ed. Charles U. Daly (Chicago: University of Chicago Press, 1968), p. 13.

For centuries the acquisition of education has been viewed as a means of improving one's lot. As early as the seventeenth century the English political economist Sir William Petty noted the link between education and income. Indeed, the assumption that education would raise the economic status of the poor was an important factor in the United States in stimulating provision of universal free schooling in the late nineteenth century and in gaining enactment of compulsory school attendance laws in the early twentieth century. Education came to be looked upon as a primary means for keeping American society open and for enabling men to break the bonds of poverty. The famous American educator, Horace Mann, showed the influence of this tenet in 1848 when, with uncommon insight for that time, he made the statement that appears at the beginning of this chapter.

Our purpose in this chapter is to explore the link between education and individual opportunity. Specifically, it is here that we examine our third proposition, that

The postschool opportunity of a pupil is related to his achievement in school, and that relationship is such that higher achievement is associated with "success" and lower achievement is associated with lack of "success."

At first glance, this would appear to be little more than a statement of the obvious. Unfortunately, the step from what seems so obvious to empirical verification of the phenomenon is not an easy one. While it may be true that schooling improves the social and economic conditions of individuals, it is much more difficult to demonstrate these relations. The prime obstacle to such systematic verification is our inability to conduct a controlled experiment in which we can observe the lifetime possibilities of the same set of persons under the same set of conditions while varying only the amount and quality of their formal education.

The everyday connections we frequently make between educational attainment and life success are based upon observations of different individuals at each level of educational attainment. Consequently, we do not know, in any controlled or scientific way, what would have happened to a particular individual had he obtained more schooling or had he not gone to school at all. Moreover, our knowledge is limited even further by the tendency of highly educated individuals to share other attributes that might explain their greater success relative to the attributes and opportunities of individuals with less schooling. The quantity and quality of one's schooling may be directly related to his ability, his family's location and wealth, his motivation, his cultural milieu, his race, and so on. Thus, the ostensible connection between schooling and success may merely reflect the greater possibilities open to persons with a number of other helpful attributes rather than being an effect of education **per se.** In all likelihood, attributing the gross improvement in an individual's lifetime opportunity to higher educational attainment probably understates the effects of his other traits. Accordingly, in reviewing evidence that links schooling to individual opportunity, we will attempt to take into account some of the other factors that frequently occur in close association with the distribution of educational attainment.

Defining "Education" and "Opportunity"
By education we refer specifically to the quality and quantity of an individual's schooling. Usually, educational **quality** will be measured by student performance on standardized tests of achievement, and **quantity** will be denoted by the years of schooling completed. In the preceding chapter we demonstrated that both these measures of schooling seem to be directly related to the quality and availability of school resources. Accordingly, in this chapter we are concerned with the following question: "If improvement in school services can increase student achievement and expand the number of years of schooling for a representative individual student, will such increases in educational performance in turn improve that same individual's lifetime opportunity?"

By "opportunity" we mean the quality and quantity of alternatives available to an individual for improving his and his family's well-being. Thus, if educational attainment is to be judged to lead to increased opportunity, it must provide an individual with a larger number of a higher quality of alternatives from which to choose in making decisions that affect his destiny and the destiny of those in his household. In applying this standard, we have chosen what we believe to be several critical dimensions of opportunity: lifetime earnings, occupational attainment, political participation, intergenerational social and economic mobility, geographic mobility, school choices, military service options, and social deviance. Available studies on each of these dimensions will be reviewed separately, with attention given both to the conceptual linkages between educational attainment and particular types of opportunity and to specific research findings.

Education and Earnings

The opportunity dimension that has received the most attention from social scientists is the relationship between educational attainment and monetary earnings. The explanation for this relatively intensive examination is threefold: first, education has been viewed traditionally as one of the most important means by which people could emerge from poverty;[2] second, earnings can be readily measured; and third, there are ready sources of data on both education and earnings (or income.)[3]

There is a sound theoretical reason for expecting education to improve an individual's earning capacity. In brief, this reasoning asserts that schooling is an investment in "human capital" that raises the productivity and work potentialities of the recipients.[4] That is, schools are expected to endow individuals with certain traits that increase their economic productivity and thus elevate their earnings. The characteristics that schools are expected to develop in students are often categorized as **cognitive** and **noncognitive.** Cognitive traits include knowledge and skills that are internalized intellectually, while noncognitive refers to assorted social skills and personality traits that are developed as a consequence of schooling. Reading ability constitutes an example within the area of cognitive traits while motivation, punctuality, and ability to work with others are examples in the noncognitive realm.[5]

If the market for labor were perfect, we would expect to find posi-

[2] The federal antipoverty efforts of the "New Frontier" and "Great Society" were aimed largely at increasing the quality and quantity of schooling available to the poor. Project Head Start and Title I of the Elementary and Secondary Education Act of 1965 are two notable examples of such programs.

[3] Personal income includes **earned income** (or earnings) and **unearned income.** The former is composed of salaries and wages, while the latter includes rents, dividends, and interest. Earned income represented about 81 percent of total reported personal income in 1964. See Harry C. Kahn, **Employee Compensation Under the Income Tax** (New York: National Bureau of Economic Research, 1968).

[4] For an early exposition of this concept see J. R. Walsh, "Capital Concept Applied to Man," **Quarterly Journal of Economics,** 49 (1935), 255–285. The theory is refined and developed substantially in Gary S. Becker, **Human Capital** (New York: National Bureau of Economic Research, 1964).

[5] For an elaboration of cognitive objectives, see Benjamin S. Bloom, **Taxonomy of Educational Objectives, Handbook I: The Cognitive Domain** (New York: McKay, 1956). Many of the noncognitive objects of the schools that relate to worker productivity are described in Alex Inkeles, "Social Structure and the Socialization of Competence," **Harvard Educational Review,** 36 (Summer 1966).

tive effects of both cognitive and noncognitive behaviors on work performance and thus on individual earnings. That is, if employment demand for workers were similar in all geographic regions and based only upon productivity characteristics developed through schooling, the relation between educational attainment and individual earnings would be straightforward. However, a number of factors render this relationship more complex. First, only a portion of the personal characteristics that determine productivity are developed in school. Second, there are market imperfections and discriminations in the demand for labor that may lead to differences in earnings for individuals with identical capacities. And, finally, to the degree that differences in individuals' productivity are also reflected in non-monetary benefits, or so-called "psychic" income (some jobs are more pleasurable than others), monetary earnings will understate true returns.

When an individual supplies labor services, he supplies abilities that are derived from a variety of background influences. Inherited traits, parents, peers, community, and communications media all represent factors that affect individual's skills and personalities. The quality and quantity of formal schooling for a typical individual are generally related to all these factors. Thus, education represents only one input into the quality of labor supplied and, similarly, accounts for only a portion of the productivity and earnings of an individual. Therefore, any analysis of the effect of schooling on earnings must attempt to separate the distinct effects of schooling from those of other influences.

But the quality of an individual's labor is not the only determinant of his earnings; **demand** for his labor is also a major determinant. To the degree that the demand structure differs among varying labor markets (rural versus urban, North versus South, and so on), correspondence between educational attainment and earnings will also differ among labor markets. Moreover, to the degree that discrimination exists against particular individuals or groups, there will be lower economic returns from education among such persons and groups.[6] Since it seems reasonable to assume that prejudicial employment practices will decrease in the future, present evidence may understate seriously the potential relation between educational attainment

[6] Stephen Michelson concludes that most of the earnings differences between whites and nonwhites are attributable to factors other than education. See "Incomes of Racial Minorities" (Washington, D.C.: Brookings, 1968), mimeographed.

and earnings for nonwhites and other groups who presently suffer the greatest economic consequences of discrimination in the labor market. Despite the existence of employment inequities, it is important to recognize that the raising of individual proficiencies through improved and prolonged schooling raises the quality of labor service supplied. Imperfections on the demand side of the marketplace may act to limit the earning opportunities of particular groups in society, when educational attainment is held constant. The point we wish to emphasize here is that equalizing labor market opportunities available to members of racial minorities will require changes in the employment demand for, as well as improvements in the productive qualifications of, nonwhites; and that, in addition to improvements in schooling, it may require greater social investment in nonschooling inputs such as health services and housing before the productive services of nonwhites are equal to those of whites.

For these reasons, we should not expect differences in education alone to explain all of the differences in earning opportunities. Yet, the evidence that has been derived from economic research in "earning functions" suggests that schooling does explain a significant share of the variation in individual income, and that equalization of levels of schooling among whites and nonwhites in combination with elimination of employment discrimination would come close to equalizing earnings between the two groups.[7] The evidence is also unequivocal in demonstrating that students who receive a higher quality or quantity of schooling show higher earnings on the average, than do those who experience poorer quality and fewer years of schooling, even after making adjustments for other factors that affect earnings.

Research Findings on Education and Earnings

The global observation that persons with more schooling receive higher earnings over their lifetimes has long been obvious even to the most casual viewer. Table 5.1 uses 1960 census data to display this simple relationship for the state of Michigan. (Of course, these dollar figures would be higher for more recent data.) In 1959, the average high school graduate was receiving almost $1,300 more annual income than the average male who terminated his education at elementary school. College graduates were receiving $2,100 more than male high school graduates who did not enter college and $3,500 more than males who did not go to high school.

[7] Ibid., especially Chapter 6.

This evidence is dramatic, but it does not meet the objection we described earlier. That is, it does not demonstrate what portion of an individual's earnings is uniquely attributable to education.[8] For evidence of this type, we turn first to the work of Becker and Denison. Both of these researchers have made downward adjustments in the returns from schooling to compensate for earnings differentials due to differences in ability, motivation, social class and so on.[9] Denison estimates that only 60 percent of the differences in individual earnings that correspond to differences in schooling is attributable to schooling itself, and 40 percent is due to the superior earnings attributes on other dimensions of persons with higher levels of

Table 5.1. Annual Income in 1959 for Michigan Males 25 Years Old and Over, by Years of Schooling

Category	Median Income
All Males	$5,269
No Schooling	1,735
Elementary	
1 to 4 years	2,479
5 to 7 years	3,910
8 years	4,591
High School	
1 to 3 years	5,358
4 years	5,881
College	
1 to 3 years	6,486
4 years or more	8,091

Source—1960 Census of Population

[8] For additional evidence of the simple relationship between education and earnings, see Paul C. Glick and Herman P. Miller, "Educational Level and Potential Income," **American Sociological Review**, 21 (June 1956), 307–312; and Herman P. Miller, "Annual and Lifetime Income Relation to Education," **American Economic Review**, 50 (December, 1960), 962–986. See also H. S. Houthakker, "Education and Income," **Review of Economics and Statistics**, 41 (February, 1959), 24–28.
[9] See Becker, **Human Capital**, and Edward Denison, **The Sources of Economic Growth in the United States and the Alternatives Before Us**, Supplementary Paper No. 13 (New York: Committee for Economic Development, 1962).

schooling. More recent studies suggest that Denision understates
the significance of schooling.[10] In fact, two statistical studies that
have examined the relative effects on income of both educational
attainment and IQ report that the introduction of the latter measure
into the analysis does not reduce the discernible impact of schooling.[11] Another study by Griliches also suggests that the impact of
individual variations in ability on incomes seems to be evident only
at higher educational levels.[12]

Given the higher earnings that accompany educational attainment,
it is interesting to explore how much of this differential is attributable
to increased learning and how much is attributable to the other (noncognitive) effects of schools. Since it appears that good schools can
improve students' achievement (as measured by standardized tests)
as well as prepare them for and motivate them to obtain more years
of schooling, it is logical to examine separately the earnings effects of
achievement and additional years of schooling. One caution from
the outset, however: to the degree that additional schooling increases
achievement, the effects of the two may be confounded.

Hansen, Weisbrod, and Scanlon report that, for low-achieving
students, the relationship between test scores and earnings swamps
the relationship between earnings and years of schooling.[13] Thus,
they conclude "that what one learns influences earnings more than
does the mere fact of spending time in school."[14] However, subsequent study on a more representative sample of males suggests that
the number of years of schooling an individual attains does have a

[10] See Mary Jean Bowman and C. Arnold Anderson, "Relationships Among
Schooling, Ability, and Income in Industrialized Societies," mimeographed
(to be published in **Edding Festschrift,** no further data available).
[11] See Zvi Griliches, "Notes on the Role of Education in Production Functions
and Growth Accounting," paper presented at the Conference on Research
in Income and Wealth, Madison, Wisconsin, 1968, pp. 34–36; published in
W. Lee Hansen, ed., **Education, Income and Human Capital,** Studies in
Income and Wealth, vol. 35 (New York: National Bureau of Economic
Research, 1970). See also John Conlisk, "A Bit of Evidence on the Income-
Ability-Education Interrelation" (University of California at San Diego, 1968),
mimeographed.
[12] **Ibid.**
[13] W. Lee Hansen, Burton Weisbrod, and William J. Scanlon, "Determinants
of Earnings: Does Schooling Really Count?" (University of Wisconsin, April,
1968), mimeographed.
[14] **Ibid.,** p. 25. They acknowledge that spending more time in school contributes to earnings, but they conclude that the cognitive rather than the
noncognitive outcomes of schooling are what influence earnings.

significant and strong association with earnings that is **in addition**
to the apparent effect of cognitive achievement.[15] Another recent
study draws together information from a variety of sources to support
the view that the noncognitive effects may even be more important
than the cognitive in explaining occupational and economic success.[16] The logic here is that schools also have the objective of pre-
paring students for particular behavioral roles (cooperating with
fellow workers, for example) and that maximizing the school's
cognitive goals may sometimes conflict with this objective.

Perhaps the most ambitious analysis to date of the relation between
education and earnings is that undertaken by Giora Hanoch.[17] Hanoch
used the "one in one thousand sample" from the 1960 census to
estimate income returns from schooling for American males by age,
race, and region while holding constant other influential variables.
Even when he employed the most stringent of statistical controls to
separate other-than-school influences, Hanoch found a strong correspondence between schooling and earnings. For example, among
white males in the North, ages thirty-five to forty-four, the estimated
effect on earnings of going beyond elementary school is substantial.
High school graduates were receiving almost $1,300 more and col-
lege graduates $3,100 more than elementary school graduates.[18] The
average earnings for all northern males in this age category was
$6,300 in 1959, so these educational differentials are significant. It is
important to stress that these represent income increments that have
been adjusted for the effects on earnings of a large number of other
individual traits that may be related to schooling.

School Expenditures, Worker Productivity, and Earnings

Three additional studies have attempted to ascertain whether individuals who attended schools in areas with higher school expenditures had higher individual earnings. That is, the quantity of schooling
was measured by the number of years completed, while the quality
was measured by expenditures (total expenditures per pupil) or
teacher salaries. Welch found that money spent on teacher salaries,

[15] Hansen and Weisbrod, work in process.
[16] See Herbert Gintis, "Production Functions in the Economics of Education
and the Characteristics of Worker Productivity" (unpublished doctoral
dissertation, Harvard University, 1969).
[17] Giora Hanoch, "Personal Earnings and Investment in Schooling" (unpublished doctoral dissertation, University of Chicago, 1965). Also see his article
of the same title in the **The Journal of Human Resources**, 2 (Summer 1967).
[18] Ibid., p. 42.

in particular, enhanced the earnings-value of each year of schooling completed among agricultural workers.[19]

Morgan and Siragelding also report that school expenditures, as distinct from number of years of schooling, appears to be an exceedingly important determinant of the earnings of individuals.[20] Using a sample of 1,525 heads of family, they examined the effect of social and educational variables on earnings. They found that the combined effect of race, urbanization of background, age, sex, and years of schooling accounted for 35 percent of the variance in earnings. By adding as an additional explanatory variable the per pupil expenditure of the state in which the respondents resided, they were able to account for 51 percent of the variance in earnings. They conclude that there exists a relatively high return from investments made to improve the quality of schools. They contend, moreover, that this finding will hold even if more elaborate efforts to remove "spurious correlations" are attempted.

Indeed, a more elaborate attempt appears to confirm their finding. Richard Morgenstein, a predoctoral fellow at The Brookings Institution, explored the earnings-education relationship for a sample of 800 males in fifteen major American cities. His initial results reveal a significant effect of school expenditures on wage levels even when controls are made for the effects of age, sex, parental social class, and years of schooling. That is, in addition to the effect of amount of schooling, there appears to be an effect on individual earnings of quality of schooling when the latter is measured by per pupil expenditures.

Summary of Education and Earnings

That schooling has an effect on earnings is substantiated by numerous studies. Better schools have higher persistence rates (fewer dropouts) and higher student achievement. Both of these schooling outcomes have been shown to be related to higher earnings or greater economic opportunity. Even when adjustments are made for individual ability and other intervening influences, the payoffs from schooling persist. Also, studies that have related school expenditures to student earnings support the view that investment in the quality of schooling is likely to improve individuals' productive capacities and earnings opportunities. While there are differences between

[19] Finis Welch, "Measurement of the Quality of Schooling," **American Economic Review**, 56 (May 1966), 379–392.
[20] James Morgan and Ismail Sirageldin, "A Note on the Quality Dimension in Education," **The Journal of Political Economy**, 76 (Sept/Oct 1968), 1069–1077.

studies in their findings on the relative magnitude of the schooling-earnings effect, virtually all studies on the subject, nevertheless, acknowledge a significant connection. There are probably few social science hypotheses that have been tested so intensively and produced such consistent findings.

Education and Occupational Choice
Another dimension of opportunity that appears to be strongly related to schooling is that of an individual's occupational choice. Employers use quantity and quality of formal educational preparation as a basis for selecting employees. Thus those individuals with more and better schooling are likely to have a larger choice of employers or occupations open to them. The possible interpretations of this effect are twofold: first, schooling credentials may be important simply for obtaining a particular position, even when these school credentials bear only a slight relationship to the proficiencies required to handle the task.[21] Alternatively, schooling requirements may be imposed as a standard for employee selection because of a direct linkage between those requirements and job performance. Either way, the significant point is that both interpretations support the proposition that the quality and quantity of a person's schooling will affect directly the range of occupational choices available to him.

Here again, research efforts have been made to separate non-school abilities that occur coincidentally with educational attainment from the unique effect of schooling. Bajema examined the interrelationships between IQ scores, educational attainment, and occupational achievement for 437 males who were forty-five years old and who had been administered the Terman Group Intelligence Test when they were in sixth grade schools in Kalamazoo, Michigan.[22] Bajema concludes that "while intelligence (as measured by intelligence tests) is associated with occupational achievement, the results of this study indicate that its effects operate wholly within the school system."[23] In other words, intelligence is important, but unless that

[21] See Ivar Berg, "Rich Man's Qualifications for Poor Man's Jobs," **Transaction**, 6 (March 1969), 45–50.
[22] Carl Jay Bajema, "A Note on the Interrelations Among Intellectual Ability, Educational Attainment, and Occupational Achievement: A Follow-Up Study of a Male Kalamazoo Public School Population," **Sociology of Education**, 41 (Summer 1968), 317–319.
[23] While Bajema's data suggest that the school's influence on occupational achievement is very strong, they do not support the assertion that intelligence has no independent effect. His method of analysis and data are inadequate for testing such a proposition.

intelligence is manifested through the skills one acquires in schools, it is not particularly useful in earning a living. Girod and Tofigh used a different sample, but also report evidence that schooling has a unique effect on ocupational choice and attainment.[24]

The most extensive study of the effect of schooling on occupational achievement is the effort of Blau and Duncan.[25] Using a large sample of twenty- to sixty-four-year-old males surveyed by the U.S. Bureau of the Census in 1962, they report that education, particularly educational achievement, has a strong effect on occupational achievement.[26]

Intergenerational Social and Economic Mobility
An interesting implication of our foregoing discussion is that increased educational attainment for an individual is likely to improve his children's opportunities. Because of this phenomenon, education represents perhaps the best means of increasing intergenerational mobility and lifting people from poverty.

As Blau and Duncan demonstrate, the higher the occupational achievement of the father, the higher that of the son.[27] In addition, the more educated a parent, the more educated the child. In a study using special data from a 1962 census survey, it was found that for every additional four years of school completed by the family head, almost one and one-half additional years were completed by the offspring.[28] Supporting evidence for this phenomenon is reported by Masters in a study of social class determinants and educational achievement.[29] He examined the simultaneous effect of several social

[24] See Roger Girod and F. Tofigh, "Family Background and Income, School Career and Social Mobility of Young Males of Working Class Origin: A Geneva Survey," **Acta Sociologica**, 9 (1965), 94–109.
[25] P. M. Blau and O. D. Duncan, **The American Occupational Structure** (New York: Wiley, 1967).
[26] **Ibid.**, Appendix H.
[27] **Ibid.**, p. 110.
[28] See Beverley Duncan, **Family Factors and School Dropouts: 1920–1960**, U.S. Office of Education, Cooperative Research Project No. 2258 (Ann Arbor: University of Michigan, 1965). Results are cited in U.S. Department of Health Education and Welfare, **Toward a Social Report** (Washington, D.C.: U.S. Government Printing Office, 1969), p. 20. A similar finding is reported in M. David H. Brazer, J. Morgan, and W. Cohen, "Educational Achievement—Its Causes and Effect" (Ann Arbor: University of Michigan, 1961).
[29] Stanley H. Masters, "The Effect of Family Income on Children's Education: Some Findings on Inequality of Opportunity," **The Journal of Human Resources**, 4 (Spring 1969), 158–175.

class variables in explaining dropout rates. He found that the probability of dropping out of school by age sixteen or seventeen is directly related to the education level of the head of household (parent or parent substitute). He also discovered that the lower the education of the head of household, the more likely it is that the child will be at a grade level behind that of his age group.

Of course, as described in Chapter 4, a child's academic performance is likely to be related to his parents' social class. The reason for this observation is that much of the education and educational motivation of a child takes place in the home. Children whose parents have more education enter their schooling careers with higher achievement scores than do their less fortunate peers.[30] This phenomenon has been confirmed in many studies of educational performance, and it is held to be the result of the quality and quantity of interaction between parents and children in the home.[31]

Thus, intergenerational upward mobility, particularly among the very poor, can be directly affected by education. Higher educational attainment improves not only the opportunity of the individual receiving the schooling but also enables him to enhance the prospects for his children.

Education and Political Participation
Since opportunity has been defined earlier as the ability to affect one's own destiny, the desire and mobility of an individual to participate in and to have an influence over governmental processes is especially important. Determination of political issues and choice of government representatives frequently have direct effects on an individual's welfare. Thus, individual opportunity in the political sphere requires political consciousness and political participation.

Among all of the significant determinants of political consciousness and political participation, schooling appears to predominate. Almond and Verba describe the overwhelming importance of education in determining political orientation and postulate several means by which education relates to political orientation.[32] The more educated person tends to exhibit a greater awareness of government's

[30] This finding is emphasized in James Coleman **et al., Equality of Educational Opportunity** (Washington, D.C.: U.S. Government Printing Office, 1966).
[31] See R. A. Peterson and L. DeBord, "Educational Supportiveness of the Home and Academic Performance of Disadvantaged Boys," IMRID Behavioral Science Monograph No. 3 (George Peabody College, 1966).
[32] Gabriel Almond and Sidney Verba, **The Civic Culture** (Princeton: Princeton University Press, 1963).

impact on the individual than is the case for persons of less education. Moreover, the more educated the individual, the greater his
awareness of political issues, the greater is the range of persons with
whom he discusses politics, the more likely he is to be a member of
a political organization, and the more positive are his attitudes about
the ability of people to govern themselves in a democratic fashion.[33]

Empirical evidence of the schools' effects on political attitudes is
found in the extensive study of Hess and Torney.[34] They examined
the backgrounds and attitudes of approximately 10,000 elementary
school students in grades two through eight selected from sixteen
middle-class and sixteen working-class schools in eight cities. On
the basis of their analysis, they conclude that "the school stands out
as the central, salient, and dominant force in the political socialization of the young child."

Given this background, it is no surprise that virtually all studies
on the subject have found a strong positive relation between educational attainment and political participation. Agger and Ostrom found
education to be even more significant than income in predicting
poltical participation.[35] Education appears to be particularly important
in explaining who is likely to cast a ballot.[36] Moreover, the greater the
individual's educational attainment, the more likely he is to become
involved psychologically in politics.[37] One of the best-known authorities on the subject concludes: "Perhaps the surest single predictor
of political involvement is number of years of formal education."[38]
In short, the link between education on the one hand and political
participation and potential efficacy on the other has been well documented. Persons with higher educational attainment are more able
and more likely to become involved in the political process and to
influence the outcomes of those issues that affect them. Persons with
lower levels of education not only are not as knowledgeable concerning political issues, and thus not as likely to be aware of matters

[33] Ibid., pp. 380–381.
[34] Robert Hess and Judith Torney, **The Development of Political Attitudes in
Children** (Chicago: Aldine, 1967).
[35] Robert Agger and Vincent Ostrom, "Political Participation in a Small
Community," in **Political Behavior,** ed. Heinz Eulau et al. (Glencoe, III.:
The Free Press, 1956), pp. 138–148.
[36] Angus Campbell, Philip L. Converse, Warren E. Miller, and Donald E.
Stokes, **The American Voter** (New York: Wiley, 1964), pp. 250–254.
[37] References to this literature are found in Lester W. Milbrath, **Political
Participation** (Chicago: Rand McNally, 1965), pp. 53–54.
[38] Angus Campbell, "The Passive Citizen," **Acta Sociologica,** 6 (Winter and
Spring 1963), 9–21.

affecting themselves, but also are less well informed about the entire political process and thus not as capable of expressing their views even when they are aware of relevant issues. Clearly, lack of schooling or lack of good schooling restricts one's ablity to exercise political rights.

Education and Crime

The direct effect of educational attainment on occupational choice, earnings, and political participation represents only some of the more prominent ways in which education is linked to opportunity. Education also has indirect effects on opportunity in that those persons with less schooling are more likely to pursue illegal activities for which they will have their freedom restricted. Low educational attainment leads to limited employment, occupational, and earning alternatives. Given limited choices, the less educated person is more likely to pursue illegal means to achieve higher status and income. The result of such illegal activity is that a person with lower educational attainment is more likely to be arrested, to be punished, and to carry a police record that further diminishes his chances of employment, his occupational choice, and his earnings. Failure in school is also likely to contribute to a rejection of the norms of the larger society, and normlessness appears to be related to crime.[39]

This is not to say that all crime or even most of it is due to low educational attainment. Rather, the evidence suggests that there is a limited range of legal alternatives for poorly-educated individuals, and consequently they are tempted to fulfill status aspirations and material needs through such illegal activities as gambling, prostitution, robbery, dealing in narcotics, and so on.

A number of empirical studies link education to crime. One of the best of these studies was recently completed in California.[40] It demonstrates that for the years between 1958 and 1967 the median years of schooling among newly imprisoned male felons remained constant at the eighth grade level. This occurred despite the fact that the median level of schooling among all California adults was 12.1 years as measured in 1960 and presumably has been rising ever since. Thus, we can see that those who commit felonies tend to possess

[39] See Elwin H. Powell, "Crime as a Function of Anomie," **The Journal of Criminal Law, Criminology, and Police Science,** 57 (June 1966), pp. 161–171.
[40] State of California, Department of Correction, **California Prisons 1967: Summary Statistics of Felon Prisoners and Parolees** (Sacramento: State Department of Correction, 1969), pp. 30–31.

substantially less than the average amount of schooling. This same study reports that in 1967 only 4.7 percent of all newly committed male felons had achieved twelve or more years of schooling. Looked at another way, 95.3 percent of all convicted felons were below the average for all California adults. Yet another finding from this study reveals that crimes of violence are associated with level of education. Homicides, assaults, and other violent felonies are tied much more closely to lower levels of education than are less violent crimes. (The preceding figures from California are supported by data from a national study.)[41] This is rather striking evidence that schooling, or lack of it, contributes to adult criminal behavior.

In addition to the foregoing studies, there is evidence that ties education to juvenile delinquency. For example, an examination of juveniles in a large city found a high negative correlation between educational attainment and the probability of being arrested for committing a juvenile crime.[42] Even when account was taken of the importance of other factors such as race, family income, family size, presence of both parents in the home, and IQ, it was found that high school dropouts were three to five times as likely to be arrested for committing a juvenile crime as were high school graduates.[43] Moreover, those juveniles enrolled in school showed the lowest probability of being arrested for committing a crime.[44] Since delinquents do not seem to show significantly lower intelligence than the general population, but are more likely to fail in school, the potential role of the schools in preventing delinquency is strongly implied.[45]

Some of the many other areas in which education affects opportunity are those relating to further schooling options and military choices. Accreditation of high schools is directly related to the breadth and quality of their instructional offerings. Low-expenditure schools are least likely to fulfill the accreditation requirements, so their students are often handicapped in obtaining college admission. Further, to the degree that poorly-endowed schools limit intellectual development, their pupils will do poorly on college entrance exam-

[41] U.S. Department of Justice, **Blue Print for Change, Annual Report of the Federal Bureau of Prisons** (Washington, D.C.: U.S. Government Printing Office, 1967), p. 9.
[42] Robert Spiegelman, **et al., A Benefit/Cost Model to Evaluate Educational Programs** (Stanford: Stanford Research Institute, 1968), pp. 32–33.
[43] **Ibid.,** p. 32.
[44] **Ibid.,** p. 85.
[45] See N. M. Prentice and F. J. Kelley, "Intelligence and Delinquency: A Reconsideration," **The Journal of Social Psychology,** 60 (August 1963).

inations. Taken together these two effects of lower-expenditure schools limit severely the options of their students for postsecondary schooling.[46]

Military choices, too, are directly affected by the quality and quantity of schooling received. Inductees are required to take the Armed Forces Qualification Test (AFQT), an instrument that purports to measure an individual's trainability. The examinee's performance on the AFQT depends in large measure on the level of his educational attainment and on the quality of his education (as reflected in the quality of school resources).[47]

A high score on the AFQT enhances an individual's opportunities in two important ways. First, inductees who do well on the examination are offered many training options, and they tend almost invariably to choose courses of study which develop abilities that have high payoffs in civilian life. Thus, the armed forces invest substantial resources in enhancing the marketable skills of those persons who have received the best pre-Army education. These persons are given expensive courses of instruction in such areas as electronics technology, diesel mechanics, aircraft maintenance, and so on. The less fortunate inductee who scores poorly on the AFQT has fewer training options. That is, the armed forces invest less in him to improve his skills and raise his occupational status and earnings in civilian life. He tends to be assigned the more menial tasks or thrown into frontline combat. That is the second means by which the poorly-educated inductee suffers in contrast with his better-educated counterpart. The more educated males avoid induction by enrolling in college and seeking employment in such critical occupations as teaching and engineering, both endeavors requiring college degrees. The less educated are drafted, so that by virtue of their lower school attainments they are, at best, more likely to be serving at a rate of meager pay while their better-educated countrymen are building careers and families. At worst, they are the ones most likely to become casualty or mortality statistics.

[46] This sacrifice in earnings attributable to this phenomenon can be calculated from knowledge of the reduced probability of being able to enroll in institutions of higher education. See Burton A. Weisbrod, "Education and Investment in Human Capital," Journal of Political Economy, 70, Supplement (October 1962), 106–123.

[47] See Peter Karpinos, "The Mental Qualifications of American Youths for Military Servce and Its Relationship to Educational Attainment," 1966 Proceedings of the Social Statistics Section of the American Statistical Association, pp. 92–111.

Finally, it is important to note that both mental health and geographic mobility tend to be educationally selective. For example, studies of social class and severe mental disorders evidence a higher incidence of such disorders among the lower social strata (where educational attainment is lowest).[48] Census data suggest that geographic mobility, and thus added job opportunity, is strongly related to education. The more highly educated individual has better knowledge of job alternatives and has more self-reliance in seeking employment in a new geographic area. Moreover, in that educational attainment is linked strongly to income, the better-educated individual is more likely to have the dollar resources necessary to move.

A Summary

Educational attainment and opportunity are linked in many ways. Abundant evidence supports the view that education affects earnings and income, occupational choice, intergenerational mobility, political participation, social deviance, and so on. Indeed, educational attainment overlaps with opportunity in so many ways that the two terms seem inextricably intertwined in the mind of the laymen and in the findings of the social scientist.

This chapter has reviewed only the individual benefits from education; however, it is important also to note that there are enormous social benefits. As a social investment, dollars spent on education yield a higher economic return than do dollars spent on buildings and physical equipment.[49] In addition, educational expenditures improve the functioning of a democratic society by increasing literacy, raising the level of public understanding on complex social issues, and increasing total political participation. Other social benefits from educational investment are also impressive.[50] In short, the quality of educational services available to an individual does influence the way in which he performs in school, and that in-school performance influences significantly the opportunities available to him and the manner in which he performs in those opportunities after leaving school.

[48] For an example of this literature see August B. Hollingshead and Frederick C. Redlick, "Social Stratification and Schizophrenia," **American Sociological Review,** 19 (June 1954), 302–306.

[49] For an example of this analysis see Becker, **Human Capital.**

[50] For an economic analysis of these see Burton A. Weisbrod, **External Benefits of Public Education** (Princeton, N.J.: Princeton University Press, 1964).

6

The Financial Roots
of Inequality

... the present plans in use
for the apportionment of school
funds in fully three-fourths of
the states of the union are in
need of careful revision. And
there is likewise need for more
careful study of the problem
than has been given it so far by
most of the states if it is desired
that future evolution shall take
place along more intelligent
lines than has been the case
in the past.[1]

[1] Ellwood P. Cubberley, **School
Funds and their Apportionment**
(New York: Columbia University,
1905), p. 253.

Up to this point in our report we have described the nature of socio-economic discrimination in the delivery of school services and the consequences of that discrimination for pupils' performance and postschool opportunity. What remains to be explained are some of the dynamics of this discrimination. How is it that, even in the face of governmental arrangements ostensibly designed to alleviate inequities, systematic disparities in the delivery of school services still occur? This question provides our focus in this chapter. Specifically, we concern ourselves here with explaining the school finance arrangements that operate in Michigan, demonstrating that financial inequities resulting from these arrangements do in fact translate into inequities in school services, and describing the manner in which these accrue primarily to the detriment of children of lower socioeconomic status.

A Return to Our Conceptual Model

In Chapter 1 we presented the conceptual components of the thesis we are pursuing. At this point we wish to inject a fourth component and two additional propositions. The three original propositions align pupils' socioeconomic status, school services, student achievement, and postschool opportunity in a model implying causal interaction. We now wish to insert **school finance arrangements** and amend the model to appear as shown in the accompanying figure.

One determinant of the quality of school services made available to students is the level of revenue generated and distributed as a consequence of the state's school finance arrangements. These arrangements act as mediators between students' osocioeconomic status and the quality of their schools. This is not to claim either

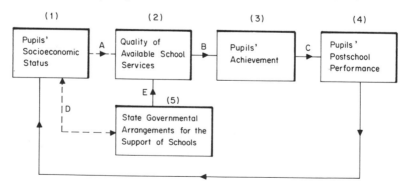

that (1) available dollars translate directly into quality of school services, or that (2) dollars are allocated to local school districts strictly on the basis of students' social and economic levels. The connection is not that simple. Rather, the quality of school services tends to be linked to students' socioeconomic status, and the state's governmental arrangements, despite absolute numbers of dollars per pupil flowing to any particular school district, do not suffice presently to disturb this linkage.

This leads us to two further propositions—D and E—which can be stated in the following fashion:

D. **Socioeconomic Status and the Level of Available Resources.** Total level of resources made available as a result of state arrangements for support of schools is related to the socioeconomic status of pupils, and that relationship is such that lower levels of resources are associated with a pupil's being from a lower socioeconomic status household.

E. **Level of Available Resources and Quality of School Services.** The total level of resources provided for the support of schools is related to the quality of school services delivered, and that relationship is such that lower levels of resources are associated with lower-quality school services.

In pursuing evidence with which to test these propositions we rely heavily upon data gathered for the Thomas Report and information made available to us by the Michigan State Department of Education. The reader should keep in mind, however, that our purpose here is not to explain school finance in a general sense or Michigan's state aid statutes specifically. Rather, the objective in this chapter is to demonstrate that the means by which revenues are distributed for schools presently reinforce socioeconomic discrimination in the delivery of school services.

Socioeconomic Status and Level of Available Resources
In seeking a simple answer as to why lower socioeconomic status students receive lower-quality school services, we need not look too far. In Table 6.1 is an illustration of the linkage between the SES of school districts from our Michigan sample and the total number of dollars per pupil those districts spent for goods and services related to instruction.

From the table it is evident that high SES districts spend more money per pupil than do others. This finding is perfectly consistent with the results of a number of school finance studies. For example,

Table 6.1[2]

Quartiles according to Variable 181			Socioeconomic Scale	
Medians from Variable 260			Expenditure per Pupil, Total Instruction	
Quartile	1	2	3	4
Median	335	331	365	420
NTRUE = 48				
STUDENT T = 2.93829				

in 1966 James, Kelly, and Garms examined determinants of school expenditures in large cities of the United States and found that the most powerful predictors of the amount spent per pupil were socioeconomic status measures such as "median years of schooling in the adult population" and "median family income."[3] The fact, however, that the linkage between SES and school dollar resources is well known among school finance experts probably renders it no less surprising or dramatic to a layman and certainly no less equitable to the school children involved.

One might inquire as to whether or not the additional dollars spent for education in high SES districts indeed purchase more and better services or are simply wasted either through administrative inefficiency or by purchasing unnecessary items. This is a reasonable question, and we address ourselves to it in the last section of this chapter. However, before explaining the relationship between dollars spent and quality of school services received, we wish to describe the rather complicated processes that tie school revenues to SES and result in the interdistrict dollar disparities displayed in Table 6.1.

[2] In this chapter we use quartiles, rather than octiles, to provide figures for illustrative purposes. STUDENT T continues to be the appropriate test of statistical significance.

[3] H. T. James, James A. Kelly, and Walter I. Garms, **Determinants of Educational Expenditures in Large Cities of the United States** (Stanford: Stanford University School of Education, 1966), Chapter IV. In this same regard see Harvey Brazer, **City Expenditures in the United States** (New York: National Bureau of Economic Research, 1959); Thomas R. Dye, "Politics, Economics, and Educational Outcomes in the States," **Educational Administration Quarterly,** 3 (Winter 1967), 28–47; Jerry Miner, **Social and Economic Factors in Spending for Public Education** (Syracuse: Syracuse University Press, 1963); and Seymour Sacks and Robert Harris, "The Determinants of State and Local Government Expenditures and Intergovernmental Flows of Funds." **National Tax Journal,** 17 (March 1964).

Resource disparities in public education occur primarily as a consequence of two factors: (1) inequities associated with the generation of revenue from local taxation of property, and (2) imperfections in state arrangements for directly distributing financial aid to school districts. In order to understand the impact of these imperfections more fully, it is necessary to explain the processes by which local school districts obtain their resources.

From Where Does School Money Come?

A precise response to this question is extraordinarily complicated. In most states only a few staff assistants in the state legislature, some administrative officers in the state department of education, and one or two assistants to the superintendent in the state's larger school districts are keenly informed about the technicalities of state school finance formulas. However, a nontechnical explanation of the general financial framework can begin with a discussion of three resource components: (1) locally generated revenues (primarily from the property tax), (2) state-provided funds, and (3) a residual category composed mostly of federal government monies. Let us describe each of these components separately and then examine them in the aggregate in relation to students' socioeconomic status and the provision of school services.

Local Property Tax Revenues
Legally speaking, almost all revenues employed for the support of public schools are **state** funds. (The only real exception to this statement is federal funds.) This is so because federal and state constitutions act in tandem to vest plenary authority for the provision of schooling in the hands of state legislatures. The state may choose to conduct the schooling function through instruments such as local school districts. However, when it does so, these instruments have been judged by the courts to be but subcomponents of the state, established for purposes of administrative efficiency. As a consequence of these arrangements, all school support funds, with the exception of privately donated money and direct federal government grants, are, legally speaking, state monies. Nevertheless, by tradition and statute, a degree of discretion in raising revenues for schools is delegated by states to local school districts and their boards of trustees. These locally generated revenues stem primarily from the

taxing of real property.[4] In general this taxing system operates as follows:

Assessed Valuation

The first step in raising money from a local property tax is to place a monetary value upon the property to be taxed. This value is typically affixed by a public official known as an "assessor." The dollar value assigned to property is known as its "assessed value." The assessed value of a piece of property is supposed to bear a constant relationship to its "true market value," the price for which the property would sell if it were actually put up for sale. This relationship is usually reflected in a dollar amount less than "true market value."

The property assessing process is subject to flaws. The assignment of a dollar value is seldom done on an annual basis and thus may not reflect increases in property value due to factors such as generalized economic inflation and greater market demand for housing. Frequently individuals doing the assessing are publicly elected and thus under political pressure to minimize assessments, particularly residential assessments. Moreover, one man does not assess every piece of property, and thus the potential exists for varying standards of value to be employed. Even under the best of conditions, the assessment is ultimately a subjective perception of a human being, and thus open to all the usual errors accompanying human frailty. All these potential imperfections may act either singly or in concert to distort the assessed value assigned to any one piece of property. These distortions may then be magnified severalfold when all the assessments within a school district are aggregated.

The total value of taxable property within the boundaries of a school district serves as the resource base for the generation of local revenues for schools. In order to compare one school district's ability to raise revenues with the ability of another, it is necessary to have a standardized unit that will take into account not only the total value of taxable resources but also the relative need of the school district to draw upon these resources. By dividing the number of students served by public schools in the district into the total value of the district's assessed property we arrive at such a unit. The label

[4] In addition to property tax income, in some school districts revenues also come from sources such as sales taxes, income taxes, bank vault taxes, and license fees. These sources, however, seldom account for more than a minor percentage of local district income.

for this unit of comparison is **assessed valuation per pupil** (AV/PP).
When efforts are made by the state government to take into
account variation in assessment practices between school districts,
as a basis for adjusting the state's direct payments to schools, we
are provided with an even more precise measure of comparison,
a unit known as **state equalized assessed valuation per pupil**
(SEV/PP).[5] These standard units of comparison are intended to
indicate a school district's "ability" to support schools.

Tax Rate

Assigning value to a piece of property, or, in the aggregate, assigning
value to all taxable property in a school district, constitutes but one
portion of the process by which local school revenues are generated.
A second step consists of determining the amount of tax to levy
against that property. The amount of the tax is referred to as the "tax
rate." Tax rates are typically expressed in mills (a mill is one-tenth
of one cent or one-thousandth of a dollar). For this reason tax rates
are sometimes known as "millage" or "millage rates." The millage
rate applied to the value of a piece of property determines the amount
of property tax to be paid. For example, in the simple case of a house
assessed at a value of $1,000, a rate of 10 mills ($1.00 per $100.00
of assessed valuation) will yield a tax revenue of $10.00. The property
tax revenue raised by a school district is equal to its total assessed
valuation multiplied by whatever tax rate is in effect for local schools.

In the same way that we described a standardized unit for comparing the relative "abilty" of school districts (assessed valuation
per pupil), we need a standardized unit for measuring the capability
and willingness of school district voters to tax themselves for purposes of supporting schools. The actual tax rate itself can serve as
such a standardized measurement unit. When used as such a measurement unit, tax rate is said to indicate a district's "effort" to
support its schools.

We can compare school districts on a combined measure of
"ability" and "effort" by multiplying the district's tax rate against its
assessed valuation per pupil and arrive at a figure that represents

[5] SEV is an attempt to arrive at a consistent assessment basis for all school
districts within a state. SEV is derived by determining the relationship in
each school district between "assessed value" and "true market value."
The ratio between these two measures is then used to calculate equalized
values. Throughout the remainder of this chapter, all references to "assessed
valuation" or AV/PP are actually for SEV.

Table 6.2

Quartiles according to Variable 181			Socioeconomic Scale	
Medians from Variable 253			Per Pupil Allocation from Local Sources	
Quartile	1	2	3	4
Median	210	203	213	368
NTRUE = 48				
STUDENT T = 3.42343				

the amount of local revenue generated per pupil.

SES, "Ability," and "Effort"

Having described the two basic ingredients in the process by which school districts generate local revenue for schools, we are now in a position to examine the relationship between a school district's results in raising local revenues and the social and economic status of its students. The results of this examination are displayed in Table 6.2. What is evident from these statistical findings is that the processes prevailing in the taxation of property accrue to a substantial revenue advantage for high SES students.

The results contained in the table begin to confirm our Proposition D regarding resource availability and student SES. It would be helpful to know more precisely why it is that property tax dynamics favor high SES students. Is it because low SES school districts are lacking in "ability," or because they cannot make an adequate revenue-raising "effort"? Our data do not lend themselves to a definitive answer to this question, but they do enable us to shed some light upon it.

Ability. Is lack of ability the revenue deficit "culprit"? It probably is, at least to a large degree. When we examine the relationship between SES indicators and assessed valuation per pupil we find that the two are significantly associated (see Table 6.3). As a consequence of this association, the lower SES school districts simply do not have the tax base wherewithal to support schools in the same fashion as do the majority of high SES districts.

The inequity is compounded, however, when the other side of the revenue coin is examined. Not only are low SES districts curtailed by lack of ability, but also they suffer from inequities associated with effort.

Table 6.3

Quartiles according to Variable 170			Average Income in Attendance Area	
Medians from Variable 265			Assessed Valuation per Pupil in Hundreds	
Quartile	1	2	3	4
Median	95	116	110	148
NTRUE = 46				
STUDENT T = 2.25114				

Table 6.4

Quartiles according to Variable 181			Socioeconomic Scale	
Medians from Variable 271			Total Millage Rate for All Purposes	
Quartile	1	2	3	4
Median	19.2	19.0	22.8	27.3
NTRUE = 48				
STUDENT T = 5.18821				

Effort. If millage rate is taken as a measure of a school district's effort to support its schools and that measure is related to district SES, we obtain the statistical results displayed in Table 6.4. A tempting explanation for this finding is simply to say: "Well, there you have it. The poor don't care. If they want good schools, they must be willing to pay for them." Now, it may be in some instances that the poor do not care. However, there exist three compelling reasons to believe that, even when they do care, it is more difficult for them to tax themselves for the support of schools than it is for high SES communities.

The three reasons are concerned with (1) the regressive nature of the property tax, (2) added public service burdens upon urban school districts (many of which contain high concentrations of low SES families), and (3) legal and political constraints against raising tax rates.

Inequities in "Effort" Due to Regressive Taxation
A fact that must be taken into account when comparing "effort" is that the property tax tends to be **regressive**; in other words, not in proportion to income. Property value is not the best measure of

·"ability" to pay; an individual's income is a better indicator. This is true primarily because "housing" represents a diminishing proportion of a person's income as he becomes wealthier. Whereas a man earning $10,000 a year may very well live in a house valued at twice that amount, the man who annually earns $100,000 is not as likely to live in a house valued at $200,000. In order to understand the regressive nature of property taxes more fully, let us cite the simplified example of a man who makes $10,000 a year and lives in a house assessed at $20,000. Near him lives a neighbor who annually earns $100,000 and lives in a home assessed at $80,000. A tax rate of $2.50 per $100 of assessed valuation (25 mills) will be a larger burden for the lower-income individual. He will pay $500 in property taxes, an amount equal to 5 percent of his annual income. His neighbor will pay $2,000 in taxes, four times as many dollars to be sure, but an amount equal to but 2 percent of his annual income.[6]

If we elevate the preceding example from the level of an individual to that of entire school districts, it can be seen that a specified tax rate applied to a relatively wealthy district will not "hurt" its residents as much as is the case when it is applied to a relatively poor district. Residents of a wealthy district might tax themselves at an even higher rate, make an even greater property tax "effort," than those of a poor district and still not feel the pinch of taxes as greatly. Moreover, if the poor district is also a heavily urban one, and thus additionally burdened with the provision of more public services than is typically the case in the suburbs and rural areas (see the following section), its tax rate for schools may be low, but its total tax rate may be high, and it is the total tax rate that has a painful impact. This general situation is particularly evident in Michigan. In a 1958 study, Musgrave and Daicoff found that the burden of the property tax rested three and a half times more heavily upon low-income than upon high-income groups.[7]

"Overburden" and Effort Inequities

A local school district's board of trustees is legally empowered to levy taxes, but it is seldom the only local government body that has access to the property tax base as a means for raising revenues. Typically, the local property rolls are also accessible for revenue

[6] A more complete explanation of the tax inequities inherent in the property tax is contained in Dick Netzer, **Economics of the Property Tax** (Washington, D.C.: Brookings, 1966).
[7] Richard Musgrave and Darwin Daicoff, "Who Pays Michigan Taxes?" Staff Papers (Lansing: Michigan Tax Study, 1958), pp. 113–151.

raising to municipal government agencies such as flood control, hospital, utilities, sanitation, recreation, and transportation. In general, the more dense the population of an area, the wider the variety of such services needed. Consequently, the residents of some school districts, particularly urban ones, are vulnerable to paying property taxes for many more purposes than simply the support of schools. (These additional taxes are frequently referred to as "municipal overburden.") Thus, a simple comparison of tax rates will not suffice of itself to give us a true measure of effort. We must also look at the other services being supported by property taxes and see the percent of all taxes that go for schools.

In tables 6.5, 6.6, and 6.7 we provide figures for the city of Detroit and some of its surrounding suburbs. These figures illustrate that

Table 6.5. Property Tax Rates—Schools, Detroit Area

City	1968–69	1967–68	1966–67
Westland	42.71(1)	37.10(4)	N/A
Madison Heights	42.28(2)	42.08(1)	33.69(3)
Oak Park	39.99(3)	38.59(3)	38.63(1)
Garden City	38.29(4)	31.80(9)	31.80(4)
Livonia	38.02(5)	36.01(5)	34.86(2)
Southfield	35.70(6)	35.68(6)	31.40(6)
Roseville	35.20(7)	33.94(7)	28.34(10)
St. Clair Shores	34.58(8)	32.90(8)	29.04(9)
Royal Oak	33.62(9)	29.00(11)	27.95(11)
Warren	32.95(10)	26.70(14)	26.34(14)
Dearborn Heights	32.53(11)	39.29(2)	29.97(7)
Pontiac	32.17(12)	25.80(16)	23.51(16)
Inkster	32.01(13)	31.80(9)	31.74(5)
Allen Park	31.94(14)	27.92(12)	26.81(13)
East Detroit	30.13(15)	30.18(10)	29.80(8)
Highland Park	29.41(16)	26.48(15)	22.71(17)
Lincoln Park	28.16(17)	25.03(17)	24.93(15)
Wyandotte	28.16(17)	28.27(13)	27.80(12)
Dearborn	23.73(18)	23.74(18)	19.31(13)
Detroit	22.53(19)	22.16(19)	16.79(19)

( ) indicate rank order
Source: State Assessed Property Division of the State Tax Commission

Financial Roots of Inequality

Table 6.6. Property Tax Rates—City Only, Detroit Area

City	1968–69	1967–68	1966–67
Detroit*	42.64(1)	34.08(7)	31.48(1)
Highland Park	29.75(2)	28.68(2)	19.91(2)
Dearborn	19.99(3)	19.50(3)	19.05(3)
Roseville	18.99(4)	15.50(9)	15.50(7)
Inkster	18.21(5)	16.74(5)	13.56(11)
Lincoln Park	17.20(6)	19.41(4)	16.74(4)
Royal Oak	16.02(7)	16.45(6)	16.72(5)
Oak Park	15.99(8)	13.99(11)	13.99(10)
Wyandotte	15.74(9)	16.42(7)	16.57(6)
East Detroit	15.22(10)	16.22(8)	14.90(9)
St. Clair Shores	15.14(11)	13.63(12)	12.32(13)
Garden City	14.22(12)	10.72(16)	11.67(15)
Madison Heights	13.73(13)	13.63(13)	12.51(12)
Pontiac	12.50(14)	15.39(10)	15.11(8)
Warren	12.44(15)	12.42(14)	12.41(14)
Livonia	12.09(16)	10.52(18)	10.55(16)
Allen Park	11.16(17)	11.20(15)	8.86(18)
Westland	11.07(18)	10.72(16)	N/A
Southfield	9.24(19)	9.38(19)	9.52(17)
Dearborn Heights	8.85(20)	8.82(20)	8.31(19)

( ) indicate rank order

*Detroit also levies a city wide personal income tax, which, for purposes of comparison, has been translated to a millage equivalent.

Source: State Assessed Property Division of the State Tax Commission

inhabitants of Detroit pay lower taxes for schools than do suburban residents, but when their total property tax rate resulting from municipal overburden is taken into account, they pay more than their nearby neighbors outside the city limits.

A further irony in considering overburden is the tendency for many municipally supported services to benefit suburban dwellers.[8] This tendency is illustrated in Michigan by the figures in Table 6.8. Here we see that Detroit provides services that are also used by suburban

[8] An excellent description of central city service to suburbs is provided in "Central City Benefits to Milwaukee Suburbs," a report of the Milwaukee Technical Committee for Fiscal Facts, to Mayor Henry W. Maier (June 1968), mimeographed.

Table 6.7. Combined City and School Tax Rates, Detroit Area

City	1968–69	1967–68	1966–67
Detroit*	65.17(1)	56.24(1)	48.27(2)
Highland Park	59.16(2)	54.35(3)	42.62(11)
Madison Heights	56.01(3)	55.57(2)	46.20(3)
Oak Park	55.98(4)	52.58(4)	52.62(1)
Roseville	54.19(5)	49.44(5)	43.84(9)
Westland	53.78(6)	47.82(8)	N/A
Garden City	52.51(7)	42.52(17)	43.47(10)
Inkster	50.22(8)	48.54(6)	45.30(4)
Livonia	50.11(9)	46.53(9)	45.41(5)
St. Clair Shores	49.72(10)	46.53(9)	41.36(13)
Royal Oak	49.64(11)	45.45(12)	44.67(7)
East Detroit	46.35(12)	46.40(10)	44.70(6)
Warren	45.39(13)	39.12(18)	38.75(15)
Lincoln Park	45.36(14)	44.44(15)	41.67(12)
Southfield	44.94(15)	45.06(13)	40.92(14)
Pontiac	44.67(16)	41.19(16)	38.62(16)
Wyandotte	43.90(17)	44.69(14)	44.37(8)
Dearborn	43.72(18)	43.24(16)	38.36(17)
Allen Park	43.10(19)	39.12(18)	35.67(19)
Dearborn Heights	41.38(20)	48.11(7)	38.28(18)

( ) indicate rank order
*Detroit also levies a citywide personal income tax, which, for purposes of comparison, has been translated to a millage equivalent.
Source: State Assessed Property Division of the State Tax Commission

dwellers. The burden of support for these services, however, is borne totally by Detroit taxpayers.

Another irony in the effort of cities to raise revenues and finance services is that the property tax base in some cities is growing less rapidly than in the surrounding suburbs, and in some instances the big-city tax base is actually decreasing. In Detroit, for example, assessed valuation dropped from $20,000 per pupil in 1960 to $16,500 in 1968. This is a consequence of a variety of factors: migration of industry to sites outside the city, urban renewal projects that replace tax-paying buildings with public structures, freeway construction that destroys taxable property, and so on. The end result is a

Financial Roots of Inequality

Table 6.8. A Display of Selected City of Detroit Institutions Serving
Metropolitan Detroit (1969–1970 Budget)

Function	Appropriations	Less Credits	Plus Fringe Costs (31.92%) Applied on Personal Services	Total Cost
Zoological Park	$2,267,638	$1,526,220	$ 481,403	$ 1,222,821
Art Institute	1,350,663	37,000	330,268	1,643,931
Historical Commission	611,788	8,250	163,607	767,145
Library	8,127,749	4,807,291	4,003,131	7,323,589
Detroit House of Correction	2,746,392	3,008,738	615,485	353,139
Total				$11,310,625

curtailed base from which to generate revenue, no matter how much tax effort is made.

Tax Rate Constraints and "Effort" Inequities

An additional factor influencing lower tax rates, and consequently contributing to a curtailment of school service quality, in low wealth, low SES school districts is the presence of legal arrangements that impose political constraints upon the tax rate. For example, in Michigan the County Allocation Board is a significant unit of government. This agency has the legal right to distribute a limit of 15 mills of property tax rate without gaining the explicit approval of voters in a tax override election. School districts do not obtain all 15 mills; the total is divided by elected representatives of the county government among various public agencies within its jurisdiction. This distribution of the 15-mill levy to the government agencies in the county is labeled "allocated tax rate." To levy taxes in excess of the allocated millage rate, a local school district must gain explicit voter approval in a tax override election. In Table 6.9 we display allocation rates for school districts in accord with AV/PP.

What can be seen from this table is that districts with the lowest amount of assessed valuation per pupil tend to receive the lowest allocation for school taxes from their counties. When we examine the allocation rate in relation to socioeconomic status of school districts we find much the same phenomenon operating. High SES districts receive a higher allocated tax rate than do low SES districts, and the

Table 6.9

Quartiles according to Variable 265			Assessed Valuation per Pupil	
Medians from Variable 266			Allocated Millage Rate	
Quartile	1	2	3	4
Median	8.6	9.0	9.1	9.2
NTRUE = 49				
STUDENT T = 3.03765				

difference between them is too great and too consistent to be likely to have occurred by chance alone.

The practical consequence of these inequities in the allocation of tax rates is that low SES and low AV/PP districts, more frequently than others, must turn to their voters in what are termed "tax override elections" in order to raise the revenue they need in excess of that generated by the allocated tax rate. The necessity to appeal to the public more frequently is a detriment because a voter majority is necessary to increase the tax rate, and such a majority is frequently difficult to obtain (who desires to have his taxes raised?). Moreover, since low SES and low AV/PP districts are also the ones in which the regressive nature of the property tax is likely to be most evident, it is there that the burden of the property tax, and thus voter resistance to overriding the allocated statutory tax rate, is likely to be highest.

From the foregoing discussion it is obvious that the circumstances surrounding the generation of school revenues from local sources are complex. Nevertheless, we wish to emphasize again the simple, but nonetheless significant consequence of these arrangements. **Less money is available from local sources for the schooling of low SES students than is the case for high SES students.**

State-Distributed Funds

If school finance arrangements surrounding the generation of revenue from taxation of local property operate to enable the rich to get richer and the poor to get poorer, then what is the effect of introducing state-distributed funds into the analysis? Before pursuing the specific answer to this question, let us first explain briefly the rationale for direct state aid and the manner in which such aid is allocated.

The Rationale for Direct State Aid to Schools

Aside from any discussion about the obvious responsibilities of
states to finance local schools as a consequence of their legal obligations, there exist three overriding economic reasons for direct state
participation in the support of local schools: (1) third-party benefits,
(2) equalization of educational opportunity, and (3) equalization of
financial burden.

Benefits. It is the nature of schooling that the benefits are not
restricted to the direct or immediate recipient. A child receiving an
education clearly benefits as his ability to understand and appreciate
the world about him and his ability to earn a living improve. But the
community also benefits from having, for example, an expanded and
improved supply of leaders, a more highly skilled work force, and a
better-educated electorate. These **spillover** or **third-party** benefits
are no longer restricted, in the main, to the community in which the
individual received his schooling. With improvements and increases
in communication and transportation, the benefits become more
widespread. With the increase in the mobility of our population, the
community that provides schooling for an individual is less likely to
be the community in which he will reside. Thus, we have a strong
rationale for having the state contribute funds for local schooling,
purely from the point of view of the benefits to be received by the
state as a whole.[9]

In passing, it should be noted that since the state is directly
affected by the quality of schooling at the local level, it may, indeed,
wish to encourage improvements in local districts. State aid grants
may attempt to achieve this by **stimulating** local districts to increase
their own revenue efforts and by providing incentives to promote
more efficient use of funds.

Equalizing Opportunity. About this topic we need not say too much
at this point. Suffice it here to refer again to our previous discussion
of disparities in local school districts' abilities to generate revenue
from property tax sources. The distribution of state funds is in part
intended to overcome such disparities so that they do not manifest
themselves boldly in unequal local school services. However, as is
our point in this chapter, the failure of the state's arrangements to
achieve this goal is the primary condition allowing school services

[9] With increased interstate mobility, the same rationale can be applied to
federal aid to education. For a more complete discussion of these arguments,
see Burton A. Weisbrod, **External Benefits of Public Education** (Princeton:
Princeton University Press, 1964).

to be associated with SES of students. In other words, if state school finance arrangements were successful in achieving the objective of equalizing resources, this study probably would not have been conducted.

Equalizing the Burden of Support. This topic is somewhat the mirror image of resource equalization. State-distributed funds are also held to be desirable because they prevent disparities in the financial burden felt by individuals who support education. The rationale here is that no citizen should have to bear a disproportionate share of the costs of schooling the children in the state. State general funds collected from all citizens should flow to school districts in a kind of upside-down, Robin Hood fashion so that poor people do not pay excessively for their children's education while the wealthy pay but a relatively small amount for theirs. The primary concern in this report is in explaining disparities that occur in the quality of school services available to students on the basis of their socioeconomic status, rather than with ways of equalizing the burden of paying for schools. Nevertheless, it is somewhat ironic to note that not only do the children of the poor have less money spent for their schooling (and consequently unequal and less adequate school services), but also that, relative to their income, their parents frequently pay more for those unequal services.

State Aid in Operation

Michigan's procedure for distributing state funds directly to local school districts operates along two broad dimensions: special-purpose finance provisions, and general-purpose aid.[10] Examples of special-purpose grants include funds to local school districts to cover costs such as transportation, remedial reading teachers, and special educational services. The general-purpose aid is given to school districts to spend at their own discretion, subject to legal restrictions, of course.

In Michigan, general-purpose aid constitutes 90 percent of all funds distributed by the state for the public schools, so this is where we will spend the major portion of our examination. In order to participate in the state aid plan a school district must tax itself at a specified millage rate (in accord with its equalized assessed valuation per pupil). Thereafter it receives state funds in inverse proportion to its fiscal capacity (AV/PP). Every district, regardless of how weatlhy

[10] There are several "pure" types of state school finance arrangements. Michigan, like most states, embodies a combination of these types.

it is, receives some state aid; and no district, regardless of how poor it is, receives more than a specified maximum.

The difficulty with this arrangement is that it does not equalize. It is true that wealthy school districts tend to receive less in state funds per pupil than do poor school districts. However, every school district gets some amount of money from the state. For example, in the 1967–1968 school year (the latest year for which complete information was available) one of the wealthiest districts in the state ($44,450 AV/PP) received $130.34 per pupil in state aid. Consequently, even though the state funds are labeled "equalizing," they do not suffice to produce equality of resources behind every child in Michigan. This imperfection is graphically displayed in Tables 6.10, 6.11, and 6.12.

In the first of these tables (Table 6.10), local school districts have been ranked in terms of their AV/PP. The amount of money generated from **local sources** is then displayed for the median school district in each quartile. This display illustrates the strong role played by "ability," or local school district wealth. Those districts with high

Table 6.10

Quartiles according to Variable 265			Assessed Valuation per Pupil	
Medians from Variable 253			Per Pupil Allocation from Local Sources	
Quartile	1	2	3	4
Median	168	212	281	323
NTRUE = 49				
STUDENT T = 7.33579				

Table 6.11

Quartiles according to Variable 265			Assessed Valuation per Pupil	
Medians from Variable 255			Per Pupil Allocations from Direct State Sources	
Quartile	1	2	3	4
Median	319	297	260	215
NTRUE = 49				
STUDENT T = −14.82545				

Table 6.12

Quartiles according to Variable 265		Assessed Valuation per Pupil	
Medians from Variable 259		Total Allocation per Pupil	
Quartile	1	2	3	4
Median	512	509	550	626
NTRUE = 49				
STUDENT T = 3.09559				

levels of assessed valuation per pupil are those that generate high levels of local revenue for their schools.

In the next table (Table 6.11), we follow the same analytical procedure, but this time we identify the amount of direct **state aid** received by the median district in each quartile. Here we find a perfect negative relationship. The lower the assessed valuation per pupil of a school district, the more state aid it receives. Superficially, it appears as though state arrangements are achieving to a high degree their objective of equalization. However, when we scrutinize this table, another fact comes to light. There is only $104 difference in state payments between the median in the quartile containing the poorest districts (quartile 1) and the median in the quartile containing the wealthiest districts (quartile 4). When we examine Table 6.12 it is evident that this small amount of money simply does not suffice to overcome the resource advantage provided to wealthy districts. Imperfections in the state's equalization efforts are such that the median district in the high assessed valuation quartile is able to generate a total allocation that is $114 more per pupil than the median district in the low AV/PP quartile.

The linkage of state aid to the socioeconomic status of a district can be seen in the next two tables. In Table 6.13 school districts in our Thomas Report sample are ranked by their SES and the state distributed funds are displayed for the median district in each quartile. Here, it can be seen that, while low SES districts do obtain more direct state aid per pupil than high SES districts, the dollar differences are not great and do not suffice to overcome the advantage of wealth. As we can see from Table 6.14, high SES districts, even in the face of state aid, still manage to spend an amount for instructional purposes that is well in excess of the money spent by low SES districts.

Table 6.13

Quartiles according to Variable 181			Socioeconomic Scale	
Medians from Variable 255			Per Pupil Allocation from Direct State Sources	
Quartile	1	2	3	4
Median	269	286	288	235
NTRUE = 48				
STUDENT T = −2.61048				

Table 6.14

Quartiles according to Variable 181			Socioeconomic Scale	
Medians from Variable 260			Expenditure per Pupil, Total Instruction	
Quartile	1	2	3	4
Median	335	331	365	420
NTRUE = 48				
STUDENT T = 2.93829				

But What about Federal Funds?

Before writing off resource quality as a present-day myth in Michigan, it is necessary to consider the effects of federal funds for education. In 1967, federal appropriations accounted for almost 8 percent of all public elementary and secondary education expenditures for the entire United States.[11] If distributed in an equalizing fashion, such an amount could substantially ameliorate revenue inequalities. However, such is not the case. In assessing the association in Michigan between school district AV/PP and receipt of federal funds, we actually found a negative correlation. That is, wealthier school districts tended to receive more federal dollars per pupil than poorer districts.

For the reader who is perplexed by this finding and surprised to hear that this occurs despite the existence of dramatically publicized pieces of federal legislation such as the 1965 Elementary and Secondary Education Act, a word of explanation is in order. Federal funds flow into a state under a wide variety of legislative authorities. It is true that ESEA Title I funds must be redistributed by a state in

[11] Kenneth B. Simon and Vance W. Grant, **Digest of Educational Statistics** (Washington, D.C.: U.S. Government Printing Office, 1967).

accord with the number of children in a district whose parents' annual income is less than $2,000. However, ESEA Title I is but one authority. As examples to the contrary, in Public Laws 815 and 874, the National Defense Education Act, the Education Professions Development Act, and a number of other ESEA Titles, no such equalizing constraint is in operation. Consequently, in general, federal funds flow in a fashion that permits high SES and wealthy (high AV/PP) districts to receive an allocation of federal money per pupil equal to, if not greater than, that received by low SES and poor (low AV/PP) districts.[12]

The aggregate consequence of all these financial arrangements, local, state, and federal, was displayed at the beginning of this chapter in Table 6.1. There we saw that the total instructional expenditures per student in school districts in the Michigan sample in relation to residents' SES. Again, in spite of state equalization arrangements and federal funds, disproportionately available resources in high SES districts persist in penetrating any efforts now being made at equalization. In order to illustrate the raw impotence of present state equalization arrangements, Table 6.15 displays the expenditure figures in 1967–1968 for the five school districts at each end of the continuum of total expenditures per pupil.

Real Resources May Be Even More Unequal
The foregoing discussion has attempted to demonstrate that school finance arrangements in Michigan do not function to achieve resource equity among local school districts. In these discussions, we have used "equity" to denote closely similar or identical levels of dollars. However, if we accurately took into account the spending power of dollars and the "need" of school districts for resources, it is likely that the absolute dollar disparities described previously would be magnified several times over. School districts with the lowest

[12] A great deal of the federal money that is redistributed by a state is done so on the basis of project proposals submitted by local districts to state authorities. It generally is the wealthier districts that have the personnel available to write the proposals. Moreover, if the program requires matching funds, such as with NDEA Title III, then poor districts are at a disadvantage to put up the local district share. For a more detailed description of the inequities involved in the redistribution of federal funds see James W. Guthrie and Stephen B. Lawton, "The Distribution of Federal School Aid Funds: Who Wins? Who Loses?" **Educational Administration Quarterly** (Winter 1969); and I. T. Johnson, "An Evaluation of NDEA Title III," **Phi Delta Kappan,** 48 (June 1967).

Table 6.15. Total Expenditures per Pupil for Five Highest-and Five Lowest-Spending Michigan School Districts, 1967–1968

Highest Spending	Total Expenditure per Pupil
1. Whitefish School	$1,038.40
2. Republic Michigamme School	1,033.35
3. Dearborn City School District	998.74
4. Oak Park City School District	973.21
5. Bloomfield Hills School	959.54
Average (mean)	$1,000.65

Lowest Spending	Total Expenditure per Pupil
1. Beaver Island Community Schools	$411.96
2. Flushing Community Schools	425.82
3. Summerfield School District	432.91
4. Three Rivers Public School District	450.88
5. Hartford Public School District	456.77
Average (mean)	$435.67

Source: Bulletin 1012, Michigan Department of Education, 1968.

levels of financial "ability" are frequently those with the greatest need for resources. This is so primarily because of two factors: (1) cost differentials and (2) disproportionate numbers of educationally disadvantaged children.

Cost Differentials

Goods and services simply do not cost the same amount in every part of the nation, every part of a state, or even in every part of a county.[13] The locations in which school-related costs tend to be highest are frequently the very places in which school resources are the lowest, in the large urban school districts and isolated rural areas. A dramatic example of the disadvantage of the urban school district is provided by the case of land prices. The school district of the city of Detroit purchases school sites in areas where land is exceedingly scarce and consequently very costly. By comparison, many of the suburbs surrounding Detroit still have access to open and undeveloped land, which they can purchase at relatively inex-

[13] Or even in every part of a single city. See David Caplovitz, **The Poor Pay More** (New York: The Free Press, 1967).

pensive rates. For example, in 1967 Detroit paid an average price per acre for school sites that was in excess of $100,000, contrasted with only approximately $6,000 per acre in surrounding suburban districts.

Land costs, however, are not the only, or even the major dimension on which differences in the buying power of a district's dollars occur. Typically, the most expensive item in a school budget is salaries for professional employees. Here again, in order to obtain the teaching manpower necessary to staff schools, Detroit offers a higher beginning salary than many of its neighboring school districts. For example, Detroit's entry-level minimum salary in 1968–1969 was $7,500. The average entry-level minimum salary for thirty-five surrounding suburban districts was $6,922. In fact, the closest suburban district in terms of entry-level salary was $300 below Detroit.[14] We wish to emphasize that Detroit was not necessarily obtaining more highly prepared or better-qualified teachers by virtue of this salary differential. The added salary is simply the amount Detroit was forced by circumstances to pay in order to obtain beginning teachers.

Big cities typically must pay higher labor rates for skilled maintenance workers; and costs of materials and supplies are generally higher for rural districts, which cannot take advantage of purchasing in large quantities. We could continue to describe cost differentials for a number of other school-related goods and services. Our point, however, is that the present arrangements by which the state allocates its funds do not adequately compensate for such cost differentials. As a consequence, the real disparities in available dollar resources, disparities in terms of what dollars purchase, are probably more unequal than they appear in absolute dollar terms.

Educationally Disadvantaged Students

A great deal of evidence exists to the effect that an impoverished early childhood environment leads to educational handicaps that are difficult to overcome.[15] The relevance of this evidence to our present concern lies in the fact that children suffering from such handicaps tend to reside in disproportionate numbers in school districts that spend lower amounts per pupil on instruction. Table 6.16 displays

[14] These data were obtained from Stanley E. Hecker, John Meeder, and Thomas F. Northey, **Teacher Salary Schedule Study,** 1968–1969 (Lansing: Michigan Education Association, 1969).
[15] See Benjamin S. Bloom, Allison Davis, and Robert Hess, **Compensatory Education for Cultural Deprivation** (New York: Holt, Rinehart and Winston, 1965).

Table 6.16

Quartiles according to Variable 182			Percent with Income under 3,000 Dollars	
Medians from Variable 260			Expenditure per Pupil, Total Instruction	
Quartile	1	2	3	4
Median	452	378	350	333
NTRUE = 48				
STUDENT T = −3.09562				

the relationship between school district instructional expenditure and percent of school district pupils from homes with annual incomes of $3,000 or less. (In reading this table keep in mind that the quartiles are arranged from left to right in accord with **increasing proportions** of poverty-impacted families.)

What is evident from the above display is that school districts with the lowest expenditures for instructional services are the very ones containing the greatest numbers of children in need of enriched, expensive school services. While Michigan's school finance statutes contain a provision whereby additional funds flow to school districts with disproportionate numbers of disadvantaged children, limitations on the total amount of funds appropriated for this provison prevent its successful operation.

Dollars and Differences in Services
In Chapter 3 we examined the relationship between SES and quality of available school services and found that lower socioeconomic status students tend to receive lower-quality services. Subsequently we demonstrated that the amount of revenue available to support school services is also associated with the SES of the school district's residents. Thus, in an indirect fashion, we have already addressed ourselves to the question of how dollars translate to services. The answer is that "they do." More dollars, in general, mean better ability to purchase high-quality educational services. However, in order to render this statement less an assertion built on logic and more a finding based on analysis, we shall present evidence in support of Proposition E, that added dollars buy added school-service quality.

In assessing the effects of resource differences we followed the basic analytical procedures employed throughout this report. We ranked school districts separately in terms of (1) the dollar amounts they spent for instructional services, and (2) their specific quality level on a number of school services. We then statistically compared the relationships between the two rank orderings. The following are examples of results obtained from this procedure.

Supplies

Contrary to what might be deemed equitable, students in high-expenditure school districts are the most likely to have their instructional materials supplied to them at no cost. Conversely, pupils in low-expenditure districts are the most likely to have to purchase such items as pencils and paper and supplementary materials out of their own funds. This finding is displayed in Table 6.17.

Instructional Arrangements

Inability to purchase high-quality school services is plainly evident in this category. Low-expenditure districts have higher percentages of students in classrooms of thirty-five or more pupils.[16] Moreover, once in a classroom, a student in a low-expenditure district is less likely to have the benefit of modern instructional aids such as audio-visual devices, teaching machines, reading laboratories, and science laboratories.[17] If the student is particularly talented in a specific subject matter field or a skill area such as music, he is much less likely to be provided with enriched instructional experiences if he attends school in a low-expenditure district.[18] Also, regardless of his academic ability, the child in a low-expenditure district is much less likely to be exposed to new instructional procedures such as team teaching, nongraded classrooms, and programmed instruction.[19]

Table 6.17

Quartiles according to Variable 260		Expenditure per Pupil, Total Instruction	
Medians from Variable 54		Supplies Available to Student at No Cost	
Quartile	1	2	3	4
Median	9	13	16	18
NTRUE = 47			
STUDENT T = 2.41752			

[16] T, 260 V. 214.
[17] T, 169 V. 188.
[18] T, 260 V. 186.
[19] T, 260 V. 255.

Instructional Staff

The quality of staff is significantly associated with expenditure levels. Low-expenditure districts employ a higher percentage of provisionally credentialed teachers.[20] Moreover, low-expenditure districts employ larger percentages of teachers either with no degree or only a bachelor's degree.[21] Conversely, higher-expenditure districts employ a larger percentage of teachers with advanced (master's) degrees.[22]

An explanation for the lower-quality staff can perhaps be found in the monetary inducements offered by low-expenditure districts. In Table 6.18 is displayed the relationship between total amount spent for instruction and amount spent per pupil for instructional salaries.

From these statistics it is obvious that the high-expenditure districts offer larger financial inducements. A specific example of this finding is illustrated in Table 6.19. The table displays the relationship of instructional expenditures to the salary paid teachers with master's degrees. Here it can be seen that low-expenditure districts simply cannot pay as much for highly qualified manpower as can other districts. As a consequence, as displayed in Tables 6.20 and 6.21, they simply do not obtain the services of as many highly qualified teachers.

Much the same results can be displayed for items such as school facilities[23] and administrative services.[24] However, the sum of such findings is that the amount of money available for the support of instructional services is related to the quality of those services.

It is possible that some low-expenditure districts are less efficient (do not maximize the amount of school service quality to be obtained

Table 6.18

Quartilies according to Variable 260			Expenditure per Pupil, Total Instruction	
Medians from Variable 263			Expenditure per Pupil for Instructional Salaries	
Quartile	1	2	3	4
Median	279	308	351	425
NTRUE = 49				
STUDENT T = 52.66247				

[20] T, 260 V. 280.
[21] T, 260 V. 281.
[22] T, 260 V. 281.
[23] T, 260 V. 196.
[24] T, 260 V. 215.

Table 6.19

Quartilies according to Variable 260		Expenditure per Pupil, Total Instruction	
Medians from Variable 273		Teacher Salary in Hundreds for M.A. Minimum	
Quartile	1	2	3	4
Median	69	69	69	74

NTRUE = 49
STUDENT T = 3.00479

Table 6.20

Quartiles according to Variable 260		Expenditure per Pupil, Total Instruction	
Medians from Variable 280		Type of Certificate	
Quartile	1	2	3	4
Median	345	348	360	353

NTRUE = 49
STUDENT T = 2.23375

Table 6.21

Quartiles according to Variable 260		Expenditure per Pupil, Total Instruction	
Medians from Variable 281		Degree	
Quartile	1	2	3	4
Median	116	120	131	139

NTRUE = 49
STUDENT T = 5.41306

at a particular dollar value) and that some others squander their money on insignificant educational frills. However, for the majority of such districts, the evidence is convincing that their lack of dollar resources handicaps them severely in acquiring the physical and human resources necessary to offer equal-quality school services. Moreover, our research cycle is made complete by the fact that low-expenditure school districts tend also to be low SES districts. In this fashion, as we stated in Chapter 1, the quality of school services available to a student becomes related to his socioeconomic status.

What remains now is to consider alternative governmental arrangements to disengage school service quality from pupils' social standing. No simplified solution is likely to suffice. It would be easy, by
manipulating a number of elementary financial formulas, to arrive at
absolute dollar equity among school districts in the amount of money
spent for the education of each child. However, absolute dollar
equity would not accomplish the goal of untying educational opportunity from social circumstances. Even if provided with equal dollars,
or even slightly more than equal dollars, low SES districts would still
be unable to deliver services of a quality commensurate with the
offerings of high SES districts. Instead of equal dollars, what is
needed is a different view of what constitutes true equality of educational opportunity. We move now to Chapter 7, where we suggest an
alternative view and describe arrangements that could translate such
a view into a reality.

7

Financing Schools for Equality

Neglecting the education of children in poorer communities in our states and in the poorer states, generation after generation, in the hope that some economic miracle will bring about the correction of the economic lag, is a pretty unrealistic point of view.[1]

[1] Paul R. Mort, **Fiscal Readiness for the Stress of Change** (Pittsburgh: University of Pittsburgh Press, 1957), pp. 27–28.

In the foregoing chapters we have demonstrated that the state of
Michigan and its school districts (1) invest more resources in the
schooling of higher socioeconomic status students; (2) that this differential investment contributes to greater educational achievement
among such students; and (3) that these achievement advantages
accrue to greater lifetime and intergenerational opportunities. It was
also shown that in Michigan, financial arrangements for supporting
schools are responsible directly for perpetuating inequalities. In this
chapter we present a set of alternative arrangements for equalizing
educational opportunity. These arrangements are based upon the
findings contained in previous chapters as well as what we consider
reasonable definitions of the educational and social goals implicit in
a democratic ideology. We will proceed in four stages: (1) to define
equality of educational opportunity, (2) to describe the discrepancy
between that definition and present reality, (3) to discuss a new
strategy for translating revenues into school services, and (4) to
suggest an alternative means for financing equal educational
opportunity.

Defining Equality of Educational Opportunity[2]
In our society's present race for "spoils" not all runners begin at the
same starting line. As we have described throughout the preceding
chapters, children from higher SES circumstances presently begin
life with many advantages. Their home environment, health care,
nutrition, material possessions, and geographic mobility provide them
with a substantial headstart when they begin schooling at age five or
six. Lower SES children begin school with more physical disabilities
and less psychological preparation for adjusting to the procedures of
schooling. This condition of disadvantage is then compounded by
having to attend schools characterized by fewer and lower-quality
services.

What must we do if schooling is to compensate for these disparities
and to provide equality of opportunity? What actions are implied in
such a goal? In responding to these questions it is important from
the outset to make clear that we are referring to equality of opportunity among **groups** of individuals, that is, by race, socioeconomic

[2] Almost the entire issue of the Winter 1968 **Harvard Educational Review**
(Vol. 38, No. 1) is devoted to the topic of "Equal Educational Opportunity."
The article entitled "The Concept of Equality of Educational Opportunity,"
by James S. Coleman, provides historical perspective on the development of
the concept.

status, residence in city or suburb, and so on. We recognize fully that genetic differences and variations in other characteristics among individuals within such groups will continue to promote **within**-group differences in attainment. However, we reject explicitly the idea of inevitable differences **among** groups with regard to the equality of their opportunity. Equality of opportunity implies strongly that a representative individual of any racial or social grouping has the same probability of succeeding as does a representative individual of any other racial or social grouping. Stated in another way, given equality of opportunity, there should be a random relationship between the social position of parents and the lifetime attainments of their offspring.

We believe strongly that the task of the school is to equalize opportunities among different social groupings by the end of the compulsory schooling period. This belief is reinforced by the fact that Michigan requires all minors to attend schools until age sixteen. Implied in this mandate is the view that formal schooling will enable representative youngsters from all social and racial groups to begin their postschool careers with equal chances of success. In a true sense, while the race for spoils will still be won by the swiftest, if schools are functioning properly, then typical individuals from all social groups should be on the same starting line at age sixteen. Our society would wish that representative children of each social grouping begin their adult lives with equal chances of success in matters such as pursuing further schooling, obtaining a job, and participating in the political system. It would seem that equality of educational opportunity could be interpreted in no other way.

But if children born at different SES levels are to have the same set of opportunities at age sixteen, though starting off with different chances of success at age five, equal amounts of school resources for children at each level will not suffice. Clearly, those children who begin their schooling with the greatest disadvantage must have disproportionately greater schooling resources in order to equalize opportunity at age sixteen. Of course, as we have documented in Chapters 2 and 6, present operation of Michigan schools leads to greater schooling resources for children from upper SES levels, a parody on the concept of equal educational opportunity. Translating school resources into dollars, more dollars must be expended on those children who typically enter school with the least initial opportunity, those from the lower socioeconomic strata.

The Opportunity Gap

Table 7.1 is a hypothetical illustration of the proportion of children at three SES levels who are likely to achieve "lifetime success." Success can be thought of as a hypothetical set of generally desired outcomes. Examples of such outcomes on which a favorable consensus might be derived include lifetime income and occupational attainment. In this illustration only about 15 percent of the low-income children are likely to achieve "lifetime success," while 50 percent and 85 percent of the medium and high SES children, respectively, should attain that goal. Yet, equality of educational opportunity requires that at the end of that period of social investment in schooling, all social and racial groups should have an equal probability of achieving success. The gap between equal opportunity and actual opportunity is represented by the white portion of the bar graph for the low and medium SES groups. That is, the opportunity gap is greatest for the low SES group, smaller for the medium SES group, and almost nonexistent for the highest group.

Capital Embodiment and Opportunity

An appropriate means of illustrating the cause and magnitude of the opportunity gap is to conduct an analysis in the context of **human capital development.** Beginning in the 1950s' economists have employed the human capital approach to understand the process of increasing social and private well-being through investing in the health, education, and training of people.[3] Briefly, economists have

Table 7.1. Proportion of Children at Three SES Levels Who Are Likely to Achieve "Lifetime Success" (A Hypothetical Representation)

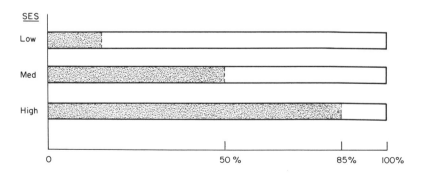

[3] For more information on the human capital concept see Gary S. Becker, **Human Capital** (New York: Columbia University Press, 1964).

found that financial investments in raising the health and proficiencies of human beings yield substantial social and economic dividends to society. Indeed, when translated into monetary terms, productivity and earnings attributable to human capital investment generally exceed the rate of return associated with investments in physical capital.[4]

The concept of human capital investment is readily applicable to our concern with the opportunity gap. To a large extent, differences in opportunity among individuals from different SES levels represent differences in the amount of capital investment embodied in them. Investment in human capital, then, is defined as resources that are devoted to an individual's growth, investments that increase his proficiencies. And, at present, both the family and our larger society invest more resources in the growth and development of high SES children than they do for low SES ones.

The low SES child is more likely than others to face prenatal malnutrition, and in his early years he is a prominent candidate for protein starvation.[5] He is less likely to receive adequate medical and dental care as well, so he is more prone to suffer from a large variety of undetected, undiagnosed, and untreated health problems. The meager income levels associated with lower SES children typically translate into less adequate shelter and a more modest overall physical environment. These factors are less likely to stimulate cognitive development than are the richer and more varied material surroundings of his higher SES peers. Limited family income also inhibits or precludes travel and exposure to the large variety of worldly experiences that increase the knowledge and sophistication of the more advantaged child. Finally, and perhaps most important, both the quality and quantity of parental services tend to be less for the lower SES child. Lower SES children are more likely to receive limited parental attention because they are frequently situated in families with many children and where one or both parents are missing.[6] Further, the low educational attainment levels of lower SES adults limits the amount of knowledge they can transmit to their children. This is a

[4] For a review of several studies in this area see Theodore W. Schultz, "The Rate of Return in Allocating Investment Resources to Education," **The Journal of Human Resources,** 2 (Summer 1967), 293–309.
[5] See Nevin S. Scrimshaw, "Infant Malnutrition and Adult Learning," **Saturday Review,** 51 (March 16, 1968), 64–66.
[6] For a discussion of the effect of family structure see Lee Rainwater and William L. Yancey, eds, **The Moynihan Report and the Politics of Controversy** (Cambridge, Mass.: M.I.T. Press, 1967).

particular drawback in the area of verbal skill development,[7] an area upon which school success depends so heavily.

Perhaps the most important component of parental investment related to SES is that of educational services provided by parents. Apparently parents with greater educational attainment themselves inculcate in their children much higher skill levels than do parents with less education. Indeed, the greater investment of human capital embodied in children from families with higher educational attainment can be estimated in terms of dollar values. That is, a parent, and particularly a mother, has the option of working or providing services to her children. The higher the educational level of the parent, the greater the value of that parent's services in the labor market, and therefore, the greater the imputed value of parental services in the home. A parent with higher educational attainment must forego a larger amount of income in order to stay home with children than a parent with lower attainment. Indeed, the educational level of parents, multiplied by the time that they invest in their children, can be converted to approximate dollar amounts of capital embodiment in each child. This can be accomplished by valuing parental educational efforts according to the market value of such services (of course, market value of services is in turn determined strongly by parents' education).[8]

Dennis Dugan, an economist, has constructed such estimates for a national sample of children. He presents calculations of the total value of parental educational services embodied in children at various age levels according to the educational level of the parents.[9] These

[7] See, for example, Ellis G. Olim, Robert D. Hess, and Virginia Shipman, "Role of Mothers' Language Styles in Mediating their Preschool Children's Cognitive Development," **School Review,** 75 (Winter 1967), 414–424; and Robert D. Hess, "Maternal Behavior and the Development of Reading Readiness in Urban Negro Children," a paper prepared for the Claremont Reading Conference, Claremont, California, February 10, 1968.

[8] It is important to make it clear that the dollar amounts derived in this fashion are only indicators of the differences in parental investment between lower and higher SES children. They are meant to be illustrative rather than conclusive. Most important, they are meant to measure the difference in capital embodiment between children at different SES levels attributable to only one component of human investment, parents' services. Differences in human capital due to differential investment in health, nutrition, physical environment, and other factors are not measured directly in our estimates.

[9] See Dennis J. Dugan, "The Impact of Parental and Educational Investments upon Student Achievement," Social Statistics Section, **Proceedings of the American Statistical Association** (1969).

Table 7.2. Value in 1965 of Mother's Educational Services for Mother's Educational Attainment by Grade of Child (All amounts in 1966 dollars)

Mother's Education	Grade 1	6	9	12
Elem. School				
0-7 years	$2724	$3412	$4126	$4989
8 years	3379	4231	5135	6235
High School				
1-3 years	3972	5012	6094	7409
4 years	6964	8898	10797	13080
College				
1-3 years	7091	9051	10995	13365
4 years	9044	11560	14076	17148
5+ years	9322	11919	14644	17978

Source: Dugan, Dennis, "The Impact of Parental and Educational Investment upon Student Achievement," **Proceedings of the American Statistical Association** (1969). Used by permission of the author.

calculations are based upon "(1) the proportion of a mother's time devoted to educationally related activities (as opposed to household chores), and (2) the number of children among whom the mother's time is divided."[10] The estimated amount of a father's time devoted to educational activities of his children is derived similarly.

For purposes of illustration, we will display only the value of mother's educational investment in children at different grade levels by educational attainment of mother. Table 7.2 contains these results for 1965. The figures shown are dollar values of accumulated educational services invested in the child by one source, the mother.

According to these estimates, the six-year-old whose mother is a high school graduate has had twice as large a maternal investment as the child whose mother terminated her education at elementary school. The child of a college graduate has 2.7 times as much investment from this source as the offspring of an elementary school graduate. These figures illustrate the substantial inequalities in human capital formation among children of different SES levels as they begin their formal schooling. Over the period of schooling, while all the values increase for all groups, the ratio of inequality remains constant.

Moreover, values of mother's and father's contributed educational services represent excellent predictors of academic success at grade one. That is, differences in human capital formation at grade one are

[10] Ibid., p. 5.

related to differences in academic performance. For example, Dugan found that measures of human capital embodiment explain approximately 95 percent of the variance in pupil verbal skills for white first graders and 88 percent of the variance for nonwhite first graders.[11] Stated in another way, there is a close correspondence between the value of embodied parental services and a child's academic achievement or between the investment in a child and the academic returns to him.

Dugan also addresses himself to the relative efficacy in raising academic performance of dollars invested in school services. That is, he estimated the combined effect of parental investment and school investment on student achievement. In this way he attempted to approximate the amount of additional school investment in lower SES children that might be needed to compensate for the greater parental investment in their higher SES peers. His results are interesting, but they are limited by the use of an inadequate expenditure measure.[12] Nevertheless, he presents a provocative finding with regard to equalizing academic performances of whites and nonwhites. Dugan found "that an additional $6,662 per nonwhite student is required to raise the nonwhite mean achievement to the level of the white achievement mean for sixth graders."[13] Distributed over the first five years of school, this translates to a mean annual expenditure of approximately $1,300 a year per nonwhite pupil above the amount that was being spent, about $400. The point is that if we are addressing ourselves to equal educational outcomes, then substantially higher dollar amounts must be spent on school services for low SES children.

An Alternative Pedagogical Strategy
Differences in dollar investment must be translated into differences in educational effectiveness if the fortunes of both low and high SES students are to be equalized at the end of the mandatory schooling process. In order to satisfy this goal, a new educational approach must be implemented, one that addresses itself to the specific needs of each child. In this respect, just as more money is presently spent on special educational arrangements for some children because of their physical capacities, so will we have to differentiate among

[11] **Ibid.**, Table 3.
[12] He used state averages for expenditure rather than districtwide or school averages. The latter are the most appropriate for this type of analysis, but they are not always available.
[13] Dugan, "Parental and Educational Investment," p. 24.

children of different SES origins. For example, more money is already
spent on children with learning problems stemming from brain damage, emotional handicaps, and severe physical disabilities. Following
the individualization of instruction for these groups, we suggest
specially tailored courses of study for other children as well.

By implication, the greater initial needs of low SES students will
necessitate greater expenditures. But how should these dollars be
spent? We begin with the general belief that additional resources
received by school districts should be employed in a manner that
will maximize their effectiveness. This concern does not focus exclu-
sively upon schooling for lower socioeconomic status children.
Rather, we believe this alternative strategy to be applicable to the
schooling of all children, and as much in need of being implemented
in Grosse Pointe as in Detroit and in Scarsdale as in New York City.
Before progressing to this rather simple proposal, however, let us
make it clear that we are not about to prescribe a specific school
program in all its full-blown operational detail. Rather, our purpose is
to propose a simplified description of a schooling strategy that would
have as its central objective the preparation of children capable of
succeeding in the out-of-school world regardless of their social
standing or racial and ethnic identity.

Who Should Adjust to Whom?
Almost regardless of the social or physical characteristics of the
child, he presently is subjected to one mode of schooling. From the
time of his first contact with school, whether it be in kindergarten or
the first grade, whether it be in the lowest-expenditure or the highest-
expenditure school district, the child is placed in a four-walled room,
with an adult teacher at the front and chalk boards around the side.
He is surrounded by other students who are much like himself, at
least in terms of matters such as size, skin color, social standing,
and so on. Upon his entry into this system the assumption is made
that he is like his classmates on almost every other dimension as
well. Unless he is somehow dramatically different from his peers,
unless he is blind or otherwise organically incapacitated, he will
receive the same kind of treatment as all his classmates. If the treatment does not fit exactly, then generally the child is asked to adjust
to it. The closer he is able to shape his attitudes and actions to con-
form to the norm of his group, the greater the benefit he is likely to
derive from the instructional system. The more he deviates from the
norm, the less likely he is to benefit. He is expected to mold himself
to fit the procedures of the school. The educational procedures are

not likely to be molded to fit his needs. If he cannot adjust himself suitably, either one of two alternatives typically transpires. He may first be provided with some sort of remedial or specialized attention, which is aimed at reshaping him to fit the system. If this does not succeed within some specified period of time, usually not a very long period, he will then, in one fashion or another, be placed outside the system. He must attend a special (read inferior) school for dropouts and other deviants.

Given the extraordinary range of human diversity, the conception of a common school mold for each child strikes us as being, at best, completely unjustified. If a physician ordered all his patients to have the same operation, take the same medicine, and pay the same amount, regardless of their ailment, we would think his performance outrageous and probably illegal. If an attorney filed the same plea for each of his clients he would very shortly find himself devoid of business. Similarly, an architect who designed the same structure for each customer regardless of the intended function would shortly go bankrupt. However, little thought is given to the fact that each child, as he enters into and progresses through school, is given treatment substantially similar to that given every other child, despite the wide variations in background, ability, interests, and ambitions. Whatever adjustments are made, he must almost always make himself. The bell rings and the teacher talks; the examinations take place in a highly standardized fashion. The child's idiosyncrasies are seldom considered; more usually they are discouraged. The operation of schools appears to be geared primarily to administrative efficiency rather than educational proficiency.

In our view, the only alternative that is feasible is to find a means by which the schooling of a child can be tailored to his particular needs and abilities. Rather than requiring that he shape himself to fit the pattern of existing services, the pattern should be fitted to him. This view calls for a vastly different conception of what constitutes a school. A means must be found whereby the desired outcomes of schooling can be better specified than is currently the case. Having such specified outcomes, it would be possible to view schooling somewhat as a diagnostic and treatment process in which individual deficiencies and abilities of students were assessed and their paths through the learning process plotted accordingly.[14] An individual

[14] For another view of how the pedagogical process might be decentralized, see H. Thomas James, "Schools and Their Leaders," the Alfred Dexter Simpson Lecture delivered at Harvard University Graduate School of Education on May 15, 1969.

path might lead periodically to classrooms filled with thirty other students, but it just as frequently might lead to museums, seashores, private tutorial sessions with teachers, an eye doctor, the City Hall, an auto assembly line, and so on. The first contact a child has with school probably should not be with a four-walled, fenced fortress, but rather with a small office in which a battery of diagnostic procedures is pursued. This process might well last for days or even weeks. In any event, it should be sufficiently thorough so as to be able to prescribe for a child a host of educational experiences tailored to his particular capabilities and deficiencies.

The process should probably begin with any treatment needed to prepare the child physically for school. Good physical condition is not sufficient in itself to guarantee learning, but physical handicaps can block learning. Consequently, children must be made healthy, and this may very well mean extensive medical treatment. Following this stage, steps need to be taken to gear the processes of formal education to the child's abilities and interests. As we have said, this might very well lead to many different learning paths, but periodically the child should return to the "clinic," where the diagnosis must be repeated, in order to assess progress and prescribe the next steps.

As the child becomes older, he should be able to assume a greater role in prescribing his own educational experiences. Moreover, if the early steps were completed successfully, there should be less need for school experiences prescribed in accord with social standing. Instead, the child's individually developed interests and innate abilities should play a larger role in determining the nature of his schooling. And, as we have held as an objective from the beginning, at least by completion of the twelfth grade children of various social groupings should be in an equal stance ready to pursue whatever postschool paths they choose with equal chances of success. Only when this condition has been achieved will equality of opportunity be a reality.

As we have stated previously, this approach will require greater educational services the lower the SES of the child. The learning performance of the low SES child is impeded by factors that vary from malnutrition and undiagnosed medical problems to the emotional damage that often accompanies a broken home. The learning environment is further handicapped by a lack of school-related educational reinforcement in the home. Under these circumstances the diagnostic and rehabilitative educational services required for lower

SES children are likely to be exceedingly more costly than those needed by their higher SES counterparts.

Implications for the Sources of Financing

The preceding proposal leads directly to a policy of higher school expenditures for low SES children. However, present financing arrangements in Michigan and other states lead directly to the opposite expenditure pattern. As Chapter 6 demonstrates, schools rely overwhelmingly for revenues on a tax base that is distributed unequally: real and personal property. Indeed, school finance in Michigan is tied primarily to local ability to support the schools rather than to the purported goal of equality. Our concern now is with identifying a means by which the strong tie between local financial ability and school-service quality can be broken, or at least weakened. But what means can be found to finance equality of opportunity?

Before outlining specific approaches for financing schools for equal opportunity, it is useful to make some general statements. Most important, we wish to emphasize that there are many possible ways of implementing true equality of educational opportunity. The actual choice of a plan is as much a function of taste and judgment as it is of technical public finance. Administrative criteria, political expediency, tradition, and other factors must all be taken into account in identifying specific arrangements for guaranteeing to all children what the law has promised. The purpose of this preliminary comment is to make the reader aware, explicitly, that the following are but illustrations of means for modifying financial arrangements. They are not presented as the only approaches nor as optima. Rather they are suggested as points of departure from which change might be initiated.

An Illustrative Approach

The ability of a local school district to generate revenue from property taxes should not be allowed to serve as the primary determinant of the quality of school services it offers to children. However, the property tax is not totally devoid of merit.[15] Indeed, some experts believe "that it would be far better to strengthen this levy than to plan for its eradication."[16] In keeping with this view, our prescription

[15] For a detailed discussion of the advantages and disadvantages of the property tax, see Dick Netzer, **Economics of the Property Tax** (Washington, D.C.: Brookings, 1966), Chapter 7.
[16] Jesse Burkhead, **State and Local Taxes for Public Education** (Syracuse: Syracuse University Press, 1963), p. 105.

is to employ a uniform and relatively low statewide property tax as a **partial** means for financing schools. This system would eliminate most of the disadvantages of the property tax while retaining the practical advantage of being able to tap a commercial source of revenue that might be left substantially untouched under other forms of taxation.[17] The revenues needed in excess of those generated from the application of a minimum statewide property tax levy would come from state general funds to be raised through means such as income taxes, sales tax, and the like. Because of the substantial equities associated with the income tax as a revenue-raising procedure, we are predisposed toward a heavy reliance upon it as the primary means for generating the state's direct dollar contribution for education.

The state would determine the per-pupil school service expenditure requirement for children at each level on the SES spectrum. In general, the per pupil requirement would vary inversely with the SES level of the students being served. Table 7.3 displays a hypothetical index of per-pupil expenditure requirements by SES level. In this table each number represents the multiple of some arbitrary dollar amount. For example, if 1 is equal to $400, 2 is equivalent to $800, and so on. Exact dollar amounts are not represented for two reasons. First, dollar requirements fluctuate over time with shifts in educational priorities and changes in price levels. Second, exact dollar figures in such a table might lend the impression that expenditure requirements are easily fixed. The truth is that these dollar relationships should be estimated initially and might have to be altered over the long run to approximate the differential costs of schooling different populations. Thus, Table 7.3 depicts a general pattern where units of expenditure and their multiples are presented as the appropriate heuristic model. Of course figures in this table are suggestive rather than ones based on precise estimates of need. However, the pattern of dollar requirements is meant to represent a scheme that would more nearly approach equality of educational opportunity than does the present one.

Because high SES children tend to receive such a high educational endowment in their home, the scheme in Table 7.3 suggests that no

[17] Admittedly, this is a matter of practicality. If business firms are to be taxed to support local or state government, it is more reasonable and theoretically more efficient to tax them on the basis of their output as measured by value added than to tax them on the basis of their real property, equipment, and inventories. On a practical basis, it is probably easier to levy and administer a property tax than one on value added. See Harvey E. Brazer, "The Value of Industrial Property as a Subject of Taxation," **Canadian Public Administration**, 4 (June 1961), 137–147.

Table 7.3. Hypothetical Expenditure Index for Equality of Educational Opportunity

SES Level	School Level Preschool	Elementary	Secondary
High	—	1.50	2.00
Medium	1.00	2.25	3.00
Low	2.00	3.00	4.00

public preschool provision is necessary to fill their needs. On the other hand, the preschool period represents an ideal time for disproportionate investment to begin for lower SES children. The efficacy of preschool investment has been widely noted in both child development literature and in practice.[18] Indeed, some particularly productive preschool programs, such as the one in Ypsilanti, Michigan, have resulted in substantial and long-lasting gains in achievement.[19] Accordingly, Table 7.3 suggests that medium SES children be provided with one-half day of preschool instruction at one unit per child and lower SES children receive a full day of preschool education at two units per student. Alternatively, the state could choose to enroll lower SES students on a half-day basis for two years while medium SES children would attend for only one year. That is, the lower SES child would begin his preschool experience at the age of three while the middle SES child would start at age four.

    Expenditures at the elementary and secondary level, as presented in Table 7.3, also reflect the pattern required for an equal opportunity approach. The higher expenditures for all groups at the secondary level are based upon the necessity for greater specialization (and thus higher qualifications for and larger numbers of personnel) at that level. Unlike many other states, Michigan does not take these differences into consideration when apportioning aid to local school districts. The salient characteristics of the requirements at all levels of

[18] For some of the research basis supporting formal educational preschool experiences for lower SES children, see Benjamin S. Bloom, **Stability and Change in Human Characteristics** (New York: Wiley, 1964).
[19] For a description of the Ypsilanti program, see David P. Weikart, **Preschool Intervention: A Preliminary Report of the Perry Preschool Project** (Ann Arbor, Michigan: Campus Publishers, 1967). For an evaluation of the Ypsilanti program and other programs for disadvantaged children, see D. Hawkridge, A. Chalupsky, and A. O. H. Roberts, "A Study of Selected Exemplary Programs for the Education of Disadvantaged Children," Final Report, U.S. Office of Education Project No. 089013 by American Institute of Research, Contract No. OEC-0-8-089013-3515 (010) (September 1968).

the matrix is that the schools must spend more money on lower SES groups in order to close the "opportunity gap."

One necessary adjustment in an SES expenditure matrix such as that presented in Table 7.3 would be for differential costs. The dollars available to a school district should be weighted so as to balance dollar differences in items such as land prices, labor costs, and salary level differentials between rural, urban, and suburban areas.[20]

Once the state's expenditure requirements are established, the task becomes that of financing those requirements. The following method, or a variant of it, could be used to generate the required financial support.[21] First, the state would require every local school

Table 7.4. An Illustration of Proposed Financing Arrangement for Achieving Equality of Educational Opportunity

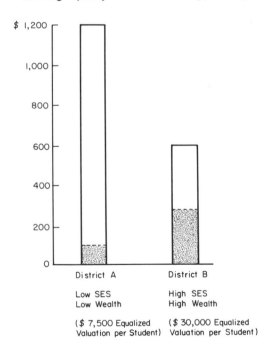

District A
Low SES
Low Wealth

($ 7,500 Equalized
Valuation per Student)

District B
High SES
High Wealth

($ 30,000 Equalized
Valuation per Student)

[20] These cost differentials were described in more detail and illustrated with actual dollar figures in Chapter 6.
[21] Thomas also suggests alternatives that might be adopted to fill the equal educational criteria described above. See J. Alan Thomas, **School Finance and Educational Opportunity in Michigan** (Lansing: Michigan Department of Education, 1968), Chapter 9.

district to levy a property tax at some uniform and relatively low rate. For example, a rate of 10 mills might be appropriate. The dollar difference between what this levy raised for the students in each school district and the state requirements for equal opportunity for those students would be allocated from state funds to each local school district. These revenues would be derived from general state sources with heavy reliance upon state income and sales taxes.

Obviously the equal educational opportunity requirement for a school district would be based upon a weighting scheme where the dollar amounts required for each district would be based upon the relative number of students in each SES group and the distribution of these across each schooling level. Now having presented the overall plan it is useful to provide an example of how it might operate. In order to simplify the illustration, we will use the hypothetical unit requirements for elementary children suggested in Table 7.3, and we will let each unit of expenditure be equivalent to $400.

Table 7.4 displays the proposed financing arrangement for two school districts, A and B. District A is assumed to contain all low SES children of elementary school age. It is also a relatively low wealth district with only $7,500 of equalized assessed valuation (of the property tax base) for each student. On the other hand, District B is inhabited by upper SES residents, and its property tax base is substantial, $30,000 of equalized assessed valuation per pupil.

Applying the uniform tax rate of 10 mills to both districts yields $300 per student in District B and only $75 per student in A. But the state requirement for low SES elementary school students (taken from Table 7.3) is $1,200 per student, and for high SES students the requirement is $600 per pupil. Therefore the state would grant $1,125 per pupil to District A and $300 per pupil to B. In this way the state would fill the gap between the local contribution, where uniform tax effort is mandatory, and the state requirement for equal educational opportunity. This approach might be termed a "variable level" foundation program, since the state requirements represent expenditure foundations below which support cannot fall.

Any suggested changes in financing the schools will be characterized by transitional problems. In such a complex area as education and its financial foundations, utopia can be approached, but it is not likely to be attained. Yet, we believe that the obstacles surrounding effective financing for equal educational opportunity are indeed surmountable. The point is that great strides forward are not costless, but they are nevertheless worthwhile if the benefits sufficiently exceed the costs, as we believe that they do in the present instance.

Inplementing Financial Arrangements

Any alternative financial arrangement that strives for equality not only must be theoretically sound; it also must lend itself to the realities of implementation. The financing model we have described appears to meet both these criteria. It is particularly important, however, to suggest guidelines for implementation.

Perhaps the most important change required in financial arrangements is for state support to be based upon individual schools as units of expenditure rather than school districts. That is, the state should provide assistance to local school districts on the basis of school-by-school calculations; school districts should spend those dollars accordingly. The reason for focusing on and emphasizing individual schools is that there frequently are enormous differences in SES levels between schools within single districts. If funds are provided to school districts on the basis of district average SES, there is too little assurance that the money will be distributed to individual schools on the basis of school SES. Indeed, where school districts have been examined on a school-by-school basis within large cities, it has been demonstrated that poor and black children attend schools that are considerably less endowed than those attended by their white, middle-class counterparts. Dollar expenditures tend to be lower; and, in some cases, even compensatory monies allocated specifically for schools serving children from low-income families have been siphoned off to support general school services throughout the districts.[22]

[22] For evidence of intradistrict financial discrimination, see Henry M. Levin, "Decentralization and the Finance of Inner-City Schools," Stanford Center for Research and Development in Teaching, R&D Memo No. 50 (May 1969), mimeographed; to be published in **Fiscal Planning for Schools in Transition: Restructure, Reform, or Revolt** (Washington, D.C.: National Education Association, in press). Poignant evidence of misallocation of funds intended for low SES schools is found in a California State Department of Education report for the City of Oakland. Oakland had received $10 million in federal funds to aid some 12,000 ghetto youngsters. Instead, much of the money was spent for services throughout the district. Thus, while financing was provided to give all ghetto elementary school children additional reading and language arts instruction, only two out of five actually received such assistance. Of 477 staff positions approved for the "target" schools, only 276 employees could be accounted for (the funds for the other positions presumably were financing personnel at other schools). Further, one-third of the total budget for instruction supported administrators working in the district's central office. This resulted in a severe understaffing of schools for

One obvious means by which funds can be conveyed directly to the schools for which they are intended, while retaining present school district boundaries, can be outlined as follows. (1) Allocate locally generated revenues from the state's mandatory millage levy to all schools within the district on a per student basis. (2) From the state requirements matrix (Table 7.3) compute the dollar amount per student needed in each school to attain equality of opportunity. (3) Grant local school districts financial support equal to the difference between the amount raised by mandatory millage and the state requirements computed for all schools in the district. (4) Require a school-by-school financial accounting each year to ensure that monies intended for particular schools were, in fact, expended in those schools. That is, unlike the present line-item accounting system in which expenditures are reported only for the district, the state must require information on a school-by-school basis in order to guarantee equity among schools. Otherwise the leakages that presently deprive low SES students of additional state and federal resources will persist. A mandatory school-by-school accounting system is necessary if the conduits between state coffers and low SES schools are efficiently to convey resources to the schools for which they are intended.

One further point in favor of using the school rather than a school district as a unit of financial analysis is that it is probably easier to obtain acurate SES information on a regular basis for the smaller units. In a study conducted for New York State, Walter I Garms and Mark C. Smith demonstrate that it is feasible to develop an SES-related measure of educational need from information that can be provided readily by school principals.[23] They suggest that an index of resource needs to be computed from information such as percentages of various specified racial and ethnic minority group students, percentage of children from broken homes, average number of schools attended by pupils in the last three years, and average number of years of schooling of the father, if present, otherwise of

---

which the federal and state governments had designed the grants. See the review of the report in **This World, San Francisco Sunday Examiner and Chronicle,** Aug. 3, 1969, pp. 5 and 6. For a broader treatment of the same topic, see Ruby Martin and Phyllis McClure, **Title I of ESEA: Is It Helping Poor Children?** (Washington, D.C.: Washington Research Project and NAACP Legal Defense and Educational Fund, 1969).

[23] See Walter I. Garms and Mark C. Smith, "Development of a Measure of Educational Need and Its Use in a State School Support Formula," Report on the Study of the New York State School Support Formula, Staff Study No. 4 (Albany, N.Y.: New York State Conference Board, June 1969).

the mother. These variables in linear combination predict approximately 70 percent of the school-to-school variation in reading and mathematics achievement.[24] Other measures might be developed at the individual school level that are also easily compiled and that are more appropriate for discerning differences in SES in rural areas. Garms and Smith also suggest ways in which the measure of school resource need can be woven into a state school finance formula.

Financing for Equality and School Administration

The state must necessarily assume the dominant role in financing schools for equality, and this fact poses a provocative question. Under the present system of school finance in Michigan, and in most other states, the state decides many of the regulations and policies relevant to local school district operation. Personnel licensing, curriculum requirements, staffing ratios, and mandatory expenditure levels are but a few of the areas in which states typically dictate educational practices. Given these procedures, it is entirely possible that if the state increases its level of financial support to the schools, it will also attempt to increase its operational influence over the schools.

More centralized administration from the state, with its almost inevitable imposition of greater operational uniformity, would be exceedingly counterproductive for two reasons. First, the variety of educational needs that confront particular schools and school districts cannot be met by increased standardization among schools. Good education is individualized, meaning that decisions affecting each child's instruction should be made as close to that child as possible. The state level is clearly an inappropriate plane upon which to make such decisions.

A second reason for resisting increased state operation is the sheer technical difficulty in administering large numbers of schools. Schooling is an activity characterized by substantial inefficiencies once a critical threshold of individual school or school district enrollment is exceeded. The nature of schools is such that large-scale bureaucracy appears incapable of managing them by any but the most mummified means. Instructional innovation and personal flexibility both seem to disappear in large school districts. With the exception of school districts so small that they cannot provide a reasonable range of services, large operational units are a deterrent

[24] Ibid., p. 47.

to good education.[25] An extensive survey of the related literature suggests that diseconomies of scale (inefficiencies and higher costs) are characteristic of school districts with enrollments in excess of 10,000 students in average daily attendance.[26] It is little wonder, then, that many school districts throughout the nation either already have been or are under pressure to decentralize their operations.

In short, there are sound reasons for allowing most local school districts to continue to administer their schools without the incumbrance of additional state regulations. Indeed, a far better case can probably be made for decentralizing decision-making for the schools beyond the degree to which is presently exists.[27]

Persons suffering from educational handicaps are caught in a downward-spiraling cycle of despair. On one hand they are tempted on almost every side by the advantages that can be achieved with the assistance of good schooling. On the other hand, their own pursuit of such objectives is frequently brought to an abrupt halt by the inadequacy of their education. For them as individuals the goals of our society become relatively meaningless. At best they are left to experience frustration and defeat. At worst, they may be propelled into a life of crime and decadence. From the perspective of the entire society, this human wastage is a double burden. Not only do the undereducated not contribute their share, but also everyone else is deprived of the benefits of those individuals who, if properly schooled, could have contributed more than their share. We have long since passed the point in our development where we can tolerate vast numbers of unskilled and underdeveloped individuals.

In this chapter we have set forth a new conception of equality of educational opportunity and described new means for pursuing that goal. We are not wedded to the specifics of our proposed approach, but we are wedded to the general need for change. The gravity of the present inequitable situation is immense, yet it is difficult to

[25] See Roger G. Barker and Paul V. Gump, **Big School, Small School** (Stanford: Stanford University Press, 1964).
[26] See H. Thomas James and Henry M. Levin, ''Financing Community Schools,'' presented at The Brookings Institution conference on the community school, December 12–13, 1968, published in **Community Control of Schools,** ed. Henry M. Levin (Washington, D.C.: Brookings, 1970). See also Henry M. Levin, ''The Case for Community Control,'' in **New Models for American Education,** ed. James W. Guthrie and Edward Wynne (Englewood Cliffs: Prentice-Hall, 1971).
[27] **Ibid.**

motivate concern among those who possess the greatest ability to remedy the situation. If allowed to persist, present disparities in school services will almost inevitably undermine our society.

Societies that have persisted longest throughout history appear to be those that have avoided vast social and economic differences among major segments of their populations. Clearly the relative success of the United States in avoiding such extremes has been fostered significantly by the past successes of our schools. Today, however, because of a shortage of resources and an inappropriate distribution of the resources that are available, schools are no longer as successful as they once were. The preservation of equal opportunity and the reality of an open society wherein individuals rise or fall in accord with their interests and abilities demands a restructuring of present arrangements for the support and provision of school services.

Appendix A
Technical Notes

Section 1. Detailed Description of the Statistical Analyses

In our analyses we deal with a set of N subjects, S_i, $i = 1, 2, \ldots, N$. Associated with each of these subjects is a set of integer variables constructed as described in the section on statistical procedures in Chapter 2. Let X_i and Y_i be two such variables. Our statistical test based on the STUDENT T is conducted as follows:

a. We construct two variables X_i' and Y_i' where $X_i' = X_i + U_i$ and $Y_i' = Y_i + V_i$. U_i and V_i are uniformly distributed pseudorandom numbers generated by computer in the usual way. Clearly, this addition does not disturb the ordering relationships of the variables; that is, if $X_i < X_j$, then $X_i' < X_j'$.

b. We rank the X_i' and Y_i' associated with each subject. Let P_i and Q_j be the ranks of X_i and Y_i, respectively.

c. Using P_i and Q_i, we compute the Spearman rank correlation coefficient, ρ_s, according to the methods outlined in Siegel.[1]

d. We compute the statistic

$$t = \rho_s \sqrt{\frac{N-2}{1-\rho_s^2}}.$$

e. We interpret the null hypothesis to be that X_i and Y_i are not related. Under this assumption X_i' and Y_i' are symmetrically distributed. Further, since X_i' and Y_i' are continuous random variables (whereas X_i and Y_i are not), the distribution for t is known[2] to be the student's t distribution with $df = N - 2$ for $N \geqslant 10$. Thus, the usual hypothesis testing procedure can be used. A two-tailed test using t is performed at the 0.05 significance level where the critical value for t, $N \geqslant 30$, is $t = 2.02$.

Table A-1 allows one to obtain the approximate value of the Spearman rank correlation coefficient ρ_s from the values of N and t. For example, if $N = 50$ and $t = 3.1$ then $\rho_s > 0.397$.

Section 2. Treatment of Data in Preparation for Analysis

Our data are derived from two sources: the Equality of Educational Opportunity Survey (EEOS) and the Michigan School Finance Study (Thomas Report). We used EEOS data to study interstudent and

[1] S. Siegel, **Nonparametric Statistics for the Behavioral Sciences** (New York: McGraw-Hill, 1956).
[2] Ibid.

Table A-1. Conversion of STUDENT T into Rank Correlation

N	T					
	2	3	4	5	6	7
10	.577	.728	.816	.870	.905	.927
20	.426	.577	.686	.762	.816	.855
30	.354	.493	.603	.687	.750	.798
40	.309	.438	.544	.630	.697	.750
50	.277	.397	.500	.585	.655	.711
60	.254	.367	.465	.549	.619	.677
70	.236	.342	.436	.518	.588	.647
80	.221	.322	.413	.493	.562	.621
90	.209	.305	.392	.470	.539	.598
100	.198	.290	.375	.451	.518	.577
200	.141	.209	.273	.335	.392	.445
300	.115	.171	.226	.278	.328	.376
400	.100	.149	.197	.243	.288	.331
500	.089	.133	.175	.219	.260	.299
600	.082	.122	.161	.200	.238	.275
700	.075	.113	.150	.186	.211	.256
800	.071	.106	.140	.174	.208	.241
900	.067	.100	.132	.165	.196	.227
1000	.063	.095	.126	.156	.187	.216
2000	.045	.067	.089	.111	.133	.155
3000	.037	.055	.073	.091	.109	.127
4000	.032	.047	.063	.079	.094	.110
5000	.028	.042	.056	.071	.085	.099

interschool relationships. Our study of interdistrict relationships drew on Thomas Report data.

Equality of Educational Opportunity Data

The EEOS data used in our analyses are divided into a principals' section, a teachers' section, and a students' section. These sections correspond to the questionnaires that were administered by the EEOS team and that are exhibited in the appendix of the report, **Equality of Educational Opportunity,** beginning on page 549. The data we used were for sixth grade students.

Our Michigan Equality of Educational Opportunity Survey data is contained on magnetic tapes. Data for sixth grade students, teachers, and principals are stored separately. We will call these tapes the "source tapes." The connecting link between these separate sets of

Table A-1. Conversion of STUDENT T into Rank Correlation (Continued)

T						
8	9	10	20	30	40	50
.943	.954	.962	.990	.996	.998	.998
.883	.905	.921	.978	.990	.994	.996
.834	.862	.884	.967	.985	.991	.994
.792	.825	.851	.956	.980	.988	.992
.756	.792	.822	.945	.974	.985	.991
.724	.763	.796	.935	.969	.982	.989
.696	.737	.772	.925	.964	.979	.987
.671	.714	.750	.915	.959	.976	.985
.649	.692	.729	.905	.954	.974	.983
.629	.673	.711	.896	.950	.971	.981
.494	.539	.579	.818	.905	.943	.963
.420	.462	.501	.757	.867	.918	.945
.372	.411	.488	.708	.833	.895	.929
.337	.374	.409	.667	.802	.873	.913
.311	.345	.379	.633	.775	.853	.898
.290	.322	.354	.604	.750	.834	.884
.272	.304	.334	.578	.728	.817	.871
.258	.288	.317	.555	.707	.800	.858
.245	.274	.302	.535	.689	.785	.845
.176	.197	.218	.408	.557	.667	.746
.145	.162	.180	.343	.481	.590	.674
.126	.141	.156	.302	.429	.535	.620
.112	.126	.140	.272	.391	.492	.577

data is the school code number, which is recorded on all tapes. This number identifies the subjects, of whatever level, associated with each school represented in the sample. From the source tapes, we prepared two others, which we will call "final tapes." They are (1) a sixth grade individual student tape, and (2) a sixth grade school average tape. Final tapes contain values of constructed variables, whereas source tapes contain untreated data. The individual student tape provided information used to study interstudent relationships, whereas the school average tape was used in examining interschool relationships.

Each student in the sample is represented by one list on the appropriate individual student tape. This list consists of the values of variables obtained from his principal, teachers in his school, and himself. The teacher variable values assigned to each student are average values for all teachers in his school. Averaging is used because it is impossible to identify specific teachers as being associated with specific students.

The school average tape is the same as the individual student tape except that values of individual student variables are replaced by school averages of these variables. Thus the tape contains a list for each school in the sample. This list consists of variable values derived from the principal, teachers, and students of that school, school averages being used for teachers and students.

Thomas Report Data

Thomas Report survey data are treated in much the same manner as EEOS data. Final tapes consist of a list for each district in the sample. These lists include values of variables constructed from data obtained from superintendents', principals', and teachers' questionnaires, state documents, and Michigan census reports.

District values obtained from principals' variables are weighted averages, the weight assigned to each principal being the number of students enrolled in his school. District values for teachers' variables are the averages of all teachers in each district.

Appendix B
Variable Descriptions and
Computer Displays

Thomas Report Variables

No.	Variable Name	No.	Variable Name
11	Percent Budget Spent on Educational Research		Past 3 Years
12	Percent Budget to Testing and Evaluative Programs	180	Provisions for Students Who Do Not Qualify for Special Education Programs
13	Percent Budget to Inservice Teacher Education	181	Socioeconomic Scale
		182	Percent with Income under $3,000
14	Days of Released Time for Inservice Activities	185	Sufficiency of Supplementary Materials
25	Percent of Nonteaching High School Principals	186	Index of Services Available to Talented Students
27	Percent Nonteaching Elementary Principals	188	Index of Instructional Aids
28	Superintendent Degree and Postdegree Units	196	Auditorium Index
		206	Number of Periods Teachers Required to Teach
46	Availability of Special Education Programs		
47	Continuance of Special Education Programs in Summer	208	Percent of Teachers with More than 3 Daily Lesson Preparations
54	Supplies Available to Students at No Cost	210	Periods per Day Department Chairman Have Free
169	Occupation of Largest Number of Residents in Attendance Area	211	Ratio of Faculty to Department Chairmen
170	Average Income in Attendance Area	214	Percent of Classes with More than 35 Students
171	Type and Value of Residences in Attendance Area	215	How Long Computer Scheduling Used
		217	Index of Science Innovation
176	Percent of Teachers with One or More College Courses since 1966	225	Index of Instructional Innovation
		231	Physics Lab Facilities
179	Percent of Students on Double Session during	241	Percent of Student Enrollment in Foreign Languages

No.	Variable Name
242	Percent of Student Enrollment in Agriculture
243	Percent of Student Enrollment in Business Education
245	Percent of Student Enrollment in Home Economics
253	Per Pupil Allocation from Local Sources
255	Per Pupil Allocation from Direct State Sources
259	Total Allocation per Pupil
260	Expenditure per Pupil, Total Instruction
263	Expenditure per Pupil for Instructional Salaries
265	Assessed Valuation per Pupil in Hundreds
266	Allocated Millage Rate in Tenths
271	Total Millage Rate for All Purposes
273	Teacher Salary in Hundreds for M.A. Minimum
280	Type of Certificate
281	Degree

Coleman Report Variables

General School Variables

No.	Variable Name
7	Acres of School
8	Age of Building
13	Library Books per 1,000 Students
28	Standardized Achievement Tests
29	Infirmary
33	Number of Days of Art

No.	Variable Name
	Teaching per 10,000 Students
34	Number of Days of Music Teaching per 10,000 Students
35	Number of Days of Speech Correction per 10,000 Students
36	Health Services per 10,000 Students
38	Number of Guidance Counselors per 10,000 Students
40	Nursing Services per 10,000 Students
41	Number of Attendance Officers per 10,000 Students
43	Total Enrollment of School
47	Percentage of Transfer Students
48	Percentage of Students Who Transfered from Your School
58	How Many Years Principal
59	How Many Years Principal in This School
60	Principal's Age
62	Index of Principal's Education
63	Major Field of Study
64	Race
77	Index of Extracurricular Activity
80	Index of Special Courses
81	RRL = Index of Teacher Load in Remedial Reading
88	Classrooms per 1,000 Students

No.	Variable Name	No.	Variable Name
	Teacher Variables		Turnover
95	Number of Years of Teaching	130	Parents Don't Take Enough Interest
98	How Assigned to This School	131	Poor Equipment
103	Academic Ability of Students	132	Too Many Interruptions During Class
105	Would You Be a Teacher Again	133	Too Much Teacher Turnover
106	Would You Be a Teacher in Another School	134	Too Much Administrator Turnover
109	General Reputation of School	135	Preparation Time
		136	Teaching Time
115	Pupils Well Fed and Clothed	137	Students per Class
		138	Hours of Counseling per Week
116	Different Races Don't Get Along Together	141	Verbal Right (Teacher)
117	Parents Attempt to Interfere with School		**Student Variables—Sixth Grade**
		142	Verbal Right (Student)
118	There is Too Much Competition for Grades	144	Nonverbal Right
		146	Reading Right
120	There Are Too Many Absences	148	Math Right
		150	Scale Score Verbal
121	The Classes Are Too Large	151	Scale Score Reading
122	Should Be a Better Mixture of Races	152	Scale Score Math
		154	Age
123	Too Much Time Spent on Discipline	155	Race
		157	Mexican American
124	Students Not Interested in Learning	158	How Many People at Home
125	Lack of Effective Leadership	159	How Many Children in Your Family
		160	Who Acts as Father
126	Parents Put Too Much Pressure on Students	161	Who Acts as Mother
		162	Father's Education
127	Teachers Don't Work Well Together	163	Father's Education
		164	Mother's Education
128	Teachers Have Too Little Freedom	168	Index of Posessions
		170	Number of Different Schools
129	Too Much Student	179	SES Level

Thomas Interdistrict

OCTILES ACCORDING TO VARIABLE 169 OCCUPATION OF LARGEST NUMBER OF RESIDEN
S IN ATTENDANCE AREA
MEDIANS FROM VARIABLE 13 PERCENT BUDGET TO IN-SERVICE TEACHER EDU
CATION

OCTILE	1	2	3	4	5	6	7	8
MEDIAN	10	10	10	50	5C	50	10	50

NTRUE = 48
STUDENT T = 2.28229

OCTILES ACCORDING TO VARIABLE 169 OCCUPATION OF LARGEST NUMBER OF RESIDEN
S IN ATTENDANCE AREA
MEDIANS FROM VARIABLE 14 DAYS OF RELEASED TIME FOR IN-SERVICE ACT
IVITIES

OCTILE	1	2	3	4	5	6	7	8
MEDIAN	1	1	1	1	3	2	3	4

NTRUE = 47
STUDENT T = 2.50348

OCTILES ACCORDING TO VARIABLE 169 OCCUPATION OF LARGEST NUMBER OF RESIDEN
S IN ATTENDANCE AREA
MEDIANS FROM VARIABLE 28 SUPERINTENDENT CEGREE AND POST-DEGREE UN
ITS

OCTILE	1	2	3	4	5	6	7	8
MEDIAN	60	55	65	65	55	70	75	70

NTRUE = 46
STUDENT T = 3.29120

OCTILES ACCORDING TO VARIABLE 169 OCCUPATION OF LARGEST NUMBER OF RESIDEN
S IN ATTENDANCE AREA
MEDIANS FROM VARIABLE 47 CONTINUANCE OF SPECIAL EDUCATION PROGRAM
S IN SUMMER

OCTILE	1	2	3	4	5	6	7	8
MEDIAN	0	0	0	0	0	25	0	25

NTRUE = 48
STUDENT T = 3.21315

OCTILES ACCORDING TO VARIABLE 169 OCCUPATION OF LARGEST NUMBER OF RESIDEN
                                   S IN ATTENDANCE AREA
MEDIANS FROM VARIABLE 188   INDEX OF INSTRUCTIONAL AIDS

OCTILE	1	2	3	4	5	6	7	8
MEDIAN	84	33	84	97	107	103	97	104

NTRUE =   49
STUDENT T =   4.54251

OCTILES ACCORDING TO VARIABLE 169 OCCUPATION OF LARGEST NUMBER OF RESIDEN
                                   S IN ATTENDANCE AREA
MEDIANS FROM VARIABLE 215   HOW LONG COMPUTER SCHEDULING USED

OCTILE	1	2	3	4	5	6	7	8
MEDIAN	0	0	0	1	0	2	2	4

NTRUE =   47
STUDENT T =   1.38449

OCTILES ACCORDING TO VARIABLE 169 OCCUPATION OF LARGEST NUMBER OF RESIDEN
                                   S IN ATTENDANCE AREA
MEDIANS FROM VARIABLE 217   INDEX OF SCIENCE INNOVATION

OCTILE	1	2	3	4	5	6	7	8
MEDIAN	0	100	200	100	300	176	300	300

NTRUE =   45
STUDENT T =   3.13646

OCTILES ACCORDING TO VARIABLE 169 OCCUPATION OF LARGEST NUMBER OF RESIDEN
                                   S IN ATTENDANCE AREA
MEDIANS FROM VARIABLE 245   PERCENT OF STUDENT ENROLLMENT IN HOME EC
                                 ONOMICS

OCTILE	1	2	3	4	5	6	7	8
MEDIAN	27	26	20	17	21	15	12	14

NTRUE =   48
STUDENT T =   -3.75013

Appendix B

OCTILES ACCORDING TO VARIABLE 170 AVERAGE INCOME IN ATTENDANCE AREA

MEDIANS FROM VARIABLE 14   DAYS OF RELEASED TIME FOR IN-SERVICE ACT
                               IVITIES

OCTILE	1	2	3	4	5	6	7	8
MEDIAN	1	1	1	3	2	1	3	3

NTRUE =   47
STUDENT T =   3.15545

OCTILES ACCORDING TO VARIABLE 170 AVERAGE INCOME IN ATTENDANCE AREA

MEDIANS FROM VARIABLE 46   AVAILABILITY OF SPECIAL EDUCATION PROGRA
                               MS

OCTILE	1	2	3	4	5	6	7	8
MEDIAN	7	10	8	15	14	15	17	18

NTRUE =   48
STUDENT T =   3.58295

OCTILES ACCORDING TO VARIABLE 170 AVERAGE INCOME IN ATTENDANCE AREA

MEDIANS FROM VARIABLE 174   STUDENTS FROM RURAL NEIGHBORHOODS

OCTILE	1	2	3	4	5	6	7	8
MEDIAN	15	100	100	0	28	0	2	0

NTRUE =   49
STUDENT T =   -2.22387

OCTILES ACCORDING TO VARIABLE 170 AVERAGE INCOME IN ATTENDANCE AREA

MEDIANS FROM VARIABLE 176   PCT OF TEACHERS WITH 1 OR MORE COLLEGE C
                               OURSES SINCE 1966

OCTILE	1	2	3	4	5	6	7	8
MEDIAN	20	23	22	28	30	28	29	28

NTRUE =   49
STUDENT T =   2.51275

OCTILES ACCORDING TO VARIABLE 170 AVERAGE INCCME IN ATTENDANCE AREA

MEDIANS FROM VARIABLE 180   PROVISIONS FOR STUDENTS WHO DO NOT QUALI
                                FY FOR SPECIAL EDUC PROGRAMS

OCTILE	1	2	3	4	5	6	7	8
MEDIAN	45	83	38	65	60	88	80	100

NTRUE =   48
STUDENT T =   2.68413

OCTILES ACCORDING TO VARIABLE 170 AVERAGE INCCME IN ATTENDANCE AREA

MEDIANS FROM VARIABLE 188   INDEX OF INSTRUCTIONAL AIDS

OCTILE	1	2	3	4	5	6	7	8
MEDIAN	84	77	88	103	98	107	102	104

NTRUE =   49
STUDENT T =   3.11042

OCTILES ACCORDING TO VARIABLE 170 AVERAGE INCCME IN ATTENDANCE AREA

MEDIANS FROM VARIABLE 208   PERCENT OF TEACHERS WITH MORE THAN 3 DAI
                                LY LESSON PREPARATIONS

OCTILE	1	2	3	4	5	6	7	8
MEDIAN	15	15	45	5	5	5	5	5

NTRUE =   48
STUDENT T =   -2.43962

OCTILES ACCORDING TO VARIABLE 170 AVERAGE INCCME IN ATTENDANCE AREA

MEDIANS FROM VARIABLE 210   PERIODS PER DAY DEPARTMENT CHAIRMEN HAVE
                                FREE

OCTILE	1	2	3	4	5	6	7	8
MEDIAN	0	0	0	0	0	0	1	1

NTRUE =   48
STUDENT T =   3.18529

OCTILES ACCORDING TO VARIABLE 170 AVERAGE INCCME IN ATTENDANCE AREA

MEDIANS FRCM VARIABLE 211   RATIO OF FACULTY TO DEPARTMENT CHAIRMEN

OCTILE	1	2	3	4	5	6	7	8
MEDIAN	3	8	8	3	8	8	8	13

NTRUE =   23
STUDENT T =   2.90626

OCTILES ACCORDING TO VARIABLE 170 AVERAGE INCCME IN ATTENDANCE AREA

MEDIANS FROM VARIABLE 215   HOW LONG COMPUTER SCHEDULING USED

OCTILE	1	2	3	4	5	6	7	8
MEDIAN	0	0	0	1	0	1	2	4

NTRUE =   47
STUDENT T =   2.51120

OCTILES ACCORDING TO VARIABLE 170 AVERAGE INCCME IN ATTENDANCE AREA

MEDIANS FROM VARIABLE 225   INDEX OF INSTRUCTIONAL INNOVATION

OCTILE	1	2	3	4	5	6	7	8
MEDIAN	100	50	100	127	100	150	137	150

NTRUE =   44
STUDENT T =   3.12795

OCTILES ACCORDING TO VARIABLE 170 AVERAGE INCCME IN ATTENDANCE AREA

MEDIANS FRCM VARIABLE 241   PERCENT OF STUDENT ENROLLMENT IN FOREIGN
                              LANGUAGES

OCTILE	1	2	3	4	5	6	7	8
MEDIAN	12	15	14	28	26	16	26	51

NTRUE =   48
STUDENT T =   4.02923

OCTILES ACCORDING TO VARIABLE 170 AVERAGE INCCME IN ATTENDANCE AREA

MEDIANS FRCM VARIABLE 242   PERCENT OF STUDENT ENROLLMENT IN AGRICUL
                                 TURE

OCTILE	1	2	3	4	5	6	7	8
MEDIAN	6	12	3	0	C	2	0	0

NTRUE =   48
STUDENT T =   -1.31078

OCTILES ACCORDING TO VARIABLE 170 AVERAGE INCOME IN ATTENDANCE AREA

MEDIANS FRCM VARIABLE 243   PERCENT OF STUDENT ENROLLMENT IN BUSINES
                                 S EDUCATION

OCTILE	1	2	3	4	5	6	7	8
MEDIAN	67	59	61	69	61	61	57	36

NTRUE =   48
STUDENT T =   -2.48128

OCTILES ACCORDING TO VARIABLE 170 AVERAGE INCCME IN ATTENDANCE AREA

MEDIANS FRCM VARIABLE 245   PERCENT OF STUDENT ENROLLMENT IN HOME EC
                                 ONOMICS

OCTILE	1	2	3	4	5	6	7	8
MEDIAN	27	26	22	20	15	20	12	14

NTRUE =   48
STUDENT T =   -4.61850

OCTILES ACCORDING TO VARIABLE 170 AVERAGE INCOME IN ATTENDANCE AREA

MEDIANS FROM VARIABLE 265   ASSESSED VALUATION PER PUPIL IN HUNDREDS

OCTILE	1	2	3	4	5	6	7	8
MEDIAN	87	102	110	121	115	105	114	182

NTRUE =   46
STUDENT T =   2.25114

OCTILES ACCORDING TO VARIABLE 171 TYPE AND VALUE OF RESIDENCES IN ATTENDA
                                CE AREA
MEDIANS FROM VARIABLE   11   PERCENT BUDGET SPENT ON EDUCATIONAL RESE
                                  ARCH

OCTILE   1   2   3   4   5   6   7   8
MEDIAN   0   0   5   0   5   5   5   5

NTRUE =   48
STUDENT T =   2.09099

OCTILES ACCORDING TO VARIABLE 171 TYPE AND VALUE OF RESIDENCES IN ATTENDA
                                CE AREA
MEDIANS FROM VARIABLE   12   PERCENT BUDGET TO TESTING AND EVALUATIVE
                                  PROGRAMS

OCTILE   1   2   3   4   5   6   7   8
MEDIAN   5   5   5   5   50   50   5   50

NTRUE =   48
STUDENT T =   2.64407

OCTILES ACCORDING TO VARIABLE 171 TYPE AND VALUE OF RESIDENCES IN ATTENDA
                                CE AREA
MEDIANS FROM VARIABLE   14   DAYS OF RELEASED TIME FOR IN-SERVICE ACT
                                  IVITIES

OCTILE   1   2   3   4   5   6   7   8
MEDIAN   1   1   1   1   2   1   3   3

NTRUE =   47
STUDENT T =   1.85393

OCTILES ACCORDING TO VARIABLE 171 TYPE AND VALUE OF RESIDENCES IN ATTENDA
                                CE AREA
MEDIANS FROM VARIABLE   215   HOW LONG COMPUTER SCHEDULING USED

OCTILE   1   2   3   4   5   6   7   8
MEDIAN   0   1   0   0   C   1   0   6

NTRUE =   47
STUDENT T =   2.48022

OCTILES ACCORDING TO VARIABLE 171 TYPE AND VALUE OF RESIDENCES IN ATTENDA
                              CE AREA
MEDIANS FROM VARIABLE 217   INDEX OF SCIENCE INNOVATION

OCTILE	1	2	3	4	5	6	7	8
MEDIAN	100	0	100	100	193	300	200	300

NTRUE =   45
STUDENT T =   3.24940

OCTILES ACCORDING TO VARIABLE 171 TYPE AND VALUE OF RESIDENCES IN ATTENDA
                              CE AREA
MEDIANS FROM VARIABLE 241   PERCENT OF STUDENT ENROLLMENT IN FOREIGN
                              LANGUAGES

OCTILE	1	2	3	4	5	6	7	8
MEDIAN	14	15	18	26	19	25	20	44

NTRUE =   48
STUDENT T =   3.20119

OCTILES ACCORDING TO VARIABLE 171 TYPE AND VALUE OF RESIDENCES IN ATTENDA
                              CE AREA
MEDIANS FROM VARIABLE 243   PERCENT OF STUDENT ENROLLMENT IN HOME EC
                              ONOMICS

OCTILE	1	2	3	4	5	6	7	8
MEDIAN	21	35	23	18	15	20	18	11

NTRUE =   48
STUDENT T =   -4.05362

OCTILES ACCORDING TO VARIABLE 181 SOCIO-ECONOMIC SCALE

MEDIANS FROM VARIABLE 14   DAYS OF RELEASED TIME FOR IN-SERVICE ACT
                              IVITIES

OCTILE	1	2	3	4	5	6	7	8
MEDIAN	1	0	1	2	1	1	5	3

NTRUE =   49
STUDENT T =   3.13732

OCTILES ACCORDING TO VARIABLE 181 SOCIO-ECONOMIC SCALE

MEDIANS FROM VARIABLE 25   PERCENT NON-TEACHING HIGH SCHOOL PRINCIP
                                ALS

OCTILE	1	2	3	4	5	6	7	8
MEDIAN	88	100	100	100	100	100	100	100

NTRUE =   49
STUDENT T =   2.72251

OCTILES ACCORDING TO VARIABLE 181 SOCIO-ECONOMIC SCALE

MEDIANS FROM VARIABLE 27   PERCENT NON-TEACHING ELEMENTARY PRINCIPA
                                LS

OCTILE	1	2	3	4	5	6	7	8
MEDIAN	62	100	88	100	100	100	100	100

NTRUE =   48
STUDENT T =   3.57341

OCTILES ACCORDING TO VARIABLE 181 SOCIO-ECONOMIC SCALE

MEDIANS FROM VARIABLE 28   SUPERINTENDENT DEGREE AND POST-DEGREE UN
                                ITS

OCTILE	1	2	3	4	5	6	7	8
MEDIAN	55	50	63	65	70	60	70	75

NTRUE =   48
STUDENT T =   2.94401

OCTILES ACCORDING TO VARIABLE 181 SOCIO-ECONOMIC SCALE

MEDIANS FROM VARIABLE 46   AVAILABILITY OF SPECIAL EDUCATION PROGRA
                                MS

OCTILE	1	2	3	4	5	6	7	8
MEDIAN	8	10	7	15	18	14	16	15

NTRUE =   50
STUDENT T =   4.36174

OCTILES ACCORDING TO VARIABLE 181 SOCIO-ECONOMIC SCALE

MEDIANS FROM VARIABLE 58   PERCENT OF TEACHERS NEW MICHIGAN GRADUAT
                               ES

OCTILE	1	2	3	4	5	6	7	8
MEDIAN	16	25	25	35	31	50	35	33

NTRUE =   51
STUDENT T =   2.77404

OCTILES ACCORDING TO VARIABLE 181 SOCIO-ECONOMIC SCALE

MEDIANS FROM VARIABLE 176   PCT OF TEACHERS WITH 1 OR MORE COLLEGE C
                               OURSES SINCE 1966

OCTILE	1	2	3	4	5	6	7	8
MEDIAN	20	20	23	25	39	29	35	24

NTRUE =   49
STUDENT T =   2.34359

OCTILES ACCORDING TO VARIABLE 181 SOCIO-ECONOMIC SCALE

MEDIANS FROM VARIABLE 180   PROVISIONS FOR STUDENTS WHO DO NOT QUALI
                               FY FOR SPECIAL EDUC PROGRAMS

OCTILE	1	2	3	4	5	6	7	8
MEDIAN	43	36	91	67	80	60	100	92

NTRUE =   48
STUDENT T =   2.47851

OCTILES ACCORDING TO VARIABLE 181 SOCIO-ECONOMIC SCALE

MEDIANS FROM VARIABLE 181   SOCIO-ECONOMIC SCALE

OCTILE	1	2	3	4	5	6	7	8
MEDIAN	35	44	49	60	64	66	79	98

NTRUE =   51
STUDENT T =   150.07889

OCTILES ACCORDING TO VARIABLE 181 SOCIO-ECONOMIC SCALE

MEDIANS FROM VARIABLE 132   PERCENT WITH INCOME UNDER 3000 DOLLARS

OCTILE	1	2	3	4	5	6	7	8
MEDIAN	376	296	274	222	204	141	88	83

NTRUE =   51
STUDENT T =   -20.62939

OCTILES ACCORDING TO VARIABLE 181 SOCIO-ECONOMIC SCALE

MEDIANS FROM VARIABLE 188   INDEX OF INSTRUCTIONAL AIDS

OCTILE	1	2	3	4	5	6	7	8
MEDIAN	73	84	83	103	104	96	99	104

NTRUE =   51
STUDENT T =   3.41064   RHO = .75450

OCTILES ACCORDING TO VARIABLE 181 SOCIO-ECONOMIC SCALE

MEDIANS FROM VARIABLE 205   NUMBER OF PERIODS TEACHERS REQUIRED TO TEACH

OCTILE	1	2	3	4	5	6	7	8
MEDIAN	6	6	6	5	5	5	5	5

NTRUE =   48
STUDENT T =   -2.09774

OCTILES ACCORDING TO VARIABLE 181 SOCIO-ECONOMIC SCALE

MEDIANS FROM VARIABLE 208   PERCENT OF TEACHERS WITH MORE THAN 3 DAILY LESSON PREPARATIONS

OCTILE	1	2	3	4	5	6	7	8
MEDIAN	15	15	5	5	5	5	5	5

NTRUE =   48
STUDENT T =   -2.55535

Appendix B

OCTILES ACCORDING TO VARIABLE 181 SOCIO-ECONOMIC SCALE

MEDIANS FROM VARIABLE 211   RATIO OF FACULTY TO DEPARTMENT CHAIRMEN

OCTILE	1	2	3	4	5	6	7	8
MEDIAN	3	8	8	3	8	8	13	13

NTRUE =   23
STUDENT T =   4.11340

OCTILES ACCORDING TO VARIABLE 181 SOCIO-ECONOMIC SCALE

MEDIANS FROM VARIABLE 217   INDEX OF SCIENCE INNOVATION

OCTILE	1	2	3	4	5	6	7	8
MEDIAN	0	100	200	100	300	176	300	300

NTRUE =   45
STUDENT T =   2.96720

OCTILES ACCORDING TO VARIABLE 181 SOCIO-ECONOMIC SCALE

MEDIANS FROM VARIABLE 225   INDEX OF INSTRUCTIONAL INNOVATION

OCTILE	1	2	3	4	5	6	7	8
MEDIAN	100	50	100	150	150	100	200	150

NTRUE =   44
STUDENT T =   2.34271

OCTILES ACCORDING TO VARIABLE 181 SOCIO-ECONOMIC SCALE

MEDIANS FROM VARIABLE 241   PERCENT OF STUDENT ENROLLMENT IN FOREIGN
                             LANGUAGES

OCTILE	1	2	3	4	5	6	7	8
MEDIAN	14	14	20	16	26	23	28	44

NTRUE =   48
STUDENT T =   4.43804

OCTILES ACCORDING TO VARIABLE 181 SOCIO-ECONOMIC SCALE

MEDIANS FROM VARIABLE 245   PERCENT OF STUDENT ENROLLMENT IN HOME EC
                               ONOMICS

OCTILE	1	2	3	4	5	6	7	8
MEDIAN	28	27	20	15	17	18	17	12

NTRUE =   48
STUDENT T =   -4.20844

OCTILES ACCORDING TO VARIABLE 181 SOCIO-ECONOMIC SCALE

MEDIANS FROM VARIABLE 253   PER PUPIL ALLOCATION FROM LOCAL SOURCES

OCTILE	1	2	3	4	5	6	7	8
MEDIAN	259	150	165	240	240	186	260	475

NTRUE =   48
STUDENT T =   3.42343

OCTILES ACCORDING TO VARIABLE 181 SOCIO-ECONOMIC SCALE

MEDIANS FROM VARIABLE 255   PER PUPIL ALLOCATION FROM DIRECT STATE S
                               OURCES

OCTILE	1	2	3	4	5	6	7	8
MEDIAN	249	239	301	271	294	281	257	212

NTRUE =   48
STUDENT T =   -2.61048

OCTILES ACCORDING TO VARIABLE 181 SOCIO-ECONOMIC SCALE

MEDIANS FROM VARIABLE 250   EXPENDITURE PER PUPIL, TOTAL INSTRUCTION

OCTILE	1	2	3	4	5	6	7	8
MEDIAN	354	316	344	318	405	324	358	482

NTRUE =   48
STUDENT T =   2.93829

OCTILES ACCORDING TO VARIABLE 181 SOCIO-ECONOMIC SCALE

MEDIANS FROM VARIABLE 271   TOTAL MILLAGE RATE FOR ALL PURPOSES

OCTILE	1	2	3	4	5	6	7	8
MEDIAN	180	203	156	214	245	200	280	265

NTRUE =   48
STUDENT T =   5.18821

OCTILES ACCORDING TO VARIABLE 182 PERCENT WITH INCOME UNDER 3000 DOLLARS

MEDIANS FROM VARIABLE 14   DAYS OF RELEASED TIME FOR IN-SERVICE ACTIVITIES

OCTILE	1	2	3	4	5	6	7	8
MEDIAN	3	4	2	2	1	1	1	0

NTRUE =   49
STUDENT T =   -3.30719

OCTILES ACCORDING TO VARIABLE 182 PERCENT WITH INCOME UNDER 3000 DOLLARS

MEDIANS FROM VARIABLE 27   PERCENT NON-TEACHING ELEMENTARY PRINCIPALS

OCTILE	1	2	3	4	5	6	7	8
MEDIAN	100	100	100	100	100	100	88	62

NTRUE =   48
STUDENT T =   -4.51274

OCTILES ACCORDING TO VARIABLE 182 PERCENT WITH INCOME UNDER 3000 DOLLARS

MEDIANS FROM VARIABLE 28   SUPERINTENDENT DEGREE AND POST-DEGREE UNITS

OCTILE	1	2	3	4	5	6	7	8
MEDIAN	70	55	70	70	65	55	65	60

NTRUE =   48
STUDENT T =   -2.64134

OCTILES ACCORDING TO VARIABLE 182 PERCENT WITH INCOME UNDER 3000 DOLLARS

MEDIANS FROM VARIABLE 48   AVAILABILITY OF SPECIAL EDUCATION PROGRA
                                MS

OCTILE	1	2	3	4	5	6	7	8
MEDIAN	18	15	19	17	15	8	8	8

NTRUE = 50
STUDENT T =   -5.44829

OCTILES ACCORDING TO VARIABLE 182 PERCENT WITH INCOME UNDER 3000 DOLLARS

MEDIANS FROM VARIABLE 51   AUXILIARY SERVICES PROVIDED NON-SCHOOL C
                                HILDREN

OCTILE	1	2	3	4	5	6	7	8
MEDIAN	100	80	80	40	60	60	40	0

NTRUE = 24
STUDENT T =   -2.42994

OCTILES ACCORDING TO VARIABLE 182 PERCENT WITH INCOME UNDER 3000 DOLLARS

MEDIANS FROM VARIABLE 176   PCT OF TEACHERS WITH 1 OR MORE COLLEGE C
                                OURSES SINCE 1966

OCTILE	1	2	3	4	5	6	7	8
MEDIAN	37	26	35	31	25	20	22	20

NTRUE = 49
STUDENT T =   -2.28519

OCTILES ACCORDING TO VARIABLE 182 PERCENT WITH INCOME UNDER 3000 DOLLARS

MEDIANS FROM VARIABLE 182   PERCENT WITH INCOME UNDER 3000 DOLLARS

OCTILE	1	2	3	4	5	6	7	8
MEDIAN	73	106	141	172	221	257	294	331

NTRUE = 51
STUDENT T =   367.86549

OCTILES ACCORDING TO VARIABLE 182 PERCENT WITH INCOME UNDER 3000 DOLLARS

MEDIANS FROM VARIABLE 210   PERICDS PER CAY CEPARTMENT CHAIRMEN HAVE
                                 FREE

OCTILE	1	2	3	4	5	6	7	8
MEDIAN	1	1	0	0	0	0	0	0

NTRUE =   48
STUDENT T =   -2.38355

OCTILES ACCORDING TO VARIABLE 182 PERCENT WITH INCOME UNDER 3000 DOLLARS

MEDIANS FROM VARIABLE 211   RATIO OF FACULTY TO DEPARTMENT CHAIRMEN

OCTILE	1	2	3	4	5	6	7	8
MEDIAN	13	8	9	13	8	8	8	3

NTRUE =   23
STUDENT T =   -3.22147

OCTILES ACCORDING TO VARIABLE 182 PERCENT WITH INCOME UNDER 3000 DOLLARS

MEDIANS FROM VARIABLE 215   HOW LONG COMPUTER SCHEDULING USED

OCTILE	1	2	3	4	5	6	7	8
MEDIAN	2	4	0	1	C	0	0	0

NTRUE =   47
STUDENT T =   -5.06185

OCTILES ACCORDING TO VARIABLE 182 PERCENT WITH INCOME UNDER 3000 DOLLARS

MEDIANS FROM VARIABLE 217   INDEX OF SCIENCE INNOVATION

OCTILE	1	2	3	4	5	6	7	8
MEDIAN	300	300	200	300	100	200	100	100

NTRUE =   45
STUDENT T =   -3.13293

Appendix B

OCTILES ACCORDING TO VARIABLE 182 PERCENT WITH INCOME UNDER 3000 DOLLARS

MEDIANS FROM VARIABLE 225   INDEX OF INSTRUCTICNAL INNOVATION

OCTILE	1	2	3	4	5	6	7	8
MEDIAN	250	137	200	127	150	50	50	100

NTRUE = 44
STUDENT T =   -3.28269

OCTILES ACCORDING TO VARIABLE 182 PERCENT WITH INCOME UNDER 3000 DOLLARS

MEDIANS FROM VARIABLE 245   PERCENT FOR STUDENT ENROLLMENT IN HOME EC
ONOMICS

OCTILE	1	2	3	4	5	6	7	8
MEDIAN	13	11	17	17	15	23	20	28

NTRUE = 48
STUDENT T =   4.33729

OCTILES ACCORDING TO VARIABLE 182 PERCENT WITH INCOME UNDER 3000 DOLLARS

MEDIANS FROM VARIABLE 250   EXPENDITURE PER PUPIL, TOTAL INSTRUCTION

OCTILE	1	2	3	4	5	6	7	8
MEDIAN	421	439	346	409	333	344	315	349

NTRUE = 48
STUDENT T =   -3.09362

OCTILES ACCORDING TO VARIABLE 260 EXPENDITURE PER PUPIL, TOTAL INSTRUCTIO

MEDIANS FROM VARIABLE 54   SUPPLIES AVAILABLE TO STUDENTS AT NO COS
T

OCTILE	1	2	3	4	5	6	7	8
MEDIAN	6	10	14	14	10	16	16	20

NTRUE = 47
STUDENT T =   2.41752

OCTILES ACCORDING TO VARIABLE 260 EXPENDITURE PER PUPIL, TOTAL INSTRUCTIC

MEDIANS FROM VARIABLE 136   INDEX OF SERVICES AVAILABLE TO TALENTED
                               STUDENTS

OCTILE	1	2	3	4	5	6	7	8
MEDIAN	118	102	203	269	129	286	217	256

NTRUE =   48
STUDENT T =   3.58193

OCTILES ACCORDING TO VARIABLE 260 EXPENDITURE PER PUPIL, TOTAL INSTRUCTIC

MEDIANS FROM VARIABLE 188   INDEX OF INSTRUCTIONAL AIDS

OCTILE	1	2	3	4	5	6	7	8
MEDIAN	75	81	98	96	84	104	102	101

NTRUE =   48
STUDENT T =   2.86063

OCTILES ACCORDING TO VARIABLE 260 EXPENDITURE PER PUPIL, TOTAL INSTRUCTIC

MEDIANS FROM VARIABLE 196   AUDITORIUM INDEX

OCTILE	1	2	3	4	5	6	7	8
MEDIAN	174	151	300	186	210	269	169	339

NTRUE =   48
STUDENT T =   2.24519

OCTILES ACCORDING TO VARIABLE 260 EXPENDITURE PER PUPIL, TOTAL INSTRUCTIC

MEDIANS FROM VARIABLE 215   HOW LONG COMPUTER SCHEDULING USED

OCTILE	1	2	3	4	5	6	7	8
MEDIAN	0	0	0	0	1	0	0	6

NTRUE =   45
STUDENT T =   1.98498

OCTILES ACCORDING TO VARIABLE 260 EXPENDITURE PER PUPIL, TOTAL INSTRUCTIO

MEDIANS FROM VARIABLE 255   PER PUPIL ALLOCATION FROM DIRECT STATE S
                                OURCES

OCTILE	1	2	3	4	5	6	7	8
MEDIAN	289	309	298	281	306	271	265	196

NTRUE =   49
STUDENT T =   -3.29661

OCTILES ACCORDING TO VARIABLE 260 EXPENDITURE PER PUPIL, TOTAL INSTRUCTIO

MEDIANS FROM VARIABLE 253   EXPENDITURE PER PUPIL FOR INSTRUCTIONAL
                                SALARIES

OCTILE	1	2	3	4	5	6	7	8
MEDIAN	264	282	300	315	329	370	384	446

NTRUE =   49
STUDENT T =   52.66247

OCTILES ACCORDING TO VARIABLE 260 EXPENDITURE PER PUPIL, TOTAL INSTRUCTIO

MEDIANS FROM VARIABLE 273   TEACHER SALARY IN HUNDREDS FOR M.A. MINI
                                MUM

OCTILE	1	2	3	4	5	6	7	8
MEDIAN	70	59	69	69	68	69	73	75

NTRUE =   49
STUDENT T =   3.00479

OCTILES ACCORDING TO VARIABLE 260 EXPENDITURE PER PUPIL, TOTAL INSTRUCTIO

MEDIANS FROM VARIABLE 280   TYPE OF CERTIFICATE

OCTILE	1	2	3	4	5	6	7	8
MEDIAN	349	340	348	348	359	361	346	359

NTRUE =   49
STUDENT T =   2.23375

OCTILES ACCORDING TO VARIABLE 260 EXPENDITURE PER PUPIL, TOTAL INSTRUCTIO

MEDIANS FROM VARIABLE 281   DEGREE

OCTILE	1	2	3	4	5	6	7	8
MEDIAN	118	119	120	120	125	136	134	141

NTRUE =   49
STUDENT T =   3.41306

OCTILES ACCORDING TO VARIABLE 265 ASSESSED VALUATION PER PUPIL IN HUNDRED

MEDIANS FROM VARIABLE 185   SUFFICIENCY OF SUPPLEMENTARY MATERIALS

OCTILE	1	2	3	4	5	6	7	8
MEDIAN	88	89	80	100	85	100	100	100

NTRUE =   48
STUDENT T =   2.45732

OCTILES ACCORDING TO VARIABLE 265 ASSESSED VALUATION PER PUPIL IN HUNDRED

MEDIANS FROM VARIABLE 215   HOW LONG COMPUTER SCHEDULING USED

OCTILE	1	2	3	4	5	6	7	8
MEDIAN	0	0	0	0	1	0	4	1

NTRUE =   45
STUDENT T =   3.24459

OCTILES ACCORDING TO VARIABLE 265 ASSESSED VALUATION PER PUPIL IN HUNDRED

MEDIANS FROM VARIABLE 253   PER PUPIL ALLOCATION FROM LOCAL SOURCES

OCTILE	1	2	3	4	5	6	7	8
MEDIAN	160	175	231	193	240	321	260	365

NTRUE =   49
STUDENT T =   7.33579

OCTILES ACCORDING TO VARIABLE 265 ASSESSED VALUATION PER PUPIL IN HUNDRE[

MEDIANS FROM VARIABLE 255   PER PUPIL ALLOCATION FROM DIRECT STATE S
                                 OURCES

OCTILE	1	2	3	4	5	6	7	8
MEDIAN	328	309	300	288	265	255	234	195

NTRUE =   49
STUDENT T =   -14.82543

OCTILES ACCORDING TO VARIABLE 265 ASSESSED VALUATION PER PUPIL IN HUNDRE[

MEDIANS FROM VARIABLE 259   TOTAL ALLOCATION PER PUPIL

OCTILE	1	2	3	4	5	6	7	8
MEDIAN	501	523	512	497	531	568	618	734

NTRUE =   49
STUDENT T =   3.09559

OCTILES ACCORDING TO VARIABLE 265 ASSESSED VALUATION PER PUPIL IN HUNDRE[

MEDIANS FROM VARIABLE 256   ALLOCATED MILLAGE RATE IN TENTHS

OCTILE	1	2	3	4	5	6	7	8
MEDIAN	81	39	89	90	89	93	90	93

NTRUE =   49
STUDENT T =   3.03765

Appendix B

EEOS Interschool

OCTILES ACCORDING TO VARIABLE 168 6-INDEX OF POSSESSIONS

MEDIANS FROM VARIABLE   7   ACRES OF SCHOOL

OCTILE	1	2	3	4	5	6	7	8
MEDIAN	3	2	5	2	7	5	9	5

NTRUE =   81
STUDENT T =   4.11999

OCTILES ACCORDING TO VARIABLE 168 6-INDEX OF POSSESSIONS

MEDIANS FROM VARIABLE 28   STANDARDIZED ACHIEVMENT TESTS

OCTILE	1	2	3	4	5	6	7	8
MEDIAN	1	1	1	1	1	1	1	1

NTRUE =   81
STUDENT T =   -.47237

OCTILES ACCORDING TO VARIABLE 168 6-INDEX OF POSSESSIONS

MEDIANS FROM VARIABLE 29   INFIRMARY

OCTILE	1	2	3	4	5	6	7	8
MEDIAN	1	0	0	0	C	1	1	1

NTRUE =   82
STUDENT T =   2.45405

OCTILES ACCORDING TO VARIABLE 168 6-INDEX OF POSSESSIONS

MEDIANS FROM VARIABLE 34   NO. OF DAYS OF MUSIC TEACHING PER 10,000
                                   STUDENTS

OCTILE	1	2	3	4	5	6	7	8
MEDIAN	35	41	43	47	41	52	48	50

NTRUE =   79
STUDENT T =   1.75761

Appendix B

OCTILES ACCORDING TO VARIABLE 168 6-INDEX OF POSSESSIONS

MEDIANS FROM VARIABLE 35   NO. OF DAYS OF SPEECH CORRECTION PER 10,
                              000 STUDENTS

OCTILE	1	2	3	4	5	6	7	8
MEDIAN	23	17	15	22	29	32	16	25

NTRUE =   79
STUDENT T =   .82083

OCTILES ACCORDING TO VARIABLE 168 6-INDEX OF POSSESSIONS

MEDIANS FROM VARIABLE 36   HEALTH SERVICES PER 10,000 STUDENTS

OCTILE	1	2	3	4	5	6	7	8
MEDIAN	23	25	19	37	42	43	44	27

NTRUE =   79
STUDENT T =   .55821

OCTILES ACCORDING TO VARIABLE 168 6-INDEX OF POSSESSIONS

MEDIANS FROM VARIABLE 40   NURSING SERVICES PER 10,000 STUDENTS

OCTILE	1	2	3	4	5	6	7	8
MEDIAN	2	5	5	5	8	7	6	7

NTRUE =   79
STUDENT T =   1.70016

OCTILES ACCORDING TO VARIABLE 168 6-INDEX OF POSSESSIONS

MEDIANS FROM VARIABLE 41   NO. OF ATTENDANCE OFFICERS PER 10,000 ST
                              UDENTS

OCTILE	1	2	3	4	5	6	7	8
MEDIAN	7	10	7	11	7	17	7	8

NTRUE =   77
STUDENT T =   .95400

OCTILES ACCORDING TO VARIABLE 168 6-INDEX OF POSSESSIONS

MEDIANS FROM VARIABLE 47   PERCENTAGE CF TRANSFER STUDENTS

OCTILE	1	2	3	4	5	6	7	8
MEDIAN	17	12	7	7	12	7	7	7

NTRUE =   80
STUDENT T =   -2.71754

OCTILES ACCORDING TO VARIABLE 168 6-INDEX OF POSSESSIONS

MEDIANS FROM VARIABLE 48   PERCENTAGE CF STUDENTS WHO TRANSFERED FR
                              OM YOUR SCHCOL

OCTILE	1	2	3	4	5	6	7	8
MEDIAN	17	12	12	12	7	12	7	2

NTRUE =   79
STUDENT T =   -2.62538

OCTILES ACCORDING TO VARIABLE 168 6-INDEX OF POSSESSIONS

MEDIANS FROM VARIABLE 58   HOW MANY YEARS PRINCIPAL

OCTILE	1	2	3	4	5	6	7	8
MEDIAN	12	7	7	7	7	7	17	7

NTRUE =   80
STUDENT T =   -.41763

OCTILES ACCORDING TO VARIABLE 168 6-INDEX OF POSSESSIONS

MEDIANS FROM VARIABLE 59   HOW MANY YEARS PRINCIPAL IN THIS SCHOOL

OCTILE	1	2	3	4	5	6	7	8
MEDIAN	7	2	2	4	4	2	12	7

NTRUE =   81
STUDENT T =   2.47786

OCTILES ACCORDING TO VARIABLE 168 6-INDEX OF POSSESSIONS

MEDIANS FROM VARIABLE 50   AGE

OCTILE	1	2	3	4	5	6	7	8
MEDIAN	50	50	50	60	50	50	50	40

NTRUE =   80
STUDENT T =   -1.06124

OCTILES ACCORDING TO VARIABLE 168 6-INDEX OF POSSESSIONS

MEDIANS FROM VARIABLE 62   INDEX OF PRINCIPAL#S EDUCATION

OCTILE	1	2	3	4	5	6	7	8
MEDIAN	56	56	56	53	56	56	56	53

NTRUE =   80
STUDENT T =   -.67647

OCTILES ACCORDING TO VARIABLE 168 6-INDEX OF POSSESSIONS

MEDIANS FROM VARIABLE 63   MAJOR FIELD OF STUDY

OCTILE	1	2	3	4	5	6	7	8
MEDIAN	0	0	0	0	0	1	0	0

NTRUE =   78
STUDENT T =   1.34194

OCTILES ACCORDING TO VARIABLE 168 6-INDEX OF POSSESSIONS

MEDIANS FROM VARIABLE 64   RACE

OCTILE	1	2	3	4	5	6	7	8
MEDIAN	1	1	1	1	1	1	1	1

NTRUE =   83
STUDENT T =   -.60702

OCTILES ACCORDING TO VARIABLE 168 6-INDEX OF POSSESSIONS

MEDIANS FROM VARIABLE 103   ACADEMIC ABILITY CF STUDENTS

OCTILE	1	2	3	4	5	6	7	8
MEDIAN	114	135	157	195	192	192	236	280

NTRUE =   86
STUDENT T =   8.57158

OCTILES ACCORDING TO VARIABLE 168 6-INDEX OF POSSESSIONS

MEDIANS FROM VARIABLE 106   WOULD YOU BE A TEACHER IN ANOTHER SCHOOL

OCTILE	1	2	3	4	5	6	7	8
MEDIAN	137	117	128	133	161	143	153	155

NTRUE =   86
STUDENT T =   3.54589

OCTILES ACCORDING TO VARIABLE 168 6-INDEX OF POSSESSIONS

MEDIANS FROM VARIABLE 109   GENERAL REPUTATION OF THE SCHOOL

OCTILE	1	2	3	4	5	6	7	8
MEDIAN	210	204	212	228	240	243	275	317

NTRUE =   86
STUDENT T =   5.11733

OCTILES ACCORDING TO VARIABLE 168 6-INDEX OF POSSESSIONS

MEDIANS FROM VARIABLE 115   PUPILS WELL FED AND CLOTHED

OCTILE	1	2	3	4	5	6	7	8
MEDIAN	58	57	33	18	10	12	9	0

NTRUE =   86
STUDENT T =   -9.02330

OCTILES ACCORDING TO VARIABLE 168 6-INDEX OF POSSESSIONS

MEDIANS FROM VARIABLE 116   DIFFERENT RACES DON≠T GET ALONG TOGETHER

OCTILE	1	2	3	4	5	6	7	8
MEDIAN	8	5	7	5	4	0	0	0

NTRUE =   86
STUDENT T =   -1.82915

OCTILES ACCORDING TO VARIABLE 168 6-INDEX OF POSSESSIONS

MEDIANS FROM VARIABLE 118   THERE IS TOO MUCH COMPETITION FOR GRADES

OCTILE	1	2	3	4	5	6	7	8
MEDIAN	0	0	0	0	7	0	4	15

NTRUE =   86
STUDENT T =   3.71301

OCTILES ACCORDING TO VARIABLE 168 6-INDEX OF POSSESSIONS

MEDIANS FROM VARIABLE 120   THERE ARE TOO MANY ABSENCES

OCTILE	1	2	3	4	5	6	7	8
MEDIAN	52	48	35	22	12	15	11	0

NTRUE =   86
STUDENT T =   -7.10255

OCTILES ACCORDING TO VARIABLE 168 6-INDEX OF POSSESSIONS

MEDIANS FROM VARIABLE 121   THE CLASSES ARE TOO LARGE

OCTILE	1	2	3	4	5	6	7	8
MEDIAN	73	81	71	67	60	52	76	23

NTRUE =   86
STUDENT T =   -3.22051

OCTILES ACCORDING TO VARIABLE 168 6-INDEX OF POSSESSIONS

MEDIANS FROM VARIABLE 123   TOO MUCH TIME SPENT ON DISCIPLINE

OCTILE	1	2	3	4	5	6	7	8
MEDIAN	45	57	50	47	37	37	30	21

NTRUE =   86
STUDENT T =   -3.38207

OCTILES ACCORDING TO VARIABLE 168 6-INDEX OF POSSESSIONS

MEDIANS FROM VARIABLE 124   STUDENTS NOT INTERESTED IN LEARNING

OCTILE	1	2	3	4	5	6	7	8
MEDIAN	55	48	36	28	25	15	23	10

NTRUE =   86
STUDENT T =   -5.63915

OCTILES ACCORDING TO VARIABLE 168 6-INDEX OF POSSESSIONS

MEDIANS FROM VARIABLE 126   PARENTS PUT TOO MUCH PRESSURE ON STUDENT
                              S

OCTILE	1	2	3	4	5	6	7	8
MEDIAN	0	2	0	3	14	5	8	33

NTRUE =   86
STUDENT T =   4.52342

OCTILES ACCORDING TO VARIABLE 168 6-INDEX OF POSSESSIONS

MEDIANS FROM VARIABLE 129   TOO MUCH STUDENT TURNOVER

OCTILE	1	2	3	4	5	6	7	8
MEDIAN	50	31	33	33	11	7	3	0

NTRUE =   86
STUDENT T =   -6.57463

OCTILES ACCORDING TO VARIABLE 168 6-INDEX OF POSSESSIONS

MEDIANS FROM VARIABLE 130   PARENTS DON≠T TAKE ENOUGH INTEREST

OCTILE	1	2	3	4	5	6	7	8
MEDIAN	73	79	74	50	40	31	37	14

NTRUE =   86
STUDENT T =   -7.40417

OCTILES ACCORDING TO VARIABLE 168 6-INDEX OF POSSESSIONS

MEDIANS FROM VARIABLE 132   TOO MANY INTERRUPTIONS DURING CLASS

OCTILE	1	2	3	4	5	6	7	8
MEDIAN	45	41	37	20	31	15	40	8

NTRUE =   86
STUDENT T =   -3.41648   RHO = -.73310

OCTILES ACCORDING TO VARIABLE 168 6-INDEX OF POSSESSIONS

MEDIANS FROM VARIABLE 133   TOO MUCH TEACHER TURNOVER

OCTILE	1	2	3	4	5	6	7	8
MEDIAN	20	23	14	7	14	9	4	4

NTRUE =   86
STUDENT T =   -3.09324

OCTILES ACCORDING TO VARIABLE 168 6-INDEX OF POSSESSIONS

MEDIANS FROM VARIABLE 138   HOURS OF COUNSELING PER WEEK

OCTILE	1	2	3	4	5	6	7	8
MEDIAN	38	43	44	30	21	20	22	20

NTRUE =   86
STUDENT T =   -6.25358

OCTILES ACCORDING TO VARIABLE 168 6-INDEX OF POSSESSIONS

MEDIANS FROM VARIABLE 168   6-INDEX OF POSSESSIONS

OCTILE	1	2	3	4	5	6	7	8
MEDIAN	61	68	72	75	78	80	83	86

NTRUE =   86
STUDENT T =   140.12569

                           EEOS INTER-SCHOOL
OCTILES ACCORDING TO VARIABLE 179 6-SES LEVEL

MEDIANS FROM VARIABLE   7   ACRES OF SCHOOL

OCTILE	1	2	3	4	5	6	7	8
MEDIAN	2	5	2	3	2	7	5	9

NTRUE =   81
STUDENT T =   3.43420

OCTILES ACCORDING TO VARIABLE 179 6-SES LEVEL

MEDIANS FROM VARIABLE   8   AGE OF BUILDING

OCTILE	1	2	3	4	5	6	7	8
MEDIAN	7	7	5	6	7	6	4	4

NTRUE =   81
STUDENT T =   -2.21513

OCTILES ACCORDING TO VARIABLE 179 6-SES LEVEL

MEDIANS FROM VARIABLE 13   LIBRARY BOOKS PER 10 STUDENTS

OCTILE	1	2	3	4	5	6	7	8
MEDIAN	37	17	50	36	35	32	31	56

NTRUE =   72
STUDENT T =   2.41279

OCTILES ACCORDING TO VARIABLE 179 6-SES LEVEL

MEDIANS FROM VARIABLE 28   STANDARDIZED ACHIEVMENT TESTS

OCTILE	1	2	3	4	5	6	7	8
MEDIAN	1	1	1	1	1	1	1	1

NTRUE =   81
STUDENT T =   -1.38965

OCTILES ACCORDING TO VARIABLE 179 6-SES LEVEL

MEDIANS FROM VARIABLE 29   INFIRMARY

OCTILE	1	2	3	4	5	6	7	8
MEDIAN	0	1	1	0	C	1	1	1

NTRUE =   82
STUDENT T =   2.44797

OCTILES ACCORDING TO VARIABLE 179 6-SES LEVEL

MEDIANS FROM VARIABLE 34   NO. OF DAYS OF MUSIC TEACHING PER 10,000
                                 STUDENTS

OCTILE	1	2	3	4	5	6	7	8
MEDIAN	41	38	31	52	48	40	47	51

NTRUE =   79
STUDENT T =   2.13531

OCTILES ACCORDING TO VARIABLE 179 6-SES LEVEL

MEDIANS FROM VARIABLE 35   NO. OF DAYS OF SPEECH CORRECTION PER 10,
                                 000 STUDENTS

OCTILE	1	2	3	4	5	6	7	8
MEDIAN	14	13	26	29	30	32	15	27

NTRUE =   79
STUDENT T =   1.48510

OCTILES ACCORDING TO VARIABLE 179 6-SES LEVEL

MEDIANS FROM VARIABLE 36   HEALTH SERVICES PER 10,000 STUDENTS

OCTILE	1	2	3	4	5	6	7	8
MEDIAN	20	19	23	55	42	30	47	38

NTRUE =   79
STUDENT T =   1.63303

OCTILES ACCORDING TO VARIABLE 179 6-SES LEVEL

MEDIANS FROM VARIABLE 41   NO. OF ATTENDANCE OFFICERS PER 10,000 ST
                              UDENTS

OCTILE	1	2	3	4	5	6	7	8
MEDIAN	7	7	13	11	8	5	12	13

NTRUE =   77
STUDENT T =   1.02271

OCTILES ACCORDING TO VARIABLE 179 6-SES LEVEL

MEDIANS FROM VARIABLE 47   PERCENTAGE OF TRANSFER STUDENTS

OCTILE	1	2	3	4	5	6	7	8
MEDIAN	12	7	12	7	12	12	7	2

NTRUE =   80
STUDENT T =   -2.19288

OCTILES ACCORDING TO VARIABLE 179 6-SES LEVEL

MEDIANS FROM VARIABLE 58   HOW MANY YEARS PRINCIPAL

OCTILE	1	2	3	4	5	6	7	8
MEDIAN	12	7	12	7	12	12	12	7

NTRUE =   80
STUDENT T =   .15985

OCTILES ACCORDING TO VARIABLE 179 6-SES LEVEL

MEDIANS FROM VARIABLE 59   YEARS AS A PRINCIPAL

OCTILE	1	2	3	4	5	6	7	8
MEDIAN	2	2	4	4	7	4	7	7

NTRUE =   81
STUDENT T =   2.20744

OCTILES ACCORDING TO VARIABLE 179 6-SES LEVEL

MEDIANS FROM VARIABLE 60   AGE

OCTILE	1	2	3	4	5	6	7	8
MEDIAN	50	50	50	50	5C	50	50	40

NTRUE =   80
STUDENT T =   -.80200

OCTILES ACCORDING TO VARIABLE 179 6-SES LEVEL

MEDIANS FROM VARIABLE 62   INDEX OF PRINCIPAL≠S EDUCATION

OCTILE	1	2	3	4	5	6	7	8
MEDIAN	56	60	53	56	53	53	53	53

NTRUE =   80
STUDENT T =   -1.19988

OCTILES ACCORDING TO VARIABLE 179 6-SES LEVEL

MEDIANS FROM VARIABLE 63   MAJOR FIELD OF STUDY

OCTILE	1	2	3	4	5	6	7	8
MEDIAN	0	1	0	0	C	0	0	1

NTRUE =   78
STUDENT T =   .17322

OCTILES ACCORDING TO VARIABLE 179 6-SES LEVEL

MEDIANS FROM VARIABLE 54   RACE

OCTILE	1	2	3	4	5	6	7	8
MEDIAN	1	1	1	1	1	1	1	1

NTRUE =   83
STUDENT T =   -1.25310

OCTILES ACCORDING TO VARIABLE 179 6-SES LEVEL

MEDIANS FROM VARIABLE 80   INDEX OF SPECIAL COURSES

OCTILE	1	2	3	4	5	6	7	8
MEDIAN	3	3	3	3	3	3	2	1

NTRUE =   83
STUDENT T =   -2.01308

OCTILES ACCORDING TO VARIABLE 179 6-SES LEVEL

MEDIANS FROM VARIABLE 103   ACADEMIC ABILITY OF STUDENTS

OCTILE	1	2	3	4	5	6	7	8
MEDIAN	135	128	174	185	200	200	238	290

NTRUE =   86
STUDENT T =   11.39110

OCTILES ACCORDING TO VARIABLE 179 6-SES LEVEL

MEDIANS FROM VARIABLE 105   WOULD YOU BE A TEACHER AGAIN

OCTILE	1	2	3	4	5	6	7	8
MEDIAN	297	307	318	319	320	325	326	345

NTRUE =   86
STUDENT T =   3.11136

OCTILES ACCORDING TO VARIABLE 179 6-SES LEVEL

MEDIANS FROM VARIABLE 106   WOULD YOU BE A TEACHER IN ANOTHER SCHOOL

OCTILE	1	2	3	4	5	6	7	8
MEDIAN	125	125	110	150	158	143	150	157

NTRUE =   86
STUDENT T =   4.45918

OCTILES ACCORDING TO VARIABLE 179 6-SES LEVEL

MEDIANS FROM VARIABLE 109   GENERAL REPUTATION OF SCHOOL

OCTILE	1	2	3	4	5	6	7	8
MEDIAN	204	200	210	215	271	242	275	319

NTRUE =   86
STUDENT T =   6.24010

OCTILES ACCORDING TO VARIABLE 179 6-SES LEVEL

MEDIANS FROM VARIABLE 115   PUPILS WELL FED AND CLOTHED

OCTILE	1	2	3	4	5	6	7	8
MEDIAN	62	42	25	37	25	18	0	0

NTRUE =   86
STUDENT T =   -6.81302

OCTILES ACCORDING TO VARIABLE 179 6-SES LEVEL

MEDIANS FROM VARIABLE 116   DIFFERENT RACES DON≠T GET ALONG TOGETHER

OCTILE	1	2	3	4	5	6	7	8
MEDIAN	4	8	5	7	6	4	0	0

NTRUE =   86
STUDENT T =   -2.26267

OCTILES ACCORDING TO VARIABLE 179 6-SES LEVEL

MEDIANS FROM VARIABLE 118   THERE IS TOO MUCH COMPETITION FOR GRADES

OCTILE	1	2	3	4	5	6	7	8
MEDIAN	0	0	2	0	0	7	5	15

NTRUE =   86
STUDENT T =   3.99809

OCTILES ACCORDING TO VARIABLE 179 6-SES LEVEL

MEDIANS FROM VARIABLE 120   THERE ARE TOO MANY ABSENCES

OCTILE	1	2	3	4	5	6	7	8
MEDIAN	53	35	14	23	16	19	3	0

NTRUE =   86
STUDENT T =   -6.90909

OCTILES ACCORDING TO VARIABLE 179 6-SES LEVEL

MEDIANS FROM VARIABLE 121   THE CLASSES ARE TOO LARGE

OCTILE	1	2	3	4	5	6	7	8
MEDIAN	76	73	45	65	65	60	26	23

NTRUE =   86
STUDENT T =   -5.38282

OCTILES ACCORDING TO VARIABLE 179 6-SES LEVEL

MEDIANS FROM VARIABLE 123   TOO MUCH TIME SPENT ON DISCIPLINE

OCTILE	1	2	3	4	5	6	7	8
MEDIAN	67	79	54	42	30	46	27	20

NTRUE =   86
STUDENT T =   -5.79238

OCTILES ACCORDING TO VARIABLE 179 6-SES LEVEL

MEDIANS FROM VARIABLE 124   STUDENTS NOT INTERESTED IN LEARNING

OCTILE	1	2	3	4	5	6	7	8
MEDIAN	55	50	45	38	22	23	20	7

NTRUE =   86
STUDENT T =   -7.75831

OCTILES ACCORDING TO VARIABLE 179 6-SES LEVEL

MEDIANS FROM VARIABLE 126   PARENTS PUT TOO MUCH PRESSURE ON STUDENT
                               S

OCTILE	1	2	3	4	5	6	7	8
MEDIAN	2	5	0	0	2	10	15	30

NTRUE =   86
STUDENT T =   4.78074

OCTILES ACCORDING TO VARIABLE 179 6-SES LEVEL

MEDIANS FROM VARIABLE 127   TEACHERS DON≠T WORK WELL TOGETHER

OCTILE	1	2	3	4	5	6	7	8
MEDIAN	10	8	2	10	5	5	0	0

NTRUE =   86
STUDENT T =   -2.15051

OCTILES ACCORDING TO VARIABLE 179 6-SES LEVEL

MEDIANS FROM VARIABLE 129   TOO MUCH STUDENT TURNOVER

OCTILE	1	2	3	4	5	6	7	8
MEDIAN	24	34	35	12	21	7	0	0

NTRUE =   86
STUDENT T =   -6.34038

OCTILES ACCORDING TO VARIABLE 179 6-SES LEVEL

MEDIANS FROM VARIABLE 130   PARENTS DON≠T TAKE ENOUGH INTEREST

OCTILE	1	2	3	4	5	6	7	8
MEDIAN	75	75	62	66	42	40	17	17

NTRUE =   86
STUDENT T =   -6.91929

OCTILES ACCORDING TO VARIABLE 179 6-SES LEVEL

MEDIANS FROM VARIABLE 131   POOR EQUIPMENT

OCTILE	1	2	3	4	5	6	7	8
MEDIAN	28	20	25	13	14	15	9	7

NTRUE =   86
STUDENT T =   -2.72788

OCTILES ACCORDING TO VARIABLE 179 6-SES LEVEL

MEDIANS FROM VARIABLE 132   TOO MANY INTERRUPTIONS DURING CLASS

OCTILE	1	2	3	4	5	6	7	8
MEDIAN	50	40	25	35	11	18	8	16

NTRUE =   86
STUDENT T =   -4.12459

OCTILES ACCORDING TO VARIABLE 179 6-SES LEVEL

MEDIANS FROM VARIABLE 133   TOO MUCH TEACHER TURNOVER

OCTILE	1	2	3	4	5	6	7	8
MEDIAN	14	25	25	6	11	7	4	0

NTRUE =   86
STUDENT T =   -3.42658

OCTILES ACCORDING TO VARIABLE 179 6-SES LEVEL

MEDIANS FROM VARIABLE 137   STUDENTS PER CLASS

OCTILE	1	2	3	4	5	6	7	8
MEDIAN	305	285	304	275	296	291	270	285

NTRUE =   86
STUDENT T =   -3.46623

OCTILES ACCORDING TO VARIABLE 179 6-SES LEVEL

MEDIANS FROM VARIABLE 138   HOURS OF COUNSELING PER WEEK

OCTILE	1	2	3	4	5	6	7	8
MEDIAN	45	44	35	27	24	23	20	20

NTRUE =   86
STUDENT T =   -8.23729

OCTILES ACCORDING TO VARIABLE 179 6-SES LEVEL

MEDIANS FROM VARIABLE 141   VERBAL RIGHT

OCTILE	1	2	3	4	5	6	7	8
MEDIAN	235	235	244	247	244	245	250	256

NTRUE =   86
STUDENT T =   3.77557

EEOS Interstudent

OCTILES ACCORDING TO VARIABLE 168 6-INDEX OF POSSESSIONS

MEDIANS FROM VARIABLE   7   ACRES OF SCHOOL

OCTILE	1	2	3	4	5	6	7	8
MEDIAN	3	3	3	4	4	5	4	4

NTRUE = 5164
STUDENT T =   8.38516

OCTILES ACCORDING TO VARIABLE 168 6-INDEX OF POSSESSIONS

MEDIANS FROM VARIABLE   8   AGE OF BUILDING

OCTILE	1	2	3	4	5	6	7	8
MEDIAN	6	6	6	6	6	4	4	4

NTRUE = 5085
STUDENT T =   -12.39241

OCTILES ACCORDING TO VARIABLE 168 6-INDEX OF POSSESSIONS

MEDIANS FROM VARIABLE   13   LIBRARY BOOKS PER 10 STUDENTS

OCTILE	1	2	3	4	5	6	7	8
MEDIAN	35	35	37	35	38	41	44	40

NTRUE = 4457
STUDENT T =   10.05733

OCTILES ACCORDING TO VARIABLE 168 6-INDEX OF POSSESSIONS

MEDIANS FROM VARIABLE   29   INFIRMARY

OCTILE	1	2	3	4	5	6	7	8
MEDIAN	0	0	0	0	1	1	1	1

NTRUE = 5136
STUDENT T =   9.87885

EEOS INTER-STUDENT

OCTILES ACCORDING TO VARIABLE 168 6-INDEX OF POSSESSIONS

MEDIANS FROM VARIABLE 33   NO. OF DAYS OF ART TEACHING PER 10,000 S
                              TUDENTS

OCTILE	1	2	3	4	5	6	7	8
MEDIAN	34	38	38	34	33	31	31	31

NTRUE = 4934
STUDENT T =   -6.15954

OCTILES ACCORDING TO VARIABLE 168 6-INDEX OF POSSESSIONS

MEDIANS FROM VARIABLE 34   NO. OF DAYS OF MUSIC TEACHING PER 10,000
                              STUDENTS

OCTILE	1	2	3	4	5	6	7	8
MEDIAN	41	41	41	43	44	47	44	47

NTRUE = 4934
STUDENT T =   7.87517

OCTILES ACCORDING TO VARIABLE 168 6-INDEX OF POSSESSIONS

MEDIANS FROM VARIABLE 35   NO. OF DAYS OF SPEECH CORRECTION PER 10,
                              000 STUDENTS

OCTILE	1	2	3	4	5	6	7	8
MEDIAN	15	15	15	16	17	18	18	17

NTRUE = 4934
STUDENT T =   6.67254

OCTILES ACCORDING TO VARIABLE 168 6-INDEX OF POSSESSIONS

MEDIANS FROM VARIABLE 36   HEALTH SERVICES PER 10,000 STUDENTS

OCTILE	1	2	3	4	5	6	7	8
MEDIAN	20	20	23	23	26	30	37	27

NTRUE = 4934
STUDENT T =   8.08725

EEOS INTER-STUDENT

OCTILES ACCORDING TO VARIABLE 168 6-INDEX OF POSSESSIONS

MEDIANS FROM VARIABLE 40   NURSING SERVICES PER 10,000 STUDENTS

OCTILE	1	2	3	4	5	6	7	8
MEDIAN	5	5	5	5	5	6	6	6

NTRUE = 4934
STUDENT T =   7.31890

OCTILES ACCORDING TO VARIABLE 168 6-INDEX OF POSSESSIONS

MEDIANS FROM VARIABLE 58   HOW MANY YEARS PRINCIPAL

OCTILE	1	2	3	4	5	6	7	8
MEDIAN	12	12	12	12	12	12	12	12

NTRUE = 5021
STUDENT T =   -4.14186

OCTILES ACCORDING TO VARIABLE 168 6-INDEX OF POSSESSIONS

MEDIANS FROM VARIABLE 59   HOW MANY YEARS PRINCIPAL IN THIS SCHOOL

OCTILE	1	2	3	4	5	6	7	8
MEDIAN	2	2	2	4	4	4	4	7

NTRUE = 5080
STUDENT T =   6.92942

OCTILES ACCORDING TO VARIABLE 168 6-INDEX OF POSSESSIONS

MEDIANS FROM VARIABLE 60   AGE

OCTILE	1	2	3	4	5	6	7	8
MEDIAN	50	50	50	50	50	50	50	50

NTRUE = 5005
STUDENT T =   -6.45764

```
                          EEOS  INTER-STUDENT
```

OCTILES ACCORDING TO VARIABLE 168 6-INDEX OF POSSESSIONS

MEDIANS FROM VARIABLE 77   INDEX OF EXTRACURRICULAR ACTIVITY

OCTILE	1	2	3	4	5	6	7	8
MEDIAN	5	5	5	5	5	4	5	5

NTRUE = 5196
STUDENT T =   -4.34778

OCTILES ACCORDING TO VARIABLE 168 6-INDEX OF POSSESSIONS

MEDIANS FROM VARIABLE 81   RRL/10

OCTILE	1	2	3	4	5	6	7	8
MEDIAN	86	86	86	86	78	78	48	74

NTRUE = 2606
STUDENT T =   -5.32036

OCTILES ACCORDING TO VARIABLE 168 6-INDEX OF POSSESSIONS

MEDIANS FROM VARIABLE 88   CLASSROOMS PER 1,000 STUDENTS

OCTILE	1	2	3	4	5	6	7	8
MEDIAN	31	30	31	31	30	31	32	32

NTRUE = 4837
STUDENT T =   9.40211

OCTILES ACCORDING TO VARIABLE 168 6-INDEX OF POSSESSIONS

MEDIANS FROM VARIABLE 98   HOW ASSIGNED TO THIS SCHOOL

OCTILE	1	2	3	4	5	6	7	8
MEDIAN	30	30	30	31	33	34	34	34

NTRUE = 5284
STUDENT T =   3.36648

EEOS INTER-STUDENT
OCTILES ACCORDING TO VARIABLE 168 6-INDEX OF POSSESSIONS

MEDIANS FROM VARIABLE 105   WOULD YOU BE A TEACHER AGAIN

OCTILE	1	2	3	4	5	6	7	8
MEDIAN	310	310	309	318	316	319	320	319

NTRUE = 5284
STUDENT T =   11.42921

OCTILES ACCORDING TO VARIABLE 168 6-INDEX OF POSSESSIONS

MEDIANS FROM VARIABLE 106   WOULD YOU BE A TEACHER IN ANOTHER SCHOOL

OCTILE	1	2	3	4	5	6	7	8
MEDIAN	128	128	135	138	141	148	148	150

NTRUE = 5284
STUDENT T =   16.45746

OCTILES ACCORDING TO VARIABLE 168 6-INDEX OF POSSESSIONS

MEDIANS FROM VARIABLE 109   GENERAL REPUTATION OF SCHOOL

OCTILE	1	2	3	4	5	6	7	8
MEDIAN	215	215	238	243	247	270	269	270

NTRUE = 5284
STUDENT T =   19.51838

OCTILES ACCORDING TO VARIABLE 168 6-INDEX OF POSSESSIONS

MEDIANS FROM VARIABLE 115   PUPILS WELL FED AND CLOTHED

OCTILE	1	2	3	4	5	6	7	8
MEDIAN	50	38	33	22	15	9	8	9

NTRUE = 5284
STUDENT T =   -29.99240

EEOS INTER-STUDENT

OCTILES ACCORDING TO VARIABLE 168 6-INDEX OF POSSESSIONS

MEDIANS FROM VARIABLE 116   DIFFERENT RACES DON≠T GET ALONG TOGETHER

OCTILE	1	2	3	4	5	6	7	8
MEDIAN	8	8	6	6	4	3	2	3

NTRUE = 5284
STUDENT T =   -13.17375

OCTILES ACCORDING TO VARIABLE 168 6-INDEX OF POSSESSIONS

MEDIANS FROM VARIABLE 117   PARENTS ATTEMPT TO INTERFERE WITH SCHOOL

OCTILE	1	2	3	4	5	6	7	8
MEDIAN	9	9	9	10	11	13	13	13

NTRUE = 5284
STUDENT T =   11.08005

OCTILES ACCORDING TC VARIABLE 168 6-INDEX OF POSSESSIONS

MEDIANS FROM VARIABLE 121   THE CLASSES ARE TOO LARGE

OCTILE	1	2	3	4	5	6	7	8
MEDIAN	73	73	71	68	67	57	55	55

NTRUE = 5284
STUDENT T =   -19.00441

OCTILES ACCORDING TO VARIABLE 168 6-INDEX OF POSSESSIONS

MEDIANS FROM VARIABLE 122   SHOULD BE A BETTER MIXTURE

OCTILE	1	2	3	4	5	6	7	8
MEDIAN	28	25	20	15	12	9	10	9

NTRUE = 5284
STUDENT T =   -19.72194

EEOS INTER-STUDENT

OCTILES ACCORDING TO VARIABLE 168 6-INDEX OF POSSESSIONS

MEDIANS FROM VARIABLE 123   TOO MUCH TIME SPENT ON DISCIPLINE

OCTILE	1	2	3	4	5	6	7	8
MEDIAN	61	61	58	47	40	31	33	33

NTRUE = 5284
STUDENT T =   -21.93787

OCTILES ACCORDING TO VARIABLE 168 6-INDEX OF POSSESSIONS

MEDIANS FROM VARIABLE 125   LACK OF EFFECTIVE LEADERSHIP

OCTILE	1	2	3	4	5	6	7	8
MEDIAN	15	16	13	9	9	9	9	8

NTRUE = 5284
STUDENT T =   -9.65476

OCTILES ACCORDING TO VARIABLE 168 6-INDEX OF POSSESSIONS

MEDIANS FROM VARIABLE 126   PARENTS PUT TOO MUCH PRESSURE ON STUDENT
S

OCTILE	1	2	3	4	5	6	7	8
MEDIAN	2	2	4	6	7	11	10	9

NTRUE = 5284
STUDENT T =   17.66247

OCTILES ACCORDING TO VARIABLE 168 6-INDEX OF POSSESSIONS

MEDIANS FROM VARIABLE 127   TEACHERS DON≠T WORK WELL TOGETHER

OCTILE	1	2	3	4	5	6	7	8
MEDIAN	8	7	7	6	5	3	3	4

NTRUE = 5284
STUDENT T =   -11.39157

EECS INTER-STUDENT

OCTILES ACCORDING TO VARIABLE 168 6-INDEX OF POSSESSIONS

MEDIANS FROM VARIABLE 128   TEACHERS HAVE TOO LITTLE FREEDOM

OCTILE	1	2	3	4	5	6	7	8
MEDIAN	26	25	25	20	19	15	15	19

NTRUE = 5284
STUDENT T =   -10.64959

OCTILES ACCORDING TO VARIABLE 168 6-INDEX OF POSSESSIONS

MEDIANS FROM VARIABLE 130   PARENTS DON≠T TAKE ENOUGH INTEREST

OCTILE	1	2	3	4	5	6	7	8
MEDIAN	71	71	62	54	42	33	34	33

NTRUE = 5284
STUDENT T =   -27.96142

OCTILES ACCORDING TO VARIABLE 168 6-INDEX OF POSSESSIONS

MEDIANS FROM VARIABLE 131   POOR EQUIPMENT

OCTILE	1	2	3	4	5	6	7	8
MEDIAN	16	16	16	16	14	13	11	12

NTRUE = 5284
STUDENT T =   -13.09770

OCTILES ACCORDING TO VARIABLE 168 6-INDEX OF POSSESSIONS

MEDIANS FROM VARIABLE 132   TOO MANY INTERRUPTIONS DURING CLASS

OCTILE	1	2	3	4	5	6	7	8
MEDIAN	41	41	37	34	34	25	25	28

NTRUE = 5284
STUDENT T =   -16.08683

EEOS   INTER-STUDENT

OCTILES ACCORDING TO VARIABLE 168 6-INDEX OF POSSESSIONS

MEDIANS FROM VARIABLE 133   TOO MUCH TEACHER TURNOVER

OCTILE	1	2	3	4	5	6	7	8
MEDIAN	18	18	14	10	8	7	7	7

NTRUE = 5284
STUDENT T =   -15.34086

OCTILES ACCORDING TC VARIABLE 168 6-INDEX OF POSSESSIONS

MEDIANS FROM VARIABLE 134   TOO MUCH ADMINISTRATOR TURNOVER -- SCHOO
                                 L PROBLEMS END

OCTILE	1	2	3	4	5	6	7	8
MEDIAN	2	2	2	0	0	0	0	0

NTRUE = 5284
STUDENT T =   -11.19344

OCTILES ACCORDING TO VARIABLE 168 6-INDEX OF POSSESSIONS

MEDIANS FROM VARIABLE 135   PREPARATION TIME

OCTILE	1	2	3	4	5	6	7	8
MEDIAN	195	195	195	200	200	200	200	200

NTRUE = 5284
STUDENT T =   5.08934

OCTILES ACCORDING TO VARIABLE 168 6-INDEX OF POSSESSIONS

MEDIANS FROM VARIABLE 136   TEACHING TIME

OCTILE	1	2	3	4	5	6	7	8
MEDIAN	550	550	550	550	550	550	550	550

NTRUE = 5284
STUDENT T =   1.10095

EEOS   INTER-STUDENT

OCTILES ACCORDING TO VARIABLE 168 6-INDEX OF POSSESSIONS

MEDIANS FROM VARIABLE 137   STUDENTS PER CLASS

OCTILE	1	2	3	4	5	6	7	8
MEDIAN	299	296	296	291	288	285	288	285

NTRUE = 5284
STUDENT T =   -9.23571

OCTILES ACCORDING TO VARIABLE 168 6-INDEX OF POSSESSIONS

MEDIANS FROM VARIABLE 141   VERBAL RIGHT

OCTILE	1	2	3	4	5	6	7	8
MEDIAN	240	240	243	243	245	245	250	247

NTRUE = 5284
STUDENT T =   13.81696

OCTILES ACCORDING TO VARIABLE 168 6-INDEX OF POSSESSIONS

MEDIANS FROM VARIABLE 154   6-AGE

OCTILE	1	2	3	4	5	6	7	8
MEDIAN	11	11	11	11	11	11	11	11

NTRUE = 5284
STUDENT T =   -12.82367

OCTILES ACCORDING TO VARIABLE 168 6-INDEX OF POSSESSIONS

MEDIANS FROM VARIABLE 155   6-RACE

OCTILE	1	2	3	4	5	6	7	8
MEDIAN	0	0	0	1	1	1	1	1

NTRUE = 5284
STUDENT T =   17.05190

OCTILES ACCORDING TO VARIABLE 168 6-INDEX OF POSSESSIONS

MEDIANS FROM VARIABLE 157   6-MEXICAN AMERICAN

OCTILE	1	2	3	4	5	6	7	8
MEDIAN	1	1	1	1	1	1	1	1

NTRUE = 5284
STUDENT T =   4.48570

OCTILES ACCORDING TO VARIABLE 168 6-INDEX OF POSSESSIONS

MEDIANS FROM VARIABLE 158   6-HOW MANY PEOPLE AT HOME

OCTILE	1	2	3	4	5	6	7	8
MEDIAN	6	6	6	6	6	5	6	6

NTRUE = 5284
STUDENT T =   -8.80105

OCTILES ACCORDING TO VARIABLE 168 6-INDEX OF POSSESSIONS

MEDIANS FROM VARIABLE 159   6-HOW MANY CHILDREN IN YOUR FAMILY

OCTILE	1	2	3	4	5	6	7	8
MEDIAN	4	4	4	4	3	3	3	3

NTRUE = 5284
STUDENT T =   -11.42714

EEOS INTER-STUDENT

OCTILES ACCORDING TO VARIABLE 168 6-INDEX OF POSSESSIONS

MEDIANS FROM VARIABLE 160   6-WHO ACTS AS FATHER

OCTILE	1	2	3	4	5	6	7	8
MEDIAN	1	0	0	0	0	0	0	0

NTRUE = 5284
STUDENT T =   -16.49598

OCTILES ACCORDING TC VARIABLE 168 6-INDEX OF POSSESSIONS

MEDIANS FROM VARIABLE 161   6-WHO ACTS AS MOTHER

OCTILE	1	2	3	4	5	6	7	8
MEDIAN	0	0	0	0	0	0	0	0

NTRUE = 5284
STUDENT T =   -5.55306

OCTILES ACCORDING TO VARIABLE 168 6-INDEX OF POSSESSIONS

MEDIANS FROM VARIABLE 162   6-FATHER≠S EDUCATION

OCTILE	1	2	3	4	5	6	7	8
MEDIAN	10	10	10	10	10	10	10	12

NTRUE = 5284
STUDENT T =   17.90533

OCTILES ACCORDING TC VARIABLE 168 6-INDEX OF POSSESSIONS

MEDIANS FROM VARIABLE 163   6-FATHER≠S EDUCATION

OCTILE	1	2	3	4	5	6	7	8
MEDIAN	10	8	8	8	9	8	8	8

NTRUE = 5284
STUDENT T =   -12.98132

EEOS INTER-STUDENT

OCTILES ACCORDING TO VARIABLE 168 6-INDEX OF POSSESSIONS

MEDIANS FROM VARIABLE 164   6-MOTHER≠S EDUCATION

OCTILE	1	2	3	4	5	6	7	8
MEDIAN	10	10	10	10	10	12	12	12

NTRUE = 5284
STUDENT T =   16.26061

Appendix B

OCTILES ACCORDING TC VARIABLE 168 6-INDEX OF POSSESSIONS

MEDIANS FROM VARIABLE 170   6-NO OF DIFFERENT SCHOOLS

OCTILE	1	2	3	4	5	6	7	8
MEDIAN	2	2	2	2	2	2	2	1

NTRUE = 5284
STUDENT T =   -18.85672

OCTILES ACCORDING TC VARIABLE 179 6-SES LEVEL

MEDIANS FROM VARIABLE   7   ACRES OF SCHOOL

OCTILE	1	2	3	4	5	6	7	8
MEDIAN	4	3	4	4	4	4	4	5

NTRUE = 5164
STUDENT T =   7.99950

EEOS INTER-STUDENT

OCTILES ACCORDING TO VARIABLE 179 6-SES LEVEL

MEDIANS FROM VARIABLE   8   AGE OF BUILDING

OCTILE	1	2	3	4	5	6	7	8
MEDIAN	6	7	6	6	6	5	4	4

NTRUE = 5085
STUDENT T =   -12.02085

OCTILES ACCORDING TO VARIABLE 179 6-SES LEVEL

MEDIANS FROM VARIABLE 13   LIBRARY BOOKS PER 10 STUDENTS

OCTILE	1	2	3	4	5	6	7	8
MEDIAN	35	30	38	35	36	38	44	47

NTRUE = 4457
STUDENT T =   14.14248

OCTILES ACCORDING TO VARIABLE 179 6-SES LEVEL

MEDIANS FROM VARIABLE 29   INFIRMARY

OCTILE	1	2	3	4	5	6	7	8
MEDIAN	0	0	0	0	1	1	1	1

NTRUE = 5136
STUDENT T =   10.48946

OCTILES ACCORDING TO VARIABLE 179 6-SES LEVEL

MEDIANS FROM VARIABLE 33   NO. OF DAYS OF ART TEACHING PER 10,000 S
                               TUDENTS

OCTILE	1	2	3	4	5	6	7	8
MEDIAN	31	38	37	38	34	34	31	27

NTRUE = 4934
STUDENT T =   -5.42763

                         EEQS   INTER-STUDENT
OCTILES ACCORDING TO VARIABLE 179 6-SES LEVEL

MEDIANS FROM VARIABLE 34   NO. OF DAYS OF MUSIC TEACHING PER 10,000
                               STUDENTS

OCTILE	1	2	3	4	5	6	7	8
MEDIAN	41	40	41	41	44	44	47	48

NTRUE = 4934
STUDENT T =   12.06232

OCTILES ACCORDING TO VARIABLE 179 6-SES LEVEL

MEDIANS FROM VARIABLE 35   NO. OF DAYS OF SPEECH CORRECTION PER 10,
                               000 STUDENTS

OCTILE	1	2	3	4	5	6	7	8
MEDIAN	15	14	17	15	18	17	20	22

NTRUE = 4934
STUDENT T =   13.71859

OCTILES ACCORDING TO VARIABLE 179 6-SES LEVEL

MEDIANS FROM VARIABLE 36   HEALTH SERVICES PER 10,000 STUDENTS

OCTILE	1	2	3	4	5	6	7	8
MEDIAN	20	19	23	20	30	30	35	38

NTRUE = 4934
STUDENT T =   12.08410

OCTILES ACCORDING TO VARIABLE 179 6-SES LEVEL

MEDIANS FROM VARIABLE 40   NURSING SERVICES PER 10,000 STUDENTS

OCTILE	1	2	3	4	5	6	7	8
MEDIAN	5	3	5	5	6	6	6	6

NTRUE = 4934
STUDENT T =   9.63650

                              EEQS INTER-STUDENT
OCTILES ACCORDING TO VARIABLE 179 6-SES LEVEL

MEDIANS FROM VARIABLE 58   HOW MANY YEARS PRINCIPAL

OCTILE	1	2	3	4	5	6	7	8
MEDIAN	7	12	12	7	12	12	12	12

NTRUE = 5021
STUDENT T =   -1.65970

OCTILES ACCORDING TO VARIABLE 179 6-SES LEVEL

MEDIANS FROM VARIABLE 59   YEARS AS A PRINCIPAL

OCTILE	1	2	3	4	5	6	7	8
MEDIAN	2	2	4	2	4	4	4	7

NTRUE = 5080
STUDENT T =   9.79575

OCTILES ACCORDING TC VARIABLE 179 6-SES LEVEL

MEDIANS FROM VARIABLE 60   AGE

OCTILE	1	2	3	4	5	6	7	8
MEDIAN	50	50	50	50	50	50	40	40

NTRUE = 5005
STUDENT T =   -4.13530

OCTILES ACCORDING TO VARIABLE 179 6-SES LEVEL

MEDIANS FROM VARIABLE 77   INDEX OF EXTRACURRICULAR ACTIVITY

OCTILE	1	2	3	4	5	6	7	8
MEDIAN	5	5	5	5	5	5	5	5

NTRUE = 5196
STUDENT T =   -4.91098

                         EEOS   INTER-STUDENT
OCTILES ACCORDING TO VARIABLE 179 6-SES LEVEL

MEDIANS FROM VARIABLE 81   RRL/10

OCTILE	1	2	3	4	5	6	7	8
MEDIAN	78	86	86	86	78	78	78	50

NTRUE = 2606
STUDENT T =   -5.23241

OCTILES ACCORDING TO VARIABLE 179 6-SES LEVEL

MEDIANS FROM VARIABLE 88   CLASSRCOMS PER 1,000 STUDENTS

OCTILE	1	2	3	4	5	6	7	8
MEDIAN	31	29	30	30	31	31	32	32

NTRUE = 4837
STUDENT T =   12.51277

OCTILES ACCORDING TO VARIABLE 179 6-SES LEVEL

MEDIANS FROM VARIABLE 98   HOW ASSIGNED TO THIS SCHOOL

OCTILE	1	2	3	4	5	6	7	8
MEDIAN	30	27	30	30	34	31	35	35

NTRUE = 5284
STUDENT T =   8.05829

OCTILES ACCORDING TO VARIABLE 179 6-SES LEVEL

MEDIANS FROM VARIABLE 105   WOULD YOU BE A TEACHER AGAIN

OCTILE	1	2	3	4	5	6	7	8
MEDIAN	310	306	315	310	319	318	325	326

NTRUE = 5284
STUDENT T =   16.04858

EEOS   INTER-STUDENT
OCTILES ACCORDING TO VARIABLE 179 6-SES LEVEL

MEDIANS FROM VARIABLE 106   WOULD YOU BE A TEACHER IN ANOTHER SCHOOL

OCTILE	1	2	3	4	5	6	7	8
MEDIAN	131	123	137	131	145	144	150	155

NTRUE = 5284
STUDENT T =   22.77127

OCTILES ACCORDING TO VARIABLE 179 6-SES LEVEL

MEDIANS FROM VARIABLE 109   GENERAL REPUTATION OF SCHOOL

OCTILE	1	2	3	4	5	6	7	8
MEDIAN	220	208	243	237	255	258	270	275

NTRUE = 5284
STUDENT T =   26.28702

OCTILES ACCORDING TO VARIABLE 179 6-SES LEVEL

MEDIANS FROM VARIABLE 115   PUPILS WELL FED AND CLOTHED

OCTILE	1	2	3	4	5	6	7	8
MEDIAN	36	50	25	28	15	15	9	4

NTRUE = 5284
STUDENT T =   -28.52804

OCTILES ACCORDING TO VARIABLE 179 6-SES LEVEL

MEDIANS FROM VARIABLE 116   DIFFERENT RACES DON≠T GET ALONG TOGETHER

OCTILE	1	2	3	4	5	6	7	8
MEDIAN	6	8	6	7	5	4	0	0

NTRUE = 5284
STUDENT T =   -15.69080

EEOS   INTER-STUDENT
OCTILES ACCORDING TO VARIABLE 179 6-SES LEVEL

MEDIANS FROM VARIABLE 117   PARENTS ATTEMPT TO INTERFERE WITH SCHOOL

OCTILE	1	2	3	4	5	6	7	8
MEDIAN	9	10	10	10	10	10	13	13

NTRUE = 5284
STUDENT T =   9.35875

OCTILES ACCORDING TO VARIABLE 179 6-SES LEVEL

MEDIANS FROM VARIABLE 121   THE CLASSES ARE TOO LARGE

OCTILE	1	2	3	4	5	6	7	8
MEDIAN	73	75	69	73	65	65	55	40

NTRUE = 5284
STUDENT T =   -26.62474

OCTILES ACCORDING TO VARIABLE 179 6-SES LEVEL

MEDIANS FROM VARIABLE 122   SHOULD BE A BETTER MIXTURE

OCTILE	1	2	3	4	5	6	7	8
MEDIAN	25	32	18	20	11	9	9	7

NTRUE = 5284
STUDENT T =   -26.02438

OCTILES ACCORDING TO VARIABLE 179 6-SES LEVEL

MEDIANS FROM VARIABLE 123   TOO MUCH TIME SPENT ON DISCIPLINE

OCTILE	1	2	3	4	5	6	7	8
MEDIAN	56	68	50	58	41	37	31	22

NTRUE = 5284
STUDENT T =   -30.08245

EEOS INTER-STUDENT
OCTILES ACCORDING TO VARIABLE 179 6-SES LEVEL

MEDIANS FROM VARIABLE 125   LACK OF EFFECTIVE LEADERSHIP

OCTILE	1	2	3	4	5	6	7	8
MEDIAN	11	20	10	15	9	9	8	9

NTRUE = 5284
STUDENT T =   -11.52689

OCTILES ACCORDING TO VARIABLE 179 6-SES LEVEL

MEDIANS FROM VARIABLE 126   PARENTS PUT TOO MUCH PRESSURE ON STUDENT
S

OCTILE	1	2	3	4	5	6	7	8
MEDIAN	3	2	5	5	6	6	10	15

NTRUE = 5284
STUDENT T =   18.27615

OCTILES ACCORDING TO VARIABLE 179 6-SES LEVEL

MEDIANS FROM VARIABLE 127   TEACHERS DON≠T WORK WELL TOGETHER

OCTILE	1	2	3	4	5	6	7	8
MEDIAN	7	8	7	7	6	5	3	0

NTRUE = 5284
STUDENT T =   -14.52824

OCTILES ACCORDING TO VARIABLE 179 6-SES LEVEL

MEDIANS FROM VARIABLE 128   TEACHERS HAVE TOO LITTLE FREEDOM

OCTILE	1	2	3	4	5	6	7	8
MEDIAN	23	28	22	25	20	18	15	15

NTRUE = 5284
STUDENT T =   -13.25460

EEOS INTER-STUDENT

OCTILES ACCORDING TC VARIABLE 179 6-SES LEVEL

MEDIANS FROM VARIABLE 130   PARENTS DON≠T TAKE ENOUGH INTEREST

OCTILE	1	2	3	4	5	6	7	8
MEDIAN	64	73	54	62	50	37	33	21

NTRUE = 5284
STUDENT T =   -32.07581

OCTILES ACCORDING TO VARIABLE 179 6-SES LEVEL

MEDIANS FROM VARIABLE 131   POOR EQUIPMENT

OCTILE	1	2	3	4	5	6	7	8
MEDIAN	16	20	15	20	13	13	12	9

NTRUE = 5284
STUDENT T =   -17.56634

OCTILES ACCORDING TO VARIABLE 179 6-SES LEVEL

MEDIANS FROM VARIABLE 132   TOO MANY INTERRUPTIONS DURING CLASS

OCTILE	1	2	3	4	5	6	7	8
MEDIAN	40	42	35	37	31	31	20	20

NTRUE = 5284
STUDENT T =   -19.16470

OCTILES ACCORDING TO VARIABLE 179 6-SES LEVEL

MEDIANS FROM VARIABLE 133   TOO MUCH TEACHER TURNOVER

OCTILE	1	2	3	4	5	6	7	8
MEDIAN	16	18	14	14	8	8	7	5

NTRUE = 5284
STUDENT T =   -19.51767

EEOS   INTER-STUDENT
OCTILES ACCORDING TO VARIABLE 179 6-SES LEVEL

MEDIANS FROM VARIABLE 134   TOO MUCH ADMINISTRATOR TURNOVER -- SCHOO
                                 L PROBLEMS END

OCTILE	1	2	3	4	5	6	7	8
MEDIAN	2	2	0	2	0	0	0	0

NTRUE = 5284
STUDENT T =   -9.59337

OCTILES ACCORDING TO VARIABLE 179 6-SES LEVEL

MEDIANS FROM VARIABLE 135   PREPARATION TIME

OCTILE	1	2	3	4	5	6	7	8
MEDIAN	195	202	195	195	200	200	200	200

NTRUE = 5284
STUDENT T =   2.43113

OCTILES ACCORDING TO VARIABLE 179 6-SES LEVEL

MEDIANS FROM VARIABLE 136   TEACHING TIME

OCTILE	1	2	3	4	5	6	7	8
MEDIAN	550	544	550	550	551	550	550	550

NTRUE = 5284
STUDENT T =   .84758

OCTILES ACCORDING TO VARIABLE 179 6-SES LEVEL

MEDIANS FROM VARIABLE 137   STUDENTS PER CLASS

OCTILE	1	2	3	4	5	6	7	8
MEDIAN	295	302	295	296	291	287	285	283

NTRUE = 5284
STUDENT T =   -13.74645

EEOS INTER-STUDENT

OCTILES ACCORDING TO VARIABLE 179 6-SES LEVEL

MEDIANS FROM VARIABLE 141   TEACHER≠S VERBAL RIGHT

OCTILE	1	2	3	4	5	6	7	8
MEDIAN	240	239	243	242	244	245	250	250

NTRUE = 5284
STUDENT T =   16.15421

OCTILES ACCORDING TO VARIABLE 179 6-SES LEVEL

MEDIANS FROM VARIABLE 154   6-AGE

OCTILE	1	2	3	4	5	6	7	8
MEDIAN	11	11	11	11	11	11	11	11

NTRUE = 5284
STUDENT T =   -6.55241

OCTILES ACCORDING TO VARIABLE 179 6-SES LEVEL

MEDIANS FROM VARIABLE 155   6-RACE

OCTILE	1	2	3	4	5	6	7	8
MEDIAN	0	0	1	0	1	1	1	1

NTRUE = 5284
STUDENT T =   34.83880

OCTILES ACCORDING TO VARIABLE 179 6-SES LEVEL

MEDIANS FROM VARIABLE 158   6-HOW MANY PEOPLE AT HOME

OCTILE	1	2	3	4	5	6	7	8
MEDIAN	6	7	6	6	6	6	6	5

NTRUE = 5284
STUDENT T =   -9.69564

OCTILES ACCORDING TO VARIABLE 179 6-SES LEVEL

MEDIANS FROM VARIABLE 159   6-HOW MANY CHILDREN IN YOUR FAMILY

OCTILE	1	2	3	4	5	6	7	8
MEDIAN	3	4	4	4	3	4	3	3

NTRUE = 5284
STUDENT T =   -9.35221

OCTILES ACCORDING TO VARIABLE 179 6-SES LEVEL

MEDIANS FROM VARIABLE 160   6-WHO ACTS AS FATHER

OCTILE	1	2	3	4	5	6	7	8
MEDIAN	0	0	0	0	0	0	0	0

NTRUE = 5284
STUDENT T =   -11.72970

Appendix B

                              EEOS   INTER-STUDENT
OCTILES ACCORDING TO VARIABLE 179 6-SES LEVEL

MEDIANS FROM VARIABLE 161   6-WHO ACTS AS MOTHER

OCTILE	1	2	3	4	5	6	7	8
MEDIAN	0	0	0	0	0	0	0	0

NTRUE = 5284
STUDENT T =   -5.34994

OCTILES ACCORDING TO VARIABLE 179 6-SES LEVEL

MEDIANS FROM VARIABLE 162   6-FATHER≠S EDUCATION

OCTILE	1	2	3	4	5	6	7	8
MEDIAN	8	10	10	10	10	10	12	16

NTRUE = 5284
STUDENT T =   63.84552

OCTILES ACCORDING TO VARIABLE 179 6-SES LEVEL

MEDIANS FROM VARIABLE 163   6-FATHER≠S EDUCATION

OCTILE	1	2	3	4	5	6	7	8
MEDIAN	8	8	8	8	8	10	8	9

NTRUE = 5284
STUDENT T =   -7.30641

OCTILES ACCORDING TO VARIABLE 179 6-SES LEVEL

MEDIANS FROM VARIABLE 164   6-MOTHER≠S EDUCATION

OCTILE	1	2	3	4	5	6	7	8
MEDIAN	10	10	10	10	10	10	12	12

NTRUE = 5284
STUDENT T =   30.97183

OCTILES ACCORDING TC VARIABLE 179 6-SES LEVEL

MEDIANS FROM VARIABLE 170   6-NO OF DIFFERENT SCHOOLS

OCTILE	1	2	3	4	5	6	7	8
MEDIAN	2	2	2	2	2	2	2	1

NTRUE = 5284
STUDENT T =   -8.82010

OCTILES ACCORDING TO VARIABLE 179 6-SES LEVEL

MEDIANS FROM VARIABLE 179   6-SES LEVEL

OCTILE	1	2	3	4	5	6	7	8
MEDIAN	42	53	61	66	81	101	124	158

NTRUE = 5284
STUDENT T =   1044.47983

Bibliography

Advisory Commission on Intergovernmental Relations — **Measures of State and Local Fiscal Capacity and Tax Effort.** A Staff Report, October 1962.

Agger, Robert, and Ostrom, Vincent — "Political Participation in a Small Community." In **Political Behavior,** edited by Heinz Eulau et al. Glencoe, Ill.: The Free Press, 1956.

Almond, Gabriel, and Verba, Sidney — **The Civic Culture.** Princeton: Princeton University Press, 1963.

Bajema, Carl Jay — "A Note on the Interrelations Among Intellectual Ability, Educational Attainment, and Occupational Achievement: A Follow-up Study of a Male Kalamazoo Public School Population." **Sociology of Education,** 41 (Summer 1968).

Barker, Roger G., and Gump, Paul V. — **Big School, Small School.** Stanford: Stanford University Press, 1964.

Barron, William E. — "Measurement of Educational Productivity." In **The Theory and Practice of School Finance,** edited by Warren E. Gauerke and Jack R. Childress. Chicago: Rand McNally, 1967.

Becker, Gary S. — **Human Capital.** New York: Columbia University Press, 1964.

Benson, Charles S. — "State Aid Patterns." In **Public School Finance,** edited by Jesse Burkhead. Syracuse, New York: Syracuse University Press, 1964.

Benson, Charles S. — **The Cheerful Prospect.** Boston: Houghton Mifflin, 1965.

Benson, Charles S. — **The Economics of Public Education,** 2nd ed. Boston: Houghton Mifflin, 1968.

Benson, Charles S., and Kelly, James A. — **The Rhode Island Comprehensive Foundation and Enhancement State Aid Program for Education.** Providence: Rhode Island Special Commission to Study the Future Field of Education, 1966.

Benson, Charles S., **et al.**   **State and Local Fiscal Rela-tionships in Public Education in California.** Report of the Senate Fact Finding Committee on Revenue and Taxation. Sacramento: Senate of the State of California, March 1965.

Berg, Ivar   "Rich Man's Qualifications for Poor Man's Jobs." **Trans-action,** 6 (March 1969).

Berkeley Unified School District,   **De Facto Segregation in the**
Board of Education, Citizens   **Berkeley Public Schools.**
Committee   Berkeley, California: Berkeley Unified School District, November 19, 1963, mimeographed.

Blau, P. M., and Duncan, O. D.   **The American Occupational Structure.** New York: Wiley, 1967.

Bloom, Benjamin S.   "International Project on the Evaluation of Educational Achievement." Bulletin No. 4, UNESCO Institute for Education. Hamburg, 1964.

Bloom, Benjamin S.   **Stability and Change in Human Characteristics.** New York: Wiley, 1964.

Bloom, Benjamin S., ed.   **Taxonomy of Educational Objectives, Handbook I: The Cognitive Domain.** New York: McKay, 1956.

Bloom, Benjamin S., Davis,   **Compensatory Education for**
Allison, and Hess, Robert   **Cultural Deprivation.** New York: Holt, Rinehart and Winston, 1965.

Bowles, Samuel S.   "Educational Production Functions." Final Report to the Office of Education under Cooperative Research Contract OEC 1-700451-2651, February 1969.

Bowles, Samuel S.   "Toward an Educational Production Function." Paper presented at the Conference on Research in Income and Wealth, November 15–18, 1968. Published in **Education, Income and Human Capital,** edited by W. Lee